Internationally Yours

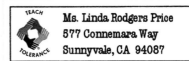
Internationally Yours

Writing and
Communicating
Successfully
in Today's
Global
Marketplace

Mary A.
De Vries

Houghton Mifflin
Company
Boston   New York

Library of Congress Cataloging-in-Publication Data

De Vries, Mary Ann.
  Internationally yours : writing and communicating successfully in today's global marketplace/Mary A. De Vries.
      p.   cm.
  Includes bibliographical references and index.
  ISBN 0-395-67026-8 (cl)   0-395-69611-9 (pa)
  1. Commercial correspondence.   2. Business writing.
3. International correspondence.   4. English language—Business
English.   I. Title.   II. Title: Writing and communicating
successfully in today's global marketplace.
HF5721.D353   1994   93–49439
808'.06665—dc20   CIP

Manufactured in the United States of America

VB 10 9 8 7 6 5 4 3 2 1

Book design by Pat Dunbar

Contents

Preface

HAVE YOU HEARD the turkey story? The setting changes depending on the storyteller, but the moral for international communicators is the same:

> An American exporter, sensing that it was time to conclude business negotiations with a counterpart in Germany, faxed a hastily composed letter suggesting that they both review the latest proposals one more time and then "talk turkey" (get serious). The German, somewhat baffled but eager to be accommodating, thereupon hired a new translator and sent a response in Turkish.

You may be thinking that no one would do something so silly, but in fact this may be one of the mildest examples of international miscommunication. Roger Axtell reported several giant faux pas in one of his books on international trade (*Do's and Taboos of International Trade,* Wiley, 1991). One concerns a slogan used by PepsiCo in Taiwan: "Pepsi Comes Alive," which was translated into Chinese as "Pepsi Brings Your Ancestors Back from the Grave." Now that's a pretty picture! General Motors, however, may have taken the prize in introducing its Chevrolet Nova in Latin America: *No va* in Spanish means "no go." Whether the bloopers are big or little, companies pay dearly in lost sales.

International correspondence is often fertile ground for language mishaps. Although most of us believe that we can avoid the really outrageous mistakes (as the PepsiCo and General Motors writers no doubt also believed), we're not so sure about the hundreds of little problems that lurk in every sentence we write. If you've ever wondered whether you were crafting your messages in the best possible way for your international readers, you're not alone. I've been receiving inquiries about this for years, and my files are bulging with letters that violate almost every known principle of good letter writing.

Someone once told me, à la Gertrude Stein, that a letter is a letter is a letter. Anyone who believes that is in BIG trouble, because writing for an international audience is a lot different from writing for a domestic audience. That's the focus of this book—what you have to do to write winning letters to people who either use English only as a second or third language or don't use it at all. Either way, your biggest challenge may be trying to *un*learn everything you learned about domestic letters.

Here's the plan: The book has nine chapters and an appendix that cover the essentials of writing international correspondence. The early chapters (1–3) introduce the complex subject of international correspondence and provide the background information you need to establish an effective writing style and a clear format for your messages.

The middle chapters (4–7) focus on the most troublesome language problems in international correspondence. The chapters use sample sentences and paragraphs as well as numerous other examples to illustrate common mistakes and how to avoid them. Each of these chapters concludes with a "Checkup" section consisting of several sample letters, good and bad. You can use these checkups to test your skills at spotting and correcting the problems that often cause misunderstandings and other mishaps in international communication.

The final chapters (8–9) deal with the differences in social, religious, and business customs around the world. It's well known that our understanding of these differences has a significant impact on the success of our contacts with people in other countries.

Here's a brief summary of each chapter and the appendix:

Chapter 1, "Two Different Worlds," looks at the situation today, including the difference between domestic and international correspondence, the role of women in global communication today, and the use of translators.

Chapter 2, "The Fine Art of Message Design," explains how to format your international messages and lists the different forms of address used in other countries.

Chapter 3, "Write It with Style," offers suggestions for an effective international writing style (capitalization, spelling, and punctuation) and summarizes the five major language pitfalls in international correspondence.

Chapter 4, "Say What You Mean—Literally," spotlights one of the most serious language pitfalls—failure to be precise and clear, including problems with modern American usage, such as trendy words; common grammatical bloopers, such as misused and misplaced modifiers; and trouble-some expressions, such as U.S. idioms.

Chapter 5, "The Language Demons Among Us," considers the hazards of using a specialized, exclusive, or tired vocabulary, particularly slang, cliches, jargon, gobbledygook, buzzwords, and other undesirable expressions that cause foreigners endless grief.

Chapter 6, "Why Short Is Beautiful," discusses the urgent need to use short, simple words and sentences (*not* simple concepts) in international correspondence, as well as other strategies for simplification and clarification to help the foreign reader translate our messages accurately.

Chapter 7, "Creating a Punctuation Roadmap," explains why we have to reverse the American trend toward using less punctuation and learn how to *over*punctuate our foreign messages so that the punctuation can serve as a roadmap that will keep the reader from getting lost.

Chapter 8, "A Matter of Respect," stresses the critical importance of respecting the many different social, business, and religious customs of people in other countries and of clearly conveying this respect in our letters to them.

Chapter 9, "Around the World from Afghanistan to Zimbabwe," continues the discussion started in Chapter 8 by taking a trip around the world through nearly two hundred country profiles and by providing important information that writers use frequently in international letters, such as nationality designations and foreign currencies.

The Appendix provides useful supplementary information, such as international mail regulations, international dialing codes to use in faxing letters to other countries, a list of U.S. embassies around the world, telephone extensions of Department of Commerce country desk officers, and additional sources of information (printed material and organizations) that may be helpful.

The many examples throughout the book were taken from or inspired by actual letters, memos, and other messages. All of the names, places, and events have been changed, however, to protect the privacy of the writers and their companies. The model sentences, paragraphs, and letters that you will see, therefore, are generic, fictional guides to composing successful international correspondence but should not be construed as instructions on how to conduct international trade.

I appreciate the generous advice and research material supplied by numerous organizations, including the Department of Commerce, Department of State, Small Business Administration, Overseas Private Investment Corporation, U.S. Information Agency, Business Council for

International Understanding (BCIU) Institute of American University, Stanford University, David M. Kennedy Center for International and Area Studies at Brigham Young University, and many other governmental, educational, and business organizations.

Among the individuals who have been especially helpful are the friends and associates who devoted many hours during the past decade collecting thousands of messages that constituted a database for this book. I'm very grateful for their valuable contribution. In particular, I want to thank Carmen Riepe, formerly a member of the Foreign Service and now a private consultant, who offered important suggestions, assisted in the research, and reviewed every page of the manuscript.

One of the things we all learned while working on the book is that it's a pioneer work. Until now, the study of international correspondence has not been a heavily traveled path. Although bookstores are full of material focusing on domestic letter writing, and I've written four such books myself, none has ventured into the complicated world of international correspondence.

As Chapter 1 explains, domestic and international correspondence are two very different worlds. By the time you finish this book, you may even decide that international correspondence is a different universe. Warp Factor 1, Mr. Sulu.

Internationally Yours

Two Different Worlds

WRITING INTERNATIONAL messages is infinitely more complex than writing domestic messages. If you want to learn how to do it right, you might begin by throwing out most of the rules you learned about domestic letter writing. However drastic that advice may seem, it's given in all seriousness. Domestic and international correspondence are two different worlds, and "never the twain shall meet."

It shocks some people to learn that the standards and practices they normally use with huge success at home could actually cause them to *lose* business in another country. Yet if you talk to businesspeople involved in global communication, you'll no doubt hear some horror stories about innocent, unintentional gaffes made by people who were just doing the same thing they always do when making contacts in the United States. Part of the problem is that we're taught how to communicate with others in our own country at a very young age, and it becomes a habit, but we aren't taught how to communicate with people in *other* countries.

Most businesspeople involved in global communications, therefore, never learned in school how to write (or talk) to someone in another country. Unless their companies provided in-house cross-cultural training or unless they took an outside course in international communication, it probably never occurred to them that there might be a crucial difference between domestic and international correspondence. Finding this out through trial and error can be expensive.

THE SITUATION TODAY

Instant Communication

A few decades ago it didn't much matter whether or not you had training in international business relations. Most jobs didn't require a global understanding. Not so today. Modern communication technologies have linked us with virtually every part of the world. Even in a small office, the morning mail is likely to include a fax from Brussels, Tokyo, or Buenos Aires. Everything is instant—or nearly so. Even traditional postal mail includes fast delivery such as Express Mail International Service and International Priority Airmail Service.

The Impact of Letters

Companies that do volume business with foreign trading partners have to make face-to-face contacts, so a lot of travel and on-site contacts are involved. Most of the books on international trade and communication therefore focus on this part of an international relationship, but they omit, or only briefly touch on, the letter-writing aspect. Yet in many countries, correspondence is the forerunner to any on-site meeting; afterward, it is the ongoing exchange of letters that solidifies and continues the business arrangements made in person. (In some parts of the world, such as Latin America, personal meetings may precede the correspondence.) It doesn't matter if a communication is transmitted by satellite, electronically, or by conventional mail. In each case the message itself—what you say and how you say it—will either strengthen or weaken the relationship.

Women in International Communication

Women entering the international business world often wonder whether the rules for men apply equally to them and whether they'll be able to work effectively in a global marketplace. The good news is that more and more countries have women in the work force, and like women in the United States, a few of them are beginning to advance in the corporate world, particularly in Western countries. This trend can only help American women find greater acceptance among their global contacts. The bad news is that the vast differences between the United States and other cultures can create communication problems if you're not well informed about your contact's culture. That's also true for men. (Chapter 8 looks at family ties and the role of women in other cultures.)

Potential Problems for Women.   An American businesswoman must craft her international letters with great care, paying particular attention to tone and word choice. If you think there's a double standard in the United States, wait until you find out what's waiting for you in some other countries. One of the first things you'll discover is that you usually have to make an exceptionally good impression to be taken seriously. Normal business etiquette often has two faces: Ordinary remarks intended to flatter a foreign reader, for example, have to be carefully worded to avoid being misinterpreted as flirtatious. Thus compliments should sound as though they come from your company or others rather than from you alone: "*We* admire . . ." "*Our department* enjoyed . . ." "*Mr. Watts and I* were impressed with . . ." Also, you can assume that in most countries men will respond unfavorably to a woman who appears to be what they consider too bold or pushy. Firm and direct words, such as *expect* or *require,* may sound too forceful in certain contexts: Comments such as "I will *expect* your reply by April 1" should be softened in most cases: "We *would appreciate* receiving your reply by April 1."

Although you may be ready for the big problems, don't overlook the little things. Even small details such as titles can be potential troublemakers. I once exchanged letters with a business contact in England, where you wouldn't expect significant cultural or language problems. But in the typed signature line of my first letter I failed to put in parentheses the title by which I wanted to be addressed. In the United States, women who want to be addressed as *Ms.* don't include the title in the signature line (only *Mrs.* if they prefer that). Big mistake. I caused my contact a lot of distress. Finally, he wrote that he had agonized over the matter and had decided not to use any title for me because he didn't want to risk offending me by choosing the wrong one. Thanks to that goof, I now remember to put *Ms.* in parentheses before my typed signature line in all of my international letters. It's obvious that many of these little things that we take for granted can create big headaches for our international contacts.

WHICH LANGUAGE TO USE—THEIRS OR OURS?

You have three choices: Use English, the accepted language of communication in the international business community; use French, which is also widely accepted worldwide; or use the language of the person you are contacting in the other country. Although it might be a nice gesture to have your letter translated into the other party's language, be certain that you have a skilled translator if you select this option.

Do You Need a Translator?

Whether or not you need a translator depends on the country you are dealing with. If businesses there do not have access to translators, you will have to send your letters in the language your contact uses. But even if you may send your messages in English, will your contact reply in English too? If not, do you know the other person's language well enough to handle any translation matters yourself?

If you decide you do need a translator, proceed with caution and be very fussy about the candidate's credentials. Choosing an inexperienced translator can be disastrous. You don't want an intended compliment to turn into an insult or a confusing curiosity because the translator isn't as expert as his or her brochure claims. Even an experienced translator can cause similar problems through a careless slip of the pen.

Consider the following apparently simple task of translating into Spanish the sentence "I intend to delve into your proposal today." In Spanish to *delve* is *cavar.* But *cavar* also means "to dig up" or "to paw." Although even an inexperienced translator wouldn't create an international incident by using that verb, your foreign contact might wonder why you wanted to paw at or unearth his proposal. Sometimes it's not a question of word choice but one of emphasis or intent. "I'd like to think about it" is often a way of stalling or politely saying no in domestic correspondence. But a translator who doesn't know that may give your foreign contact the impression that you're favorably inclined and just need a day or so to put together your reply.

Be prepared to educate your translator in advance. Tell him or her not only why you're sending the message and what you want it to accomplish but also what impression you want the reader to receive. Describe the reader to the translator and mention any possible language confusion or other problems that the reader might experience. Most blunders come from misunderstandings or unintentionally mistranslated comments. Remember when former president Jimmy Carter's interpreter in Poland announced that the president was pleased to be there grasping their secret parts? If a president's interpreter could make such a blunder, it's reasonable to assume that your translator could do as much damage.

It doesn't take much imagination to see that if you don't use precisely the right word in precisely the right context, you could unwittingly make some bizarre, embarrassing, or misleading statements. At best, you could sound like a fool; at worst, you could kill a pending deal. So if your foreign contact either knows English or is apt to have access to translation services, it might be safer to stick with English, at least in the beginning.

If you must use a translator, keep in mind that the language in other countries changes from time to time, just as it does in the United States. Regional differences are also important. Your translator, therefore, should be completely up to date on contemporary usage and, if possible, familiar with the particular part of the country you're contacting.

Always review your translator's work. Although languages differ in capitalization of nouns and adjectives, you know that personal and company names should be capitalized. Since you'll be more familiar with names, statistics, and other specific matters than your translator is, examine such facts carefully. Check whether accents not available on your typewriter or computer software have been handwritten in. Finally, if your letter or enclosures are especially sensitive, have them back-translated; that is, have a different translator put the letter back into English to see if it has remained true to your original. The added cost of double translation may be a small price to pay for discovering a crucial error.

Where to Find a Translator

Businesses that handle a lot of international correspondence often employ their own translators. If the country you deal with has minimal (or no) translation services available and does not accept English, you may have to send your messages in the language of that country or, possibly, in French, which is frequently accepted where English is not. Even if you send many or all of your messages in English, you still may have to translate the incoming messages written in another language.

If your firm doesn't have a staff translator for the language you need, look for translation services in the yellow pages of your telephone directory. Or contact the American Translators Association in Ossining, New York, for suggestions. Better yet, contact other companies that do business in foreign lands and ask where they found their translators and if they're satisfied. In all cases, ask candidates for references and check them out.

Eventually, computerized language translation systems will provide an electronic alternative to human translation services. The vocabulary of early models, however, has been too limited and the cost of the systems too high for practical use.

If you're traveling, you may be able to locate reliable translators in some countries through your travel agent, through major hotels where you stay, through U.S. consulates or embassies, or through the firms you plan to visit. Since some countries do not have interpreters or translators, it's important to determine what's available before you leave the

United States. Even if such services do exist in another country, you may not want to use them. If you tend to be suspicious or at least cautious, as you should be, you may prefer to find a translator at home who can accompany you on your trip. That way you'll be more confident that the translator's loyalties are clearly with you and your firm.

BUSINESS CUSTOMS AND PRACTICES

Know Your Reader

The ageless admonition to know your audience has especially significant implications in international correspondence, far more so than in domestic situations, where it doesn't take much effort to understand the needs, interests, and customs of your contacts. Just as you can usually assume that your contacts in the United States share your general business customs and practices, you can assume that those customs and practices are not the same in other countries.

You already know the U.S. national holidays by heart, so you are automatically aware when business offices are likely to be closed. You know the predominant stylistic trends, such as the almost exclusive use of the title *Ms.* for women in business. You know how the U.S. government operates, and you're probably familiar with most of the major domestic trade regulations in your industry. You no doubt meet other businesspeople through referrals, at conferences, and over dinner or at lunch. So before you even write to your contacts, you may be backslapping and calling them Jane and Jim. That's all fine in the United States, but it would earn you a black mark under the rules of etiquette in most other countries.

How much do you really need to know about your contact's country? "Everything" would be nice. It's surprisingly easy to make dreadful mistakes. In spite of all the trade between the United States and the Far East, for example, Americans fail to study even common Asian customs and business practices. Consider one of the most popular words in the English language—*you*. In the United States we try to personalize our writing by taking the "you approach." Authors of domestic letter-writing books, in fact, enthusiastically promote this approach. But in certain other countries, such as Japan, people don't like this personal touch. They believe that writers should refer to their company: "Would *your company* be interested in this plan?" Not: "Would *you* be interested in this plan?"

Where to Find Information

Before you write a single word to someone in another country, find a book on that country or region. Read it thoroughly and then reread it, looking for hints about the country's customs and business practices. Some books profile all of the major countries of the world. *The World Factbook, The Statesman's Year-Book,* and the *World Travel Guide,* for example, contain a variety of information on every country in the world, and each is updated annually. Popular world almanacs, such as *The Universal Almanac,* also profile the nations of the world. Specific information on social and business matters, such as attitudes, greetings, and the use of names, is often provided in books discussing a particular country or region (check the index and table of contents in a book before you buy it). For information that will help you improve the quality of your international correspondence, look for books that cover business protocol, customs, and manners.

Don't limit yourself to books, however. The Department of State's *Background Notes,* which resembles a newsletter, provides profiles of individual countries that cover everything from geography to communications to relations with the United States. Brigham Young University's *Culturgram* series, also resembling a small newsletter, lists greetings, attitudes, business hours, language, and other information about each country. A much larger newsletter-style publication is the Department of Commerce's *Overseas Business Reports,* which provides marketing and investment information on various countries.

Chapters 8 and 9 of this book contain important information about cultural and business practices around the world, including religious customs, which have a very strong impact on business practices in many parts of the world. The country profiles in Chapter 9 include the major religions and languages, the principal holidays, and the common business hours in each country. Chapter 9 also includes a list of the proper nationality and ethnic designations around the world and the currency used in each country.

The Appendix provides information on postal and private mail as well as time differences to observe in fax transmissions. It also lists books and other sources of information that will help you expand your knowledge of the various countries.

2

The Fine Art of Message Design

HERE'S SOME GOOD NEWS: The format you use for international correspondence should be the same as the format you use for domestic correspondence. This suggestion assumes that your regular format meets the basic criteria of a standard business letter. "Anything goes" won't do. A businessperson in Virginia once wrote to me that "around here, all the letters I see look like hell!" He was right. From the samples he enclosed, I could immediately see that the margins were too small, the position of certain elements was wrong, and the spacing between some of the elements was incorrect. Unfortunately, those samples reminded me of many letters I have received.

HOW TO FORMAT
AN INTERNATIONAL MESSAGE

Importance of Format

The format of a message is almost as important as the text, because it gives readers their first impression of you and your company. If your format violates accepted letter-writing standards in the business world, it makes you appear unprofessional and uninformed or out of touch with contemporary practices. Who wants to start a relationship with a bad first impression?

The format of an international message is especially important because you want to do everything possible to ensure that your message is clear. An overcrowded, messy letter will make it harder for the recipient or the translator to wade through the text. To make this task easier, give the format a clean, neat, open appearance.

Common Formats

International messages sent by postal mail or fax are usually prepared in one of the standard business-letter formats described in this chapter. Other fast messages, such as telexes, should be sent in a condensed format appropriate for the particular method. E-mail, for example, is usually prepared in a memo format with a heading of guide words (*To, From, Subject,* and so on) instead of a letter-style inside address and salutation. For setup and transmission procedures, follow the requirements and instructions of your company's system or subscriber service.

Three common letter formats in international correspondence are the full-block, block, and modified-block formats (see the illustrations in this chapter). In the full-block format, all elements begin flush left. In the block format, the date, reference line, complimentary close, and signature line begin slightly to the right of the center of the page. The modified-block format is the same as the block format except that the paragraphs are indented, usually one-half to one inch.

Once you've selected a suitable format for your company, put the specifications in your word processing program so that you can standardize your correspondence style. Your letters will look better, and using a recorded format will save your word processing operators time and effort.

Business Stationery. Everything you can gain with an attractive format may be lost if your stationery lacks permanence and dignity. Although to control costs your firm may prefer airmail-weight paper for international correspondence, a letter shouldn't fall apart in the reader's hands at the destination.

The so-called dignity that stationery conveys by the paper and letterhead design you use is largely a subjective consideration. Generally, companies choose a style that is representative of their product or service and fits the image they want to project, whether modern or traditional. Specifically, a company that deals with an international audience needs to know whether that audience is more conservative and traditionally oriented than the firm's domestic contacts. If so, the foreign audience would be likely to favor a white, off-white, or other light-colored paper and a conservative letterhead design with a clean, readable typeface. However, if a company cannot choose to have one design for domestic use and another for international use, both markets must be considered in selecting paper and letterhead design.

INTERNATIONAL SUIT DISTRIBUTORS
100 KENNEDY CIRCLE
CAMDEN, NJ 08103
U.S.A.

phone 609-555-0101 / fax 609-555-0102

May 1, 1994

Your reference 00012

Mr. Li Hao Chung, President
Taipei Suit Company Ltd.
2121 Fu Hsing Road, 6th Floor
Taipei 11549, Taiwan

Dear Mr. Li:

Thank you for your kind invitation to visit the
Taipei Suit Company June 6 and 7, 1994.

Mr. Roier and I are pleased to accept your
invitation to learn more about your company's
products. Taipei apparel is admired both in the
offices of International Suit Distributors and
throughout the United States.

We look forward to meeting you on June 6 and will
send you details about our arrival when our travel
arrangements are complete.

Sincerely yours,

(Ms.) Deanne Sidwell
General Manager

jr

Full-Block Letter Format

INTERNATIONAL SUIT DISTRIBUTORS
100 KENNEDY CIRCLE
CAMDEN, NJ 08103
U.S.A.

phone 609-555-0101 / fax 609-555-0102

May 1, 1994

Your reference 00012

Mr. Li Hao Chung, President
Taipei Suit Company Ltd.
2121 Fu Hsing Road, 6th Floor
Taipei 11549, Taiwan

Dear Mr. Li:

Thank you for your kind invitation to visit the
Taipei Suit Company June 6 and 7, 1994.

Mr. Roier and I are pleased to accept your
invitation to learn more about your company's
products. Taipei apparel is admired both in the
offices of International Suit Distributors and
throughout the United States.

We look forward to meeting you on June 6 and will
send you details about our arrival when our travel
arrangements are complete.

Sincerely yours,

(Ms.) Deanne Sidwell
General Manager

jr

Block Letter Format

INTERNATIONAL SUIT DISTRIBUTORS
100 KENNEDY CIRCLE
CAMDEN, NJ 08103
U.S.A.

phone 609-555-0101 / fax 609-555-0102

May 1, 1994

Your reference 00012

Mr. Li Hao Chung, President
Taipei Suit Company Ltd.
2121 Fu Hsing Road, 6th Floor
Taipei 11549, Taiwan

Dear Mr. Li:

Thank you for your kind invitation to visit the Taipei Suit Company June 6 and 7, 1994.

Mr. Roier and I are pleased to accept your invitation to learn more about your company's products. Taipei apparel is admired both in the offices of International Suit Distributors and throughout the United States.

We look forward to meeting you on June 6 and will send you details about our arrival when our travel arrangements are complete.

Sincerely yours,

(Ms.) Deanne Sidwell
General Manager

jr

Modified-Block Letter Format

The letterhead for both foreign and domestic use should include the official company name and complete mailing address, as well as telephone, fax, or other numbers. (If your letterhead does not have the fax number printed on it, type it below the printed telephone number.)

Regardless of the design, standard business stationery should measure 8½ inches wide by 11 inches long and be folded in thirds to fit a standard business envelope of the same stock. The format you use for the message (margins, layout of elements, and so on) must be appropriate for these dimensions.

Business Cards.   Business cards have their own special requirements for an international audience, and members of your firm may use different cards for different countries. Have your international cards printed on the reverse side in the language of the country with which you deal—always in type of equal quality to that on the English side. People in many countries place great emphasis on the exchange of business cards, so it's important to pay special attention not only to what a card says but to how it looks.

Include your name, your company's name, your position (job title), your company's address, and your telephone, fax, and other fast-message numbers. Don't use abbreviations, such as *St.* (Street) or *E.* (East) on cards going to people in other countries. Examine samples at printing establishments and office supply stores, and notice the different layouts for different executive levels. The name of an officer or very high-level executive, for example, is often centered and more prominent than the company name. The opposite is true for a lower-level executive. Just as contacts in countries with traditional customs may respond more favorably to a conservative letterhead design, they also may respond more favorably to a conservative business-card design.

Principal Letter Elements

A standard business letter may have as many as fifteen parts, and the way that you style and position these elements on your stationery will influence the overall effectiveness of the format. In the order they are used or positioned on a page, the key elements are the date, reference line, confidential notation, inside address, attention line, salutation, body, complimentary close, signature line, identification line, enclosure notation, mail notation, copy notation, and postscript. However, not all of the above elements are used as much in international correspondence as they are in domestic correspondence. Attention lines, confidential notations, and postscripts, for example, are not familiar to many foreign readers, and you should avoid them unless you know that your contact will not be puzzled or confused by them.

Date.   Place the date flush left in the full-block format and slightly right of the page center in the block and modified-block formats, two to four line spaces below your letterhead. To avoid confusion, always spell out the month. In some countries, 5/3/94 means March 5, 1994; in the United States, it means May 3, 1994.

December 1, 19—

Reference Line.   Place the reference line two line spaces below the date, aligned on the left under the date. If the letterhead has a printed line, such as "In reply refer to," insert your reference after that printed line (which may be printed *above* the date). Place your own reference above any reference of your contact. Always spell out *reference* (not *ref.*) in international correspondence.

Contact's reference only:	December 1, 19—
	Your reference IC-3456
With printed line:	*When replying, refer to:* IC-3456
	December 1, 19—
Two references:	December 1, 19—
	Our reference AB-78910 Your reference IC-3456

Confidential Notation.   Although not common in international correspondence, a confidential notation is used if you don't want anyone but the addressee to open the letter. Place it flush left in all formats, either (a) about four line spaces above the inside address or (b) about two line spaces below the reference line. Use all capital letters or an initial capital and underlining.

CONFIDENTIAL

Confidential

Inside Address.   Place the inside address flush left in all formats. Depending on the size of the letter, it may be two to twelve line spaces below the date or reference line. Address the person with the appropriate personal or professional title (*Mr., Mrs., Miss, Dr.*) for the particular country. Some countries use quite different titles from those used in the United States, and the last section in this chapter describes such variations in address forms. Write the person's name exactly as he or she writes it. Place a long job title on a separate line. Include the country on the same line as the city or on a separate line in all capitals, as on the envelope.

Mr. Hondeval Premadasa
Director of Foreign Trade
Colombo Plan Bureau
12 Melbourne Avenue
Colombo 4-169, Sri Lanka

Mr. Hondeval Premadasa
Director of Foreign Trade
Colombo Plan Bureau
12 Melbourne Avenue
Colombo 4-169
SRI LANKA

Attention Line. An attention line, used infrequently in international correspondence, is meant to ensure that a letter addressed to a company is directed to a specific person. You should also use it when you want a letter addressed to one person to be opened by another person if the addressee is absent. (Notice the suggestion in the last section of this chapter about using an attention line to get faster responses.) Place the attention line flush left in all formats, with one line space before and after it. Add a title or department if your contact works in a large company.

Attention Beatrix Van Zant, Office of the President

Attention Oji Oduber, General Manager

Salutation. Place the salutation flush left in all formats, two line spaces below the inside address or attention line. When the letter is addressed to a person, use the opening *Dear* followed by the person's name (by title when the name and gender are unknown). If you have any doubts about the proper use of a person's name, it's better to ask what is correct than to risk repeated misuse. In some countries, the last-stated name is actually the person's first name. In Japan, Toshiki Yoshikawa would be addressed as Mr. Toshiki. But Jerry Chan, whose first name is Western, would be addressed as Mr. Chan. In a few countries, titles such as *Engineer* and *Architect* are used, but in most countries the principal titles are *Mr., Mrs.,* and *Miss* or the scholastic title *Dr.* The title *Ms.* is not common in other countries. For women, use *Dr.* if appropriate or otherwise *Mrs.* or *Miss* (or the foreign equivalent, such as *Gospozha* for *Mrs.*

or *Gospozhitsa* for *Miss* in Bulgaria and Russia). For more about titles and names, read the forms-of-address guidelines at the end of this chapter.

To individuals:	Dear Mr. Andreotti:
	Dear Mrs. Krzysztof:
	Dear Mr. Andreotti and Mrs.
	Krzysztof:
	Dear Dr. Mswati:
	Dear Dr. Mswati and Mr. Andreotti:
	Dear Messrs. Mswati and Andreotti:
	Dear Mesdames Krzysztof and Prinna:
	Dear Sir: (*man—name unknown*)
	Dear Madam: (*woman—name unknown*)
To companies:	Ladies and Gentlemen: (*firm—*
	men and women)
	Ladies: (*firm—women only*)
	Mesdames: (*firm—women only*)
	Gentlemen: (*firm—men only*)

Subject Line.   A subject line can be helpful when appropriate, although it is uncommon in some countries. Place the subject flush left or indented, depending on the paragraph style, two line spaces below the salutation. The word *Subject,* which may be all capitals or initial capital only, is followed by a colon. Underlining may be used if desired.

HIGH-VELOCITY WELDER

High-Velocity Welder

SUBJECT: HIGH-VELOCITY WELDER

SUBJECT: High-Velocity Welder

High-Velocity Welder

Body.   Begin your message two line spaces below the salutation or the subject line. Single-space the text and leave one line space between paragraphs. Use margins from one and one-quarter to two inches, depending on the size of the letter. Indent paragraphs in the modified-block format. Use short paragraphs, numbered lists, indented (blocked) examples, tables, or anything else that will simplify the textual information for a foreign reader (more about this in Chapter 6). If the letter is too long for one page, put at least two lines of the body on the second page.

Complimentary Close.   Place the closing two line spaces below the body, flush left in the full-block format and slightly right of the page center in the other formats. Capitalize the first word and place a comma after the last word. Avoid the familiar closings used in domestic letters, such as *Cordially* and *Warmest regards.* Some foreign readers would be offended by such familiarity.

Sincerely,

Sincerely yours,

Very sincerely yours,

Respectfully, (*very formal*)

Respectfully yours, (*very formal*)

Signature Line.   Place the typed signature line four to five line spaces below and aligned at the left with the complimentary close. Place a short title after your name and a long title on the line below it. Type your name precisely as you sign it, for example J. B. Parks or Jonathan B. Parks. Do not precede a man's name with the title *Mr.,* but do put *Ms.* or *Mrs.* in parentheses before a woman's name. The title *Ms.* is not used in the signature line in domestic correspondence, but since many countries do not know this form, it is helpful to include it for foreign readers, who might otherwise not know how to address you. Academic degrees should follow the name.

Eldon B. McKay
Senior Trade Representative

(Ms.) Arlene Dixon, President

(Mrs.) Dana Whittley
Vice President, New Product Development

Paul C. Devanti, Sc.D.
Director, Sales and Marketing

Identification Line.   Place the identification line flush left in all formats, two line spaces below the typed signature line. Follow the policy of your firm if this line is omitted on the original and used only on file copies. If the person dictating the letter, the one signing it, and the one typing it are all different, use three sets of initials in that order. The writer's initials, however, are not necessary if his or her name appears on the signature line. Place a colon between each set of initials.

ADM:wc

ADM:FB:wc

wc

Enclosure Notation.   Place the enclosure notation flush left in all formats, one or two line spaces below the identification line. In non–English-speaking countries it is helpful to the reader if *enclosure* is spelled out, since the abbreviation *enc.* may not be familiar in that country.

Enclosure

Enc.

Encs.

Enclosures: 3

Enclosures: Map
            Annual Report

Mail Notation.   Place the mail notation flush left in all formats, one or two line spaces below the enclosure notation.

Registered

By Express Mail International Service

Copy Notation.   Place the copy notation flush left in all formats, one or two line spaces below the mail notation. In non–English-speaking countries it is helpful to the reader if you spell out *copy* rather than use an abbreviation, such as *c*, which may not be used in that country.

Copy: Henck Kraag

Copies: Henck Kraag
             Johan Aaron

c: Henck Kraag

Postscript.   Place the postscript flush left or indented, depending on the paragraph style, two line spaces below the last notation. Use a postscript only to state something unrelated to the body of the letter, not to add something that you forgot to include in the body. Generally, postscripts should be avoided in correspondence to non–English-speaking countries. Readers there may not know what the abbreviation *P.S.* means.

P.S. I'll send details on January 7 about our proposed meeting. MMK

Continuation-Page Heading.   When a letter runs over to an additional page, place the continuation-page heading three to four line spaces after any printed continuation-page company name and address. Otherwise, use a blank sheet that matches the letterhead paper and begin four to six line spaces from the top. Do not use the word *continued* on this page or the first page. Write the addressee's name, the date, and the page number stacked, in a single line flush left, or centered across the page. The person's title may be used or omitted.

Gen. Yang Peng
March 6, 19—
page two

Gen. Yang Peng, March 6, 19—, page two

Gen. Yang Peng   March 6, 19—   page 2

Envelope.   The words *PAR AVION* (or Label 19, Airmail *PAR AVION*) must appear on the front and back of a postal envelope being sent airmail. On the address side, place the words to the left of the address block. Place the country name in all capitals on the last line of the address block. Refer to the material on international mail in the Appendix for more about addressing envelopes, and check a current edition of the *International Mail Manual* for additional regulations and addressing requirements.

Mr. Dennis F. Stowe
Royal Industries Ltd.
52 Grosvenor Gardens
London SW1W OYA
ENGLAND

FORMS OF ADDRESS

This is going to be one of those there's-no-easy-answer topics. When you're dealing with nearly two hundred countries, each with its own set of rules, a single, general answer would be useless. The situation is even more complicated if you consider regional, ethnic, religious, and language differences within each country.

If you're looking for reference material, you'll find lots of published information on other countries and regions but not nearly enough on the correct forms of address in each country. You can, however, pursue the usual government channels, such as consulates and embassies, check with language schools and translation services, and generally consult books and other literature dealing exclusively with the countries that concern you. Select sources that discuss matters of protocol, such as the proper use of names and titles.

Correct Forms for Titles and Names

What should you look for? You'll need to know what personal or professional titles to use in the inside address and salutation and how to state a person's name correctly. Most people in other countries object to too much familiarity, so you should never address someone by his or her first name unless asked to do so. Also, keep in mind that in some countries the style of names is very different from that in the United States.

Although not all Western nations use precisely the same forms-of-address style as that used in the United States, the following rules apply in countries such as Canada that are very similar:

> *Titles:* Address a person by the scholastic title of *Dr.* if the person has a doctorate: *Dr. Benjamin O'Donnell, Dear Dr. O'Donnell.* Otherwise, use the personal title *Mr.* for a man and *Mrs.* or *Miss* for a woman (*Ms.* is rarely used in other countries). If *Esq. (Esquire)* is used as a courtesy title after the name of a prominent professional man or woman, no title precedes the name: *Benjamin O'Donnell, Esq.* Most common in England, where it is used only for men, *Esq.* is seldom used in the United States or in other countries.

> *Names:* Address a person by his or her last name, which is the last-stated name in American- or English-style usage: *Mrs. Carol Dennison, Dear Mrs. Dennison.*

If you apply these rules in the wrong country, however, you'll be doing a lot to further the view that Americans are lazy and insensitive.

People who do a lot of business in other countries complain about how slowly things move. Not only does a foreign company often take a long time to translate a letter written in English into its own language, it may also take a long time to answer some letters because the foreign contact is away on business or vacation for long periods. If you're experiencing delays in getting a response, you may want to address your letter generally to the firm (use *Ladies and Gentlemen* for the salutation) and put the name of your contact in an attention line. Or you may prefer to address the letter to your contact as usual but address the envelope only to the firm. With either practice, your letter is more likely to be opened, read, and acted on when your contact is absent.

Variations in Address Forms

Here are some examples of the wide variation in address forms from one country to another. Abbreviations of titles are given in English, but keep in mind that the foreign version will differ in some cases: *Engineer,* for example, is abbreviated *Eng.* in English but is *Ing.* in certain other languages, such as Italian, German, and Spanish.

Asia and the Far East.　Watch for numerous differences from American-style forms of address, particularly in the order of stating first (given) names and last names (surnames).

> In some countries, such as China, Japan, Taiwan, and Vietnam, the family name is often stated first. *Mr. Yasushi Mieno, Dear Mr. Yasushi.* Sometimes the person has an English first name preceding the family name and the traditional first name: *Miss Jenny Zhang Wa, Dear Miss Zhang.* To add to the confusion, some people are changing the order of their given name and surname to conform to Western style: *Mr. Mieno Yasushi, Dear Mr. Yasushi.* If you can't determine which is the given name and which is the surname, ask. Within the country, a suffix may be attached to the last name. Instead of using the title *Mr.,* for example, the Japanese themselves attach the suffix *san* to the family name: *Yasushi-san.*

> In Thailand, the Thais use the form *Khun* before the first name: *Nitya Jotikasthira, Khun Jotikasthira.* Westerners may use *Mr., Miss,* or *Mrs.* before either the given name or the surname: *Nitya Jotikasthira, Dear Mr. Nitya* (surname) or *Dear Mr. Jotikasthira* (given name).

Europe.　Although many countries in Europe use the same forms of address as those used in the United States, variations occur even among Western nations.

> In Great Britain, given names are commonly used without a title, as they are in the United States, soon after initial contact: *Mr. Robert Kingsley, Dear Robert* or *Bob.* To avoid offending anyone, however, it is always pru-

dent to wait until you are asked to use a first name. Unlike in the United States, in Great Britain, surgeons and dentists are addressed with a personal title: *Mr., Miss,* or *Mrs.* rather than the scholastic title *Dr.: Mrs. Margaret Andrews, Dear Mrs. Andrews.* Academic doctors are very often addressed as *Dr.* professionally but not socially.

In Spain, the surname consists of the father's family name followed by the mother's family name: *Mr. Juan Antonio Yáñez-Barnuevo.* (Portugal uses the same system, but the mother's family name comes first.) Both names are used in correspondence (only the father's family name in conversation): *Dear Mr. Yáñez-Barnuevo.*

In the Netherlands, professional titles, such as *Director (Bestuurder),* are commonly used with the last name: *Dir. Beatrix Van Zant, Dear Dir. Van Zant.* A personal title is used for a medical doctor: *Mr. (Mijnheer), Miss (Juffrouw),* or *Mrs. (Mevrouw): Mr. Johann De Reus, Dear Mr. De Reus.*

In Germany, single women under age twenty are addressed as *Miss (Fräulein);* those over twenty, as *Mrs. (Frau).* The Germans themselves often address a person in upper management by a position title without a name: *Herr Direktor.* Other professional people also use this form, for example, *Herr Doktor* and *Frau Ingenieur.*

In Italy, professional titles, such as *Architect* (m.: *Architetto,* f.: *Architettura)* and *Lawyer* (m.: *Avvocato,* f.: *Avvocatessa)* are commonly used with the surname: *Arch. Sophia Andreotti, Dear Arch. Andreotti.* The scholastic title *Dr.* (m.: *Dottore,* f.: *Dottoressa)* is used for anyone else with a B.A. degree or higher: *Dr. Luigi Penelli, Dear Dr. Penelli.*

In Russia, the personal titles of *Mr. (Gospodin), Miss (Gospozhitsa),* and *Mrs. (Gospozha),* not used under Communist rule, are now acceptable. Russian names often consist of a given name, a middle patronymic name, and a last name: *Mr. Boris Lukin Vernadsky, Dear Mr. Vernadsky.*

Africa and the Middle East. This is one part of the world where first names are commonplace—but not always out of informality.

In the Arab world, for example, many of the countries use the given name preceded by a title for practical reasons. The full name is lengthy, consisting of the given name, the father's name, the paternal grandfather's name, and, in certain countries, the family name. The prefixes *ibn* (son of) and *bint* (daughter of) sometimes precede an ancestral name: *Mr. Nassib ibn Haidalla, Dear Mr. Nassib.* In northern Africa, *ben* or *ould* (son of) and *bon* (father of) may be used. *Sheikh* is a title of respect for an influential or elderly man.

In Israel, unlike most of the other countries in this region, given names used without a title are common, as they are in the United States, soon after initial contact: *Mr. Yoram Biran, Dear Yoram.*

In Lebanon, titles in Arabic are used with the given name: *Duktoar Mahmoud Hammoud, Dear Duktoar Mahmoud.* Titles in English may be used with the surname: *Dr. Mahmoud Hammoud, Dear Dr. Hammoud.*

Latin America.   Most of the countries in this region use professional titles such as *Architect* and *Engineer* as well as the scholastic title *Dr.* But differences exist between the individual countries.

In some countries, such as Mexico and Bolivia, *Miss (Señorita)* is used for a woman unless it is known that the woman is married, when the title *Mrs. (Señora)* is required: *Miss J. A. Montaño, Dear Miss Montaño.*

In some countries, such as Mexico, Paraguay, Guatemala, and Panama, the title *Licenciado* is used for anyone with a B.A. degree or higher: *Lic. Francisco Lopez, Dear Lic. Lopez.*

In Colombia, *Dr.* (m.: *Doctor,* f.: *Doctora*) is used for anyone with a B.A. degree or higher: *Dr. Fernando Cepeda, Dear Dr. Cepeda.*

In Uruguay, *Dr.* (m.: *Doctor,* f.: *Doctora*) is used for anyone with a B.A. degree or higher except for an engineer (*Ingeniero*) or professor (m.: *Profesor,* f.: *Profesora*): *Ing. Ramiro Romeo, Dear Ing. Romeo.*

In Ecuador, Venezuela, and Costa Rica, *Dr.* (m.: *Doctor,* f.: *Doctora*) is used for an M.D. and a Ph.D.: *Dr. José Lasso, Dear Dr. Lasso.*

In Bolivia, Paraguay, Panama, Guatemala, and Belize, *Dr.* (m.: *Doctor,* f.: *Doctora*) is used for an M.D., a Ph.D., and a lawyer: *Dr. Jorge Velasco, Dear Dr. Velasco.*

In Brazil, titles are used with given names for a doctor (*Doutor*), professor (m.: *Professor,* f.: *Professora*), and priest (*Padre*): *Professor Paulo de Lima, Dear Professor Paulo.* Titles such as *Mr.* (*Senhor*), *Miss* (*Menina*), and *Mrs.* (*Senhora*) are used with family names: *Mr. Ronaldo Largas, Dear Mr. Largas.*

These few examples should give you an inkling of the complexity surrounding forms of address in other countries. Providing complete details for all the countries would require a book in itself. However overwhelming the information may seem, there is no way to brush it aside. People everywhere, including Americans, expect others to use their names and titles correctly. Most of the cultures of the world, in fact, place very strong emphasis on business protocol, and ignorance or carelessness in this area is usually taken as a sign of lack of respect. An exporter once told me that just as insensitivity will get you nowhere, sensitivity will get you everywhere.

3

Write It with Style

STYLE IS ONE of those big umbrella terms. To some writers it covers just about everything, including format and the stationery on which your letters are typed or printed out. In particular, it refers to the distinctive way you treat the words and phrases in your letters, such as how you capitalize, spell, and punctuate them.

Your company may have prepared its own style guide, or it may have adopted the style provided in a recognized style book, such as the *Chicago Manual of Style, Prentice Hall Style Manual,* or *Gregg Reference Manual.* Or your firm may use a more specialized guide, such as the American Institute of Physics' *Style Manual,* the Council of Biology Editors' *CBE Style Manual,* or the American Mathematics Society's *Mathematics into Type.*

AN EFFECTIVE WRITING STYLE

Everyone hates rules, but no one has ever found a way to develop an effective writing style without them. But I know the feeling. My stress level rises whenever I work with software documentation, because every time I get a new program, I dread having to memorize the new instructions. So I don't. I page through the book once, but I study and memorize only the rules that apply to the document I'm preparing at the moment. Eventually, as I prepare more and more documents, I learn all the rules, but it's less painful if I don't overwhelm myself trying to learn all of them at once.

To ease the pain here, let's start with an easy general rule about writing style: You should use an American capitalization, spelling, and punctuation style when writing to a foreign contact in English. If you're quoting from a foreign document, however, keep the style of that document. Also, follow the style your foreign contact uses in writing his or her personal name, company name, and company address.

The capitalization, punctuation, and spelling style that you use isn't as important as the consistency with which you use it. A foreign reader who knows English only as a second or third language may have enough trouble translating your message without wondering why you wrote *macroeconomics* closed in the first paragraph and hyphenated (*macroeconomics*) in the second paragraph. Although consistency is also necessary to avoid appearing careless and unprofessional to a domestic audience, it is *mandatory* to avoid creating confusion and misunderstanding when writing for a foreign audience.

Capitalization

If you don't have a company style guide or a specialized professional style book, you can apply the guidelines in this chapter to comments in the body, or text, of your letters. For detailed information about modern capitalization style, however, you'll find that a good style book is indispensable.

In matters of style, it often seems that for every rule there's an exception. Most software languages, for example, are written in all capitals (*BASIC*), but a few have only an initial capital (*Pascal*). This matter of exceptions to the rules is an annoying fact of letter-writing style that doesn't discriminate—we all have to put up with it.

People.   Capitalize the names of real and fictional people. Lowercase articles and prepositions according to the preferred style of the individual or the style common in a particular country. (Study letters you receive from contacts in each country as well as style books and any other published material you can collect.)

> E. I. du Pont de Nemours
> Friedrich von Steuben
> Abdel-Aziz ibn Saud (son of Saud)
> Uncle Sam
> Harold "Kip" Kingsley
> Pope John Paul III; the pope; the papacy

Titles.   Capitalize personal titles, academic titles, titles of high officials, titles of nobility, religious titles, titles in the judiciary, and military titles when they precede a name. Use a small (lowercase) letter when they follow a name or are used alone. Always lowercase ordinary job titles. Although the use of the abbreviation *Esq. (Esquire)* is fading, it may still be used after a man or woman's name in the United States and after a man's name in certain other countries, notably Britain. When it is used, there should be no title before the name.

Mr. Jeremy Webster; Jeremy Webster, Esq.

Professor Abid Singhvi; Abid Singhvi, professor of business administration; the professor

Secretary of State Warren Christopher; Mr. Secretary; Warren Christopher, secretary of state; the secretary of state

the Reverend Martin Kerruish; Rev. Martin Kerruish; Martin Kerruish, minister of the United Lutheran Church; the minister

Judge W. O. Kilmer; W. O. Kilmer, the judge; the judge

General Nathan Addington; General Addington; Nathan Addington, the general (*Note:* The U.S. titles *General of the Army* and *Fleet Admiral* are capitalized both before and after a name or when used alone.)

Elizabeth II, queen of England; Her Majesty, Queen Elizabeth; Her Majesty; the queen

Ona Apuuli, CPA; accountant Ona Apuuli; the accountant

Organizations, Groups, and Structures.   Capitalize the important words in the official name of an organization, group, or structure. Lowercase general references.

Axell and Midland Exporters, Inc.; the export company

North Atlantic Treaty Organization (NATO); the organization

Allied forces; the Allies

Red Army; the Russian army

United States Navy; the navy

United States Marine Corps; the Marine Corps; the marines

Royal Air Force; the British air force

Sisters of Mercy; the order; the sisters

Roman Catholic church; the church

St. Luke's Episcopal Church; the church

Champs-Elysées

the Capitol (U.S.); Capitol Hill

Geography.   Capitalize important words in the names of particular places. Lowercase adjectives and general locations.

Northern Hemisphere; one of two hemispheres

the West; Western world; western United States; west of the Mississippi

Northern Ireland; northern Africa; northern United States
New York State; state of New York; the state
South Seas
English Channel; the Channel
Niger River; the river
Niger and Benue rivers; the rivers

Derivatives.   Do not capitalize words and terms derived from proper nouns.

India; india ink
Roman; roman type
China; china (dishes)

Government.   Capitalize the important words in the names of governmental or political bodies, countries, and documents. Lowercase general references except in special cases.

Commonwealth of Australia; the commonwealth
British Empire; the empire
U.S. Constitution; the Constitution of the United States; the Constitution
Pennsylvania Constitution; the constitution of Pennsylvania; the constitution
Civil Rights Act of 1964
U.S. Congress; the Congress; congressional
U.N. Security Council; the Security Council; the council
House of Commons; the Commons; the lower house
Japanese Diet (Parliament); the Diet (Parliament); a parliament; parliamentary
Communist party; Communists; the party
Clinton administration; the administration
U.S. Supreme Court; the Supreme Court; the Court
Arizona Supreme Court; the state supreme court; the court

History.   Capitalize the important words in the names of historical and cultural periods (except recent periods), special occasions and events, and wars and battles. Lowercase general references.

Dark Ages
antiquity
Stone Age

nuclear age
Christian Era; the era
Victorian era; the era
Yalta Conference; the conference
cold war (*or* Cold War)
World War I; the Great War; First World War; the war
Korean conflict
Vietnam War, the war
Israeli occupation
invasion of Kuwait

Languages and Nationalities.   Capitalize languages and nationalities.

a Spaniard; the Spanish language
a Russian; Russian culture

Time and Days.   Capitalize proper nouns in time zones. Use
capitals or small capitals for *A.D.* and *B.C.* Lowercase *a.m.* and *p.m.*
Capitalize special days. Lowercase general references to an occasion
such as a general election.

eastern standard time (est)
Pacific standard time (Pst)
Greenwich mean time (Gmt)
a.m.; p.m.
A.D., B.C.; A.D., B.C.
10 o'clock (*or* ten o'clock) in the morning; 10:30 a.m.
spring
summer solstice
Monday
January
Christmas Eve
Passover
Fourth of July; the Fourth; Independence Day
election day
inauguration day

Numbers.   Capitalize numbers in a proper name unless figures
are used. Lowercase general references.

Third Reich
Second World War; World War II; the war
the second battle
twentieth century
Thirteenth Precinct; the precinct
Flight 201; the flight
volume 2 (*or* Volume 2)
paragraph seven
Room 21

Vehicles. Capitalize the names of vehicles, craft, and vessels. Lowercase general references to a type of vehicle. (Italicize the name of a ship but not the initials preceding it.)

HMS *Century;* the *Century;* the ship
Sputnik II; the satellite
Challenger; the space shuttle
the Concorde; the airplane
a Boeing 727; the airplane
ICBM; the missile
Amtrak; the train
Greyhound; the bus

Products and Services. Capitalize the important words in brand names and trademarks. Lowercase general references to a type of product or service. Business correspondence style also lowercases trademarks that are clearly established as common nouns because of widespread use and familiarity.

Kleenex; tissue
Coca-Cola; Coke; cola drink; the soft drink
Levi's; overalls
Bufferin; aspirin
Datatech Systems II; the system; the computer
time-sharing

Headings and Titles. Capitalize the important words in artistic, musical, and literary material. Lowercase general references.

How to Write International Correspondence (book)
Business Week (magazine)

"Short Is Beautiful" (chapter)
Exporting Careers (documentary film)
The World Today (television series)
"The Last Christmas" (television episode)
Cats (play), act 1, scene 3
Nobel Prize; the prize; the award
William Tell Overture
Jenson's *Woman Possessed* (painting)
Mona Lisa (traditional work of art)
Hands Across the Sea (slogan)
Koran; Koranic (sacred book)
Talmud; talmudic (sacred book)
Mass (the eucharistic sacrament)
high mass (an individual service)

Spelling

In international correspondence you always have to assume that your contact may not know English very well, if at all. Also, the skill of the translator used by a foreign company may be less than perfect, and the tools your contact relies on, such as a dictionary and, less likely, an English grammar book, may be old or generally inadequate. Imagine, then, how your contact may have to struggle to translate a word you mis-spell or a typographical error you fail to catch before the letter goes out. Although your domestic contacts would likely assume in such an instance that you're careless or lazy, they at least would probably know what you meant. But what would a foreign contact do?

Don't count on your computer spell checker to solve this problem. I have a relatively powerful spell checker, but it still leaves a lot to be desired. Even if it contained all the words I use or even if I had the time to keep adding new words to its databank, it wouldn't be able to correct a sentence with a word omitted, which could turn the sentence into gib-berish. Nor could it fix a word in which a letter or two are omitted, creat-ing another legitimate, though incorrect, word (*the* instead of *then*).

The rules for spelling are numerous and complex. What's worse, they're riddled with exceptions. Many people would prefer to grab a good dictionary now and then rather than try to learn not only the rules but all of those exceptions. Learning a few guidelines, however, may improve your spelling skills, for which your foreign contacts will no doubt be very grateful.

Names. To form the plural of a name, add *s* or *es* without changing the original spelling of the name.

Teegens, Teegenses
Jreiki, Jreikis

Titles. Use plurals only in formal situations.

Mr., Messrs.	Miss, Misses
Ms., Mss.	Mrs., Mmes.

Possessives. If a singular noun doesn't end with an "s" sound, add an apostrophe and *s*.

company's policy
New York's skyscrapers

If the word ends with an "s" sound and the possessive creates a new syllable, also add an apostrophe and *s*. If it is awkward to pronounce the new syllable, however, just add the apostrophe alone.

boss's letter
for conscience' sake

Add an apostrophe alone to most plural words, except for a few irregular nouns that change the spelling of the entire word; in those cases, add both an apostrophe and an *s*.

children's program
three days' work

Add an apostrophe alone when a word ending is pronounced "eez."

L. B. Surtees' design
Yerkes' law

Use separate apostrophes to show separate possession and a single apostrophe to denote combined possession.

A. C. Fergiani and D. L. Rabanovich's letter (joint letter)
Fergiani's and Rabanovich's letters (two different letters)

Compounds. A *compound* is a combination of two or more words used as a single term. The modern American practice is to write most compounds closed. Check your dictionary, however, if you're uncertain whether it should be closed, hyphenated, or open (two separate words, no hyphen).

backup   paperwork
checklist   sidetrack

Other compounds are written with a hyphen, including those in which one part precedes a proper noun and those that cause two of the same vowels to come together.

cross-reference   non-Asian
know-how   semi-independent

A hyphen may also be needed to avoid confusion in meaning.

re-form (form again)
re-lease (lease again)

Hyphenate a compound adjective before a noun, but write it open after the noun.

The well-informed person has an advantage.
The person who is well informed has an advantage.

Some compounds are written open as two separate words without a hyphen.

Latin America   vice president
master plan   work force

Prefixes.   A *prefix* is a form added to the beginning of a word to change its meaning. Most prefixes are written closed unless they precede a proper noun or create a double vowel that is hard to read; a few, such as *ex-*, are always hyphenated.

audiovisual   nonstandard
biochemical   postwar
countermeasure   prewar
ex-president   pro-European
intercity   semi-insulated
microunit   transnational
minicomputer   ultrasensitive
multilingual   understaffed

Suffixes.   A *suffix* is a form added to the end of a word to change its meaning. In some cases, the final consonant must be doubled before the addition of a word ending.

beginning   management

cancellation	monochrome
childlike	motorcade
fearful	nationwide
foolproof	passerby
heartfelt	statehood
hemisphere	troublemaker
homeless	trustworthy

Foreign Words.   Many words of foreign origin have plurals that differ from the regular English plural. Many of these words have Anglicized plurals as well. Consult a dictionary when in doubt. The following Anglicized terms are examples of preferred English plurals.

focus, focuses

formula, formulas

tempo, tempos

appendix, appendixes

Foreign words may use one or more of the nine principal diacritical marks.

acute ´	grave `
breve ˘	haček
cedilla ˛	macron ¯
circumflex ^	tilde ~
dieresis ¨	

Usually, when an occasional foreign term is used in a primarily English-language text, the foreign term is italicized or, in typed copy, underlined. According to the U.S. Government Printing Office *Style Manual*, the following terms have become Anglicized and, therefore, do not need to be italicized or accented. Other guides, such as *The American Heritage Dictionary of the English Language, Third Edition*, retain the accents. Follow the preferred style of your company.

aba ca	applique
aide memoire	apropos
a la carte	auto(s)-da-fe
a la king	blase
a la mode	boutonniere
angstrom	brassiere
aperitif	cabana

cafe
cafeteria
caique
canape
cause celebre
chateau
cliche
cloisonne
comedienne
comme ci comme ca
communique
confrere
consomme
cortege
coulee
coup de grace
coup d'etat
coupe
crepe
crepe de chine
critique
critiquing
debacle
debris
debut
debutante
decollete
dejeuner
denouement
depot
dos-a-dos
eclair
eclat
ecru
elan
elite

entree
etude
facade
faience
fete
fiance
frappe
garcon
glace
grille
gruyere
habitue
ingenue
jardiniere
litterateur
materiel
matinee
melange
melee
menage
mesalliance
metier
moire
naive
naivete
nee
opera bouffe
opera comique
papier mache
piece de resistance
pleiade
porte cochere
porte lumiere
portiere
pousse cafe
premiere

protege	seance
puree	smorgasbord
rale	soiree
recherche	souffle
regime	suede
risque	table d'hote
role	tete-a-tete
rotisserie	tragedienne
roue	vicuna
saute	vis-a-vis

Numbers and Symbols.   The general (nontechnical) business style for numbers is to spell out *one* through *ninety-nine* and all large round numbers. If a large uneven number appears in a paragraph, however, use figures for all numbers related to that discussion. The word *million* may be used instead of six zeros unless an uneven amount in the millions appears in the same paragraph.

Each of the three shipments included four manuals and eight tests.

> Each of the three shipments included 4 manuals and 116 tests.
> I read that a thousand people heard the speech.
> I read that 1,250 people heard the speech.
> The population is over 3 million, with about 1 million women and 2 million men.
> The population is over 3,000,000, with 1,234,709 women and 1,765,291 men.
> It cost two dollars.
> It cost $2.31.
> The pen cost $2.00, and the book cost $29.98.

Add *s* to figures to form the plural. Add *s* or *es* to a spelled-out number.

1990s	sixes and sevens
low 30s	eighties

When referring to inclusive numbers, some writers put a hyphen between the figures. The first digits of the concluding number can be dropped, as illustrated below, unless the beginning number ends in a double zero or unless the numbers will be incorrect if the digit is dropped. In some countries, particularly in non–English-speaking countries, it will be clearer to your readers if you state inclusive numbers with words such as *from* and *to* (*from 110 to 114*) rather than use a hyphen

(*110–14*). In any case, if the numbers are introduced by the word *from,* always substitute *to* for the hyphen; if the numbers are introduced by the word *between,* always substitute *and* for the hyphen.

> pp. 100–109, 109–10, 247–561, 1100–1161, 1221–22, 1307–9
> the years 1800–1900, 1880–1916, 1900–1920, 1990–91
> from 900 to 950 (*not* from 900–950)
> between 900 and 950 (*not* between 900–950)

Figures are routinely used with the word *percent* in general business writing, even if the number is less than one hundred.

> 15 percent
> 20.1 and 30.0 percent

If a decimal fraction might exceed one, put a zero in front of the decimal; otherwise, omit it.

> 0.13 and 2.40
> R = .17 (will not exceed 1.00)

In domestic correspondence writers often put a colon between the two figures in a ratio but spell out a general reference. In international correspondence it is always preferable to spell out the ratio in case the foreign reader doesn't understand what the colon means.

> seven to one (7:1)
> chances of one in a million

Weights and Measures.   Treat weights and measures like other numbers. If symbols or abbreviations are used, however, figures must be used even for numbers under one hundred. But you can be most certain that your foreign contact will understand you if you spell out abbreviations and symbols whenever possible.

ten kilometers	10'2"
thirty-five degrees	35°
fourteen pounds	14 lbs.
101.2 feet	

Some foreign writers make greater use of roman numerals than English writers do. To form a numeral, follow these guidelines: Repeating a letter increases its value (XXX = 30). Placing a letter after one of greater value also increases its value (LXX = 70). Placing a letter before one of greater value subtracts from it (XC = 90). Placing a line over a letter multiplies the value by a thousand ($\overline{\text{X}}$ = 10,000).

I	1	LXXX	80
II	2	XC	90
III	3	C	100
IV	4	CC	200
V	5	CCC	300
VI	6	CD	400
VII	7	D	500
VIII	8	DC	600
IX	9	DCC	700
X	10	DCCC	800
XX	20	CM	900
XXX	30	M	1,000
XL	40	MM	2,000
L	50	MMM	3,000
LX	60	M$\overline{\text{V}}$	4,000
LXX	70	$\overline{\text{V}}$	5,000

Abbreviations.   Although your foreign contacts may be familiar with international abbreviations or acronyms, such as *NATO,* they may not know other English forms. Unless a foreign company has very modern translation services, it may not have an up-to-date book of English abbreviations. The safest policy is *never* to use general abbreviations, such as *mgr.,* for manager and to use technical abbreviations only if unavoidable. (For more about abbreviations, read the discussion about acronyms in Chapter 4.)

A foreign contact may be familiar with metric measures, although some countries still use traditional systems of weights and measures (refer to the list of countries in Chapter 9). It's always better to spell them out to be certain they aren't misinterpreted. The following abbreviations represent the metric base units.

meter	m	steradian	sr
kilogram	kg	hertz	Hz
second	s	newton	N
kelvin	k	joule	J
ampere	A	watt	W
candela	cd	coulomb	C
mole	mol	volt	V
radian	rad		

Multiples of the base units are as follows:

one quintillion	E (exa)	one-tenth	d (deci)
one quadrillion	P (peta)	one-hundredth	c (centi)
one trillion	T (tera)	one-thousandth	m (milli)
one billion	G (giga)	one-millionth	μ (micro)
one million	M (mega)	one-billionth	n (nano)
one thousand	k (kilo)	one-trillionth	p (pico)
one hundred	h (hecto)	one-quadrillionth	f (femto)
ten	da (deka)	one-quintillionth	a (atto)

Generally, avoid the use of hecto, deka, deci, and centi and instead stick to prefixes of multiples in increments of a thousand.

You may also see abbreviations of organizational names in letters from your foreign contacts. If you use any such abbreviations in your letters, be certain to spell out the name the first time it is mentioned and put the abbreviation in parentheses after the spelled-out version (more about this in Chapter 4).

> I contacted the International Monetary Fund (IMF) on March 5, 19—. On April 7 the IMF sent me the enclosed chart.

Troublesome Words.   Have you ever thought that no matter how hard you try, you just can't remember how to spell some words? You're not alone. It's not uncommon to misspell hundreds of words—the same ones—over and over. You may have trouble remembering whether a word ends in *ible* or *able,* or perhaps your fingers have a mind of their own at the keyboard. Here are some words that are known to be troublemakers for business writers and are likely to increase translation difficulties for your foreign readers if they are misspelled.

accede	acquiesce	allotted
accessible	admirable	allowable
accessory	advantageous	all right
accidentally	affect	altogether
accommodate	(v: *influence*)	analysis
accompanying	affidavit	analyze
accumulate	aggravate	anticipate
acknowledgment	agreeable	anxious
acquaintance	allotment	apologize

apparel
apparent
applicable
appreciable
archaeology
architect
argument
ascertain
assessment
assured
attendance
attorneys
baccalaureate
bankruptcy
beneficial
benefited
calendar
campaign
cancellation
casualty
catalog(ue)
clientele
collateral
commitment
comparable
compelled
competent
complement
   (*complete*)
compliment
   (*flatter*)
concede
concession
concurred
congratulate
conscience

conscientious
conscious
consensus
consequence
consistent
courteous
creditor
debtor
deceive
deductible
defendant
deferred
deficit
dependent
depositor
desirable
deteriorate
discrepancy
dissatisfied
effect (n: *result*)
effect (v: *cause to
   happen*)
eligible
eliminate
embarrass
endeavor
enthusiasm
equipped
etiquette
exaggerate
exceed
excessive
existence
extraordinary
extremely
familiarize

forcible
forfeit
formerly
forty
forward
fourth
fulfillment
gauge
genuine
grievance
guarantee
harass
hazardous
identical
illegible
inasmuch as
incidentally
inconvenience
incurred
indispensable
inducement
influential
intercede
interfere
irrelevant
itinerary
jeopardize
judgment
justifiable
knowledge
laboratory
legitimate
liaison
license
likable
maintenance

manufacturer	particularly	ridiculous
menus	permanent	satisfactorily
mileage	permissible	seize
miscellaneous	persuade	serviceable
mischievous	phase	siege
modernize	practically	simultaneous
mortgage	precede	sincerity
negligible	preferable	sufficient
negotiate	preference	superintendent
ninety	preferred	supersede
ninth	proceed	transferred
noticeable	prominent	unanimous
occurrence	questionnaire	vacuum
offense	recurrence	valuable
omitted	regrettable	yield
pamphlet	repetition	
parallel	responsibility	

Punctuation

You may think that punctuation is mostly a nuisance, but it serves a very good purpose—to make your letters clear and easy to read. You'd never believe this from the way some writers misuse punctuation. If you really want to drive a foreign reader crazy, try leaving out an important comma or sticking it in the wrong place. That can change the entire meaning of a sentence, as illustrated in Chapter 7. In fact, punctuation is one of the five crucial problem areas for writers of international correspondence. (The others are listed at the end of this chapter.)

Here's an easy rule to remember: Always *over*punctuate letters to foreign readers. This advice goes exactly contrary to the modern trend in domestic letter writing to use less punctuation, in the belief that a letter with fewer punctuation marks looks less cluttered and is easier to type. But international correspondence has a completely different objective— to guide a reader carefully through each sentence.

The principal marks of punctuation are the apostrophe, brackets, colon, comma, dash, ellipsis points, exclamation point, hyphen, parentheses, period, question mark, quotation marks, semicolon, and virgule.

Apostrophe.   Use an apostrophe to show possession.

> the manager's office
> the employees' benefits

Use an apostrophe to form plurals when confusion might result without it.

> the a's and b's
> the M.A.'s in business and economics

Although you may use an apostrophe to indicate omitted letters, doing this isn't a good idea in international correspondence. Many foreign readers don't understand contractions and can't find them in their dictionaries.

> it's (it is)
> '90s (1990s)

Brackets.   Use brackets within a parenthetical quote rather than double parentheses.

> (*Note:* The figures for the beginning of the decade [1991, 1993–94] are estimates.)

Use brackets as required in mathematical copy.

> $a + 7[(r - 1)y]$
> $[x - y + a(t + 2)]$

Also use brackets to insert your own comments within quoted material.

> According to Henry Olson, "By using a simple math operation [multiplication], you can update the chart to current rates."

Colon.   Use a colon when you want to introduce a comment or other information, such as a list. But omit the colon if the list follows a form of the verb *to be* or is the object of a verb or preposition.

> The text includes the following topics: management, budgeting, and report preparation.
> The topics are management, budgeting, and report preparation.
> The text includes management, budgeting, and report preparation.

Use a colon if special emphasis is desired. Usually, however, a semicolon or period is sufficient.

> We would prefer a firm contract: Everyone's responsibilities will then be clear.

Use a colon after various elements in a letter.

> Dear Mr. Legwaila:
> Please refer to: COM-2139
> KDC:jf

Also use a colon to express time and to indicate ratios that aren't spelled out. Usually, however, it is preferable to spell out ratios in international correspondence.

> 12:25 p.m.
> ten to one odds (10:1 odds)

Comma. Use commas with great care to help foreign readers avoid misreading and to lead them through a sentence by clearly showing pauses and divisions, such as clauses, phrases, and words in a series.

> The reply, without regard to our decision, was appealing.
> After you received the official document, we sent a copy to our branch office.
> The newspapers, journals, and television reports were consistent.

Use a comma to set off elements such as appositives, adjectives, and interjections.

> Yes, we received your letter of April 9.
> Our manager, Wendall Schultz, is in Europe this week.
> The contract dated September 17, 1993, will soon expire.
> On January 5, 21,942 signatures were submitted.

Use a comma to introduce quoted material presented as an independent sentence.

> In the letter he said, "We would like to receive details about your X-M laser printer." *But:* In the letter he said that they "would like to receive details about your X-M laser printer."

Although you may use a comma to denote omitted words, it is better to write out a sentence in full to be certain your foreign reader will understand it.

> Our position is, we must satisfy government regulations. *Better:* Our position is that we must satisfy government regulations.

Dash. Use a dash to set off parenthetical material instead of using parentheses. But treat this alternative with caution: It might create a confusing translation in another language.

The multination trip—7,192 miles—was exhausting.

The staff meeting—should we include support staff?—is set for November 6.

Use a dash for emphasis.

You already know what I think of the plan—it is useless.

Also use a dash to introduce lists (instead of a colon).

She mentioned four important qualities—loyalty, sincerity, friendliness, and helpfulness.

Ellipsis Points. Ellipsis points are seldom used in international correspondence except to show omitted words in quoted material. Use three dots (periods), with a space around each one, for missing words in the middle of a sentence and four dots, with a space around the last three, for missing words (or sentences) at the end of a sentence.

According to the report, "The imports . . . sold by franchised dealers beginning in 1990 include sales of trucks over 10,000 pounds. . . . These figures are based on the Intercity Council of America. . . ."

Ellipsis points are used in domestic writing to show an incomplete thought or emphasis similar to that provided by a dash. But this use could confuse a foreign reader and should be avoided.

It seems like a good idea, but . . .

Consider the facts . . . a steadily declining market.

Exclamation Point. Use an exclamation point to show strong feeling.

What a wonderful machine!

Please be careful!

Although you may use an exclamation point in domestic correspondence to suggest that your remark shouldn't be taken seriously, don't attempt such facetious comments or forms of irony with foreign readers. They may not realize what the exclamation point is meant to signal and might take your remarks seriously (more about this in Chapter 4).

I almost died when I read your letter!

Oh, how nice; they lost your luggage!

Hyphen. Use a hyphen in certain compounds, prefixes, and suffixes.

owner-operator
well-known businessperson
ex-senator
bell-like structure

Although a hyphen is properly used to divide a word at the end of a line, this practice isn't recommended. Foreign readers usually aren't familiar enough with English to know if a divided word is two separate words hyphenated to form a compound or if it's actually a single word divided temporarily because it won't fit on the line. It slows the translation process and hence the reader's comprehension. Unless a word already contains a hyphen, such as a hyphenated compound, and you divide it precisely at that point, it's better to keep your letters ragged right (without divided words and hyphens).

> *Acceptable:* I believe that the government is very pro-American.
>
> *Avoid:* I believe that the government is very pro-American.

Parentheses. Use parentheses to enclose miscellaneous material that you insert in a sentence but do not want to be part of the main sentence.

> Two members of our staff (John Nichols and Ella Stevens) attended the technology fair in Osaka.
>
> In 1990 the president signed the Revenue Reconciliation Act (RRA).

Also use parentheses as required in mathematical contexts.

$$x(1 + y) \times b(1 + y) = 12$$

Period. Use a period to mark the end of a sentence. In American-style punctuation, it appears inside the closing quotation marks; in British-style punctuation, it appears outside.

> The association between aligned companies and the parent corporation is unclear.
>
> According to the journal, "The association between aligned companies and the parent corporation is unclear."

Also use the period after certain abbreviations and initials and after numbers in a list.

p. 72

4:05 a.m.

D. R. Sebele, Ph.D.

Estimated vehicle registration includes the following:

1. Automobiles
2. Trucks
3. Buses
4. Motorcycles

Question Mark.   Use the question mark to conclude a direct question but not a statement in which no question is intended.

"Do you have the customs declaration?" he asked.

He asked if you have the customs declaration.

Although you may use a question mark after a word or expression to question its accuracy, this practice should be avoided in international correspondence. Attempt to use facts that you know or write out any doubt that you want to express.

His employment began on January 4(?), 1991. *Better:* His employment began in January 1991. (We cannot confirm the date but believe it may have been January 4.)

The (unanimous?) vote was affirmative. *Better:* The vote was affirmative. (We believe it may have been unanimous too.)

Quotation Marks.   Use quotation marks to enclose precise quotes. For a quotation within a quotation, use single quotation marks. In American-style punctuation, commas and periods are placed inside the closing quotation marks; in British-style punctuation, they appear outside.

According to B. R. Rutherford III, "The new almanac states that 'federal, state, and local governments spent more than $300 million this year on higher education,' but television reports suggest the figure is higher."

If you have a long quote (more than four or five lines), type it indented from the left margin as a block quotation (extract). Beginning and ending quotation marks are not used in a block quotation. Therefore, any single quotation marks that would otherwise be used (for a quote within the quotation) should be changed to double quotation marks.

According to B. R. Rutherford III:

> The new almanac states that "federal, state, and local governments spent more than $300 million this year on higher education," but television reports suggest the figure is higher. One conflicting report appeared in the *New York Sentinel* on May 5, 1993. It stated that more than $350 million had been spent on higher education by midyear.

Use quotation marks to enclose words being defined or referred to as words if italics (underlining in typed copy) are not used for this.

> "Puls" is a subdivision of the afghani monetary unit. *Or:* *Puls* is a subdivision of the afghani monetary unit.
>
> The term "age-mate" refers to someone about the same age as another. *Or:* The term *age-mate* refers to someone about the same age as another.

Use quotation marks around titles of book chapters, articles, unpublished papers, television and radio episodes, and songs. But italics (underlining in typed copy) are preferred for titles of books, magazines, reports, plays, films, operas, and paintings.

> "Punctuation Pointers" (chapter)
>
> "The Growth of Global Communication" (article)
>
> "A Historical Perspective on Exports to Developing Nations" (unpublished paper)
>
> "Marty's Return" (television episode)
>
> *Cheers* (television series)
>
> "Star-Spangled Banner" (song)
>
> *Trade in the Far East* (book)
>
> *Time* (magazine)
>
> *Petroleum Use in EEC Markets* (report)
>
> *Phantom of the Opera* (play)
>
> *The Computer Chip Market* (film)
>
> *Madame Butterfly* (opera)
>
> *The Tower* (painting)

In domestic correspondence quotation marks may be placed around a term that is intentionally misused. But avoid this practice in international correspondence. Foreign readers might miss your intent and take the usage literally.

> The company "reinvented" tax shelters each time it filed a tax return.

Semicolon.   Use a semicolon instead of a period to separate two sentences when a less abrupt break is desired or when the second sentence begins with a transition word such as *therefore*.

> Ghana has more than a half dozen languages; the official one is English.
>
> The Faeroe Islands are an autonomous part of Denmark; that is, they have home rule and send representatives to the Danish Folketing.

Use a semicolon to separate items in a series that already have other punctuation.

> The sales territory includes Kobe, Japan; Taipei, Taiwan; and Seoul, Korea.

Virgule.   A virgule (also known as diagonal, solidus, and slash) may be used between inclusive figures or words of equal weight, although a hyphen is more common for this purpose. In international correspondence, however, it is preferable to use words for inclusive figures (*1992 to 1993; April to May 1994*).

> 1992/1993 (*or* 1992–93)
>
> April/May 1994 (*or* April–May 1994)
>
> owner/operator (*or* owner-operator)

Use a virgule to take the place of the word *per* and *to* in tables and other technical compilations. But spell out *per* and *to* in general correspondence.

> 10 gal./min. (10 gallons per minute)
>
> $2,250/yr. ($2,250 per year)

Also use a virgule as required in mathematical copy.

> $a + b/x - y$

STYLE PITFALLS

The Impact of Language Problems

Since this is a book about international correspondence, common language pitfalls in writing are a major concern. This is the area that requires us to *un*learn everything we think we know about composing correspondence.

During the past two decades I have collected and evaluated thousands of letters, memos, and electronic messages, both domestic and international. The majority of them have had obvious language problems. Although poor word choice and clumsy composition can lead to unproductive domestic communication, the problem increases dramatically in global contacts since readers are often unfamiliar with English. Costly misinterpretations and misunderstandings are inevitable. A study by the Parker Pen Company, in fact, revealed that language problems are at the root of many, if not most, international business misunderstandings.

Five Crucial Problems

It wouldn't take much time to compile a long list of mistakes that create havoc in international correspondence. To make it easy, though, you can fit most of the mistakes into five categories. All of these problems are described briefly here and discussed in more detail in later chapters.

First, business writers fail to be literal in their letters. Being literal means that you have to be painfully specific, as Chapter 4 illustrates. Don't count on your contact knowing what you *really* mean. It never turns out that way. You have to say—in very simple, straightforward language—exactly what you mean.

Second, business writers use slang, jargon, buzzwords, cliches, and other language variants that foreign readers simply don't understand and often can't find in their English dictionaries. Chapter 5 tells you what to do about this problem. Your company, for example, may have decided to change course to avoid the rat race in a certain area of business. But don't say that or some perplexed reader on the other side of the globe will be picturing your maneuvers to avoid a stampede of furry little gray creatures.

Third, business writers fail to use short words and sentences. It's tempting to let other people know how brilliant and highly educated we are, but the exercise backfires in international correspondence. The best advice is to make it short and keep it simple. Follow the examples in Chapter 6.

Fourth, business writers fail to punctuate their letters carefully and heavily, as international correspondence requires. Punctuation is like a roadmap to foreign readers. Take away the map and they'll probably be lost by the end of the first paragraph. Notice some of the examples in Chapter 7.

Fifth, business writers fail to respect the customs of the reader's country. This one will earn you a prominent spot on someone's blacklist. Most foreign readers attach a lot of importance to custom and don't appreciate thoughtlessly insensitive remarks or American laziness in not bothering to learn about other cultures—and there's a lot to learn, as you'll see in Chapters 8 and 9. Whether you misuse someone's name, get too friendly too fast, or forget that something may be a religious taboo, it will get you off to a bad start—or worse.

If the do's and don'ts of writing international correspondence suddenly seem a lot more complex than you ever imagined they might be, keep reading. There's nothing that can't be learned. International communication is a fascinating subject, because in every country you're dealing with a different culture. The rest of the chapters in this book should clear up some of the worst misconceptions about writing international correspondence and help you develop a new sensitivity toward other countries and cultures.

4

Say What You Mean— Literally

THIS IS THE PROBLEM: Your foreign contacts will translate everything you write literally, no matter how ridiculous that practice might seem. Therefore, you have to take pains to avoid any embellishments in your letters and to keep your remarks simple, clear, and exact, just as if you were trying to teach a young student how to fly a plane. You and the student and the plane could end up in pieces on the ground if you weren't absolutely precise in your instructions.

Making clear, precise statements means using English that isn't subject to more than one interpretation. If you write that you're going to "bend over backwards" to find a way to modify a plan, don't be surprised if your foreign contacts wonder how such remarkable physical agility could possibly affect your ability to alter the plan. Keep reminding yourself that everything you say will be taken literally.

A very busy importer learned all about being precise when he asked for certain goods to be delivered in the "early spring," rather than in a particular month or on a particular day. Spring came and went, and no goods appeared. He was about ready to complain vigorously when he suddenly realized that his contact lived in the Southern Hemisphere, where the seasons are reversed. Foolishly, he had written his original letter in haste, and it had somehow slipped his mind that in other parts of the world, customs, business practices, and even climate may be very different from that in the United States. Now, whether or not he's in a rush, he takes plenty of time to give precise dates and other information, even when the details are of minor importance.

Some of the communication mishaps that occur in international correspondence are amusing, even hilarious; others are just silly. But some—too many—become almost tragic when the resulting confusion and misunderstanding torpedo a vital business relationship. Careless use of language in both correspondence and personal meetings is widely recognized as one of the two most serious impediments to effective international communication; the other is insensitivity to different cultures and customs. Whether your personal composition weakness is using trendy words and idioms that your contacts don't understand or whether other unfortunate habits weaken your messages, the result is always the same—lost time and business.

This chapter and the next describe the most dangerous language pitfalls—those unsuspecting traps that have all the superficial innocence of a minefield. You might, in fact, think of your international correspondence as just that: a minefield that you need to negotiate successfully so that a serious mistake won't cause everything to blow up in your face.

INTERNATIONAL ENGLISH

English Around the World

Not only is English the universal language of business, but it's also the official language in nearly three dozen countries and the second most important language taught in Europe, Japan, China, Africa, and the Middle East; in addition, it's spoken in the major business and tourist areas of more than half the countries of the world. Such pervasiveness may sound reassuring, but American businesspeople need to remind themselves that English is not the *only* language. Just look at the numerous languages listed in the country profiles in Chapter 9. In fact, English is the native language in only a dozen of the nearly two hundred countries in the world.

In spite of the worldwide recognition of English as the language of international business, Americans who don't know the language of the countries in which they trade are at a disadvantage. In international trade you have to compete with companies in other countries as well as those in the United States, and businesspeople in other countries are frequently multilingual. So by using the languages of their contacts' countries, they are often accepted in other countries faster than a monolingual American would be.

Even if your contacts in other countries can understand your letters or successfully translate them from English into their own language, the question is *which* English do they know—U.S.(American) English, U.K. (British) English, or the English used in another country? If you thought U.S. English and U.K. English were the only two forms that you had to worry about, you've been suffering from a misconception shared by millions of other Americans.

It's time to get rid of the notion that English is English wherever you are in the world. It's not. Pick up a copy of *International English Usage* (New York University Press, 1987), and you'll learn about English around the globe, from Africa to Latin America to Europe to the Far East. You'll discover strange variations in English usage from country to country.

Japanese English, for example, often doesn't distinguish between the singular and the plural of words (*company, companies*), because the Japanese don't have singular or plural in their own language and they're not used to making such distinctions: "We enjoyed meeting your ten *representative*[s]." Egyptian English deviates from U.S. English by treating certain adjectives as nouns: "He is from the *Egyptian* [delegation]." Sometimes the meanings of words differ from U.S. definitions. Australian English terms, for instance, may reveal an aboriginal influence, as in *forestland*, which refers to "grass," not "trees." In South Africa another word for "meeting" is *indaba*.

You're probably wondering if you should imitate the particular brand of English used in each country. Fortunately, you don't have to do that. You should write your letters in U.S. English. But you still need to use your knowledge of the differences in international English to avoid expressions in your correspondence that might confuse the recipient.

If you know, for example, that someone in Australia is going to think you mean "grass" if you refer to *forestland*, rephrase your sentence:

> We understand that most of the land where the new factory will be built contains primarily trees [*not* forestland].

If you know that South African English has borrowed a term from another language, put the adopted word in parentheses after the U.S. English version:

> We are happy that you can attend the June 4 meeting (indaba).

All of this focus on differences in English around the world may seem like a lot of work—and it is. But the purpose is obvious: The more precise and clear that your letters to foreign contacts are, the less chance there will be for costly misinterpretations and misunderstandings.

U.S. English Versus U.K. English

You've heard the many jokes about Americans and Britons speaking different languages. The suggestion isn't entirely facetious, and it concerns both the spoken and written word. Americans often envy the British, who can make a grammatically incorrect, simplistic statement sound absolutely brilliant just from the way they say it. In many places, people are impressed with the British accent and often are unimpressed with American enunciation and pronunciation. While traveling in Europe, in fact, one businesswoman was complimented in several countries because her speech *didn't* "sound American."

The written word puts us on a more equal footing—or does it? Yes and no. Although businesspeople around the world would probably prefer corresponding with a Briton, it's not because U.K. English is grammatically or linguistically superior; it's because Americans are so informal in their use of English. Sometimes we tend to avoid the clear, literal statement as being too stuffy, too . . . British. So we try to relax the language, bending the rules of grammar and composition along the way. In international correspondence, that's a certain path to disaster.

The difference between U.S. English and U.K. English largely involves different spellings of the same word, different meanings for the same word, and different words for the same meaning. Confused? Look at the following examples, and you'll immediately see why people joke about two different languages.

American	British
apartment	flat
bathroom	lavatory
billion	milliard
bombed (failed)	bombed (succeeded)
center	centre
defense	defence
elevator	lift
gas(oline)	petrol
labor	labour
lease	let
license	licence
liter	litre
long-distance call	trunk call
pavement	road

police car	panda
program	programme
railroad	railway
realize	realise
sidewalk	pavement
stocks	shares
table (put aside)	table (act on immediately)
tuxedo	dinner jacket

If you expect to do business in England or one of the other U.K. countries, ask your local bookstore to order a book that describes the differences between U.S. and U.K. English. Also order a regular British dictionary and a British dictionary of slang so that you can look for different spellings and meanings. Also get a British grammar book, which should help you spot the principal differences in grammatical usage and practice.

You'll notice, for instance, that U.K. English sometimes uses different prepositions from U.S. English: "He filled *in* [out] the application." U.K. English also uses different plural and singular words: "Have you checked the *maths* [math]?" Some words that we consider singular are treated as plural in U.K. countries, which means that there is a different form of verb-pronoun agreement: "The government *are* [is] meeting in *their* [its] chamber." Something that seems odd to Americans is the omission of the articles *a, an,* or *the* in certain phrases: "We will place another order in [the] future."

Most of the grammatical differences won't give you heartburn, since you'll continue to use American rules of grammar and shouldn't have any trouble understanding the U.K. version. But in some cases differences in either grammar or terminology could easily get you in trouble or embarrass you at some very inopportune moment. Based on the examples given in this chapter alone—and hundreds more are lurking somewhere—the "two" languages merit further study. This is not only a good idea but a requirement if you intend to communicate successfully with people in other countries who are more fluent in U.K. English than in U.S. English.

MODERN AMERICAN USAGE

Americans hate to be behind the times, and domestic letter books prod writers to use a modern style. In U.S. usage a modern style means a friendly, relaxed, conversational tone and a certain tolerance of neologisms, clever word play, acronyms, and other contemporary forms. But in international correspondence this practice will usually work against you. People in other countries often aren't familiar with new words, modern American tongue-in-cheek humor, and other contemporary practices. So you need to worry less about being up to date and more about being clear and precise.

Neologisms

Americans love new words and quickly and easily add them to their vocabularies. But how new is "new"? Most language authorities consider a word new if it hasn't been used in its present form for more than two to three decades. That may not sound very new to you, but remember that words don't become known nationwide overnight.

Often a neologism begins as a slang expression or a vulgarism used in a limited geographic area by a particular segment of society. Young people—high school age or younger—can't resist creating their own language, and many of the new words come from them. Others come from businesses that develop specialized terminology to fit their products and services. As usage spreads from one location to another and from one segment of society to another, it gains limited acceptance as a neologism. Finally, if it hangs on long enough and enters the vocabulary of the so-called literate professional world, it becomes an accepted part of the English language (often very much against the wishes of language purists).

If you've ever listened to a specialist using unfamiliar technical language or children who sound as though they've just arrived from another galaxy, you should be able to sympathize with your foreign contacts. They find it difficult enough trying to translate English words and expressions that have been around for a century and more. If you dilute your traditional English with neologisms, a foreign reader is going to wonder what language you're using. Consider this example from a U.S. businessperson's letter to a foreign client:

> We believe the suggested exchange of technology and services will *teflon-coat* our respective organizations. Without this type of mutually beneficial arrangement, your competitors may well find themselves *tapped out* during a recession.

You can almost see the readers shaking their heads in dismay: "Where do Americans get these words?"

Here are a few neologisms gleaned from my file of sample letters. Treat them like a deadly virus.

access: Retrieve data from computer storage; now applied to the process of getting any information from any place of storage and often used merely to suggest entering a particular place.

add-on: Something that can be added to basic equipment, such as an external hard disk; now used to refer to anything added to something that already exists—a piece of equipment, a house, a car, or virtually anything else.

A-list: The most important candidates being considered for something; see also "short list."

arb: An arbitrageur; someone who quickly buys and sells stocks for profit when companies are preparing to merge.

Automation Alley: The Michigan robotics production area between Detroit and Ann Arbor.

baseland: A local area network in which the computers are wired together for communication.

bells and whistles: Nonessential features added to a product simply to make it more appealing to consumers.

blow off: Cancel or fail to attend something or appear somewhere.

Bowash: The Boston-Washington (D.C.) corridor.

cafeteria plan: An option offered to employees in a company that allows them to design their own benefits program.

camel: Act in a dull, unimaginative way.

couch potatoes: People who spend most of their free time watching television.

critical path: The technique of controlling complex events effectively with a computer.

damage control: The effort to limit or minimize damage from a mistake, an accident, or another problem.

DRIP: A dividend reinvestment program in which shareholders take their dividend in stock.

econometrics: The application of statistical methods to solve economic problems.

E-mail: Electronic mail, such as computer mail or facsimile transmission.

English creep: The increasing use of English as an international language.

exit: Leave a computer program or operation; now also used to refer to leaving any activity.

facadism: The technique of retaining the fronts of old buildings on the new structures.

fast burn: A reduction in fuel consumption with rapid ignition; now also used to mean getting angry.

fast track: The fastest and most direct route taken by a person or product.

fifth-generation computer: A robotic computer programmed to simulate human activity in problem solving.

flanker: A spinoff product with a similar name that capitalizes on the name of the original successful product.

focus group: A small target population considered typical of a larger group.

gamer: Someone who finishes a game or project in spite of pain or setbacks.

golden handcuffs: A contract under which executives will lose attractive benefits if they leave the company.

hangup: A mental block.

hell camp: A tough Japanese leadership-training program.

hooked: Addicted to narcotics or anything else.

insider trading: The illegal use of inside knowledge of a company stock to make money.

Joe Six-Pack: A typical American.

just-in-time: A production system designed to eliminate inventory stockpiles whereby everything arrives "just in time" for production and sale.

killer technology: Technology so radical that everything before it becomes obsolete.

meltdown: The melting of part of a nuclear-reactor core; now used to refer to any type of deterioration or decline.

net-net: The final amount or last word.

niche market: A new market that develops between or in addition to existing markets.

overkill: Too much of anything.

peewee tech: Small-company technologies.

power trip: An obvious display and enjoyment of personal power.

prosumer: An older person who continues to be productive but without financial compensation.

sandwich generation: People who have to care for both children and parents.

shark repellent: Efforts to fend off the aggressor in a corporate take-over.

short list: The final candidates most likely to be selected; see also "A-list."

slammer: A high-pressure salesperson; formerly slang for "jail."

sleaze factor: Evidence of unethical behavior.

smart card: A small plastic card containing a microprocessor.

sound bite: A short excerpt of a videotape.

spin control: The effort to cast a potentially unfavorable event in a favorable light.

strapped: Short of funds.

tapped out: Out of money or other resources.

Teflon: Capitalized when referring to the nonstick coating on a product; lowercased when used to refer to anyone or anything immune to damage from external forces.

Trojan horse: Something appearing to provide normal activity but actually designed for illegal or secret activity.

turn on: Become excited or interested.

uptight: Anxious or nervous about something.

user-friendly: Easy to learn and use.

wannabee: Someone who aspires to a particular position.

A client once asked how to handle the problem of neologisms in international correspondence. My recommendation was simply to rephrase the language in ordinary, traditional English. He was understandably troubled by the fact that it often takes more words to describe something in traditional English, and letter writers are frequently criticized for being unnecessarily wordy. That's true, but in international correspondence the main concern is reader understanding, not brevity. Although a short message mailed or faxed to another country may cost less to send than a long one, how much is the saving worth if the reader doesn't understand the content?

Another common question is how to reword a statement with a neologism without sounding fourth-gradish or condescending. If you keep in mind that your objective is to use simple, clear words, *not* simple concepts, no one will consider you uneducated or amateurish. Also, simple, clear words in themselves will not sound condescending, but statements such as "Let me give you a lesson on . . ." or "To educate you about . . ." *will*. If you just say what you mean without an added phrase implying that the reader is an idiot, no one will be offended.

Consider some of the neologisms just described. The following examples include the original statement and a suggested rewrite.

Original: I will *access* our design specifications to determine if the performance ratio can be modified as you requested.

Rewrite: I will *examine* [or *study*] our design specifications to determine if the performance ratio can be modified as you requested.

Original: The following paragraph is suggested as an *add-on* to Section 14.C.a on page 10 of the proposal.

Rewrite: We suggest *adding* the following paragraph to Section 14.C.a. on page 10 of the proposal.

Original: Our agent William Thornton has been representing companies in *Automation Alley* for twenty years.

Rewrite: Our agent William Thornton has been representing companies in *Detroit and Ann Arbor, Michigan,* for twenty years.

Original: Teenagers in the United States have been *hooked on* our products for many years.

Rewrite: Teenagers in the United States have been *eager* [or *avid*] buyers of our products for many years.

Original: Our program is inexpensive and *user-friendly.*

Rewrite: Our program is inexpensive and *easy to learn and use.*

Trendy Words

Some words come and go. These faddish expressions are new words that don't last long enough to become acceptable English. They never get out of the dictionaries of cliches or slang and into the standard English dictionaries. You may not remember the ones that have almost disappeared, such as *bummer* (bad experience), *boondoggle* (to spend public money on a futile activity), and *blue blazes* (to an extreme).

What's trendy today? Listen to politicians and businesspeople being interviewed over television, and you'll hear many trendy words and expressions. Here are a few examples:

grow the economy: Make the economy grow.

revenue enhancement: New taxes.

nuke: Bomb or destroy, usually by using nuclear weapons.

cocooning: Staying home or retreating.

Fortune 500: Big business (leading industrial companies).

homeboy: Close friend.

New Age: Beyond or abandoning the traditional.

PSI: Pollution Standard Index, used by the Environmental Protection Agency to measure air quality.

carjacking: Stealing a car while the owner is still in it.

spin doctor: One who tries to make potentially unfavorable events and actions appear favorable.

vanilla: Dull or bland.

zero out: Pay no taxes.

Even if today's trendy words are here tomorrow, they shouldn't be used in international correspondence. It will be a long time before they become universally known as part of the standard English vocabulary.

Humor

You may think the one about so and so is hilarious, but will your foreign contact be equally convulsed in laughter? Not likely. Humor is a personal matter. Think about the people who laugh hysterically over an old Three Stooges movie. Then there are those who can watch a "MASH" rerun for the fiftieth time and laugh until they cry. How about those who prefer the drier, more sophisticated humor of some politicians (I mean the ones who are *intentionally* funny)?

What about you? Do you like slapstick, tongue-in-cheek anecdotes, irony, sarcasm, innuendos, or ethnic jokes (bad taste)? Or do you secretly enjoy teasing people mercilessly, turning everything they say and do into a joke? In a way, it doesn't matter, because the odds that your contact will appreciate exactly the same type of humor that you like are not very good. The odds that your contact will even realize that you're trying to be funny or clever are almost nil.

When I reviewed my collection of sample letters while writing this book, one of the things that surprised me was how many people apparently have a sense of humor. Although most of us admire that quality in a person, many of the attempts to be clever or funny on paper were flops. So in domestic correspondence we might give people an A for effort but an F for delivery; in international correspondence it has to be an F all the way. Here's the first example I found.

> I missed my latest deadline, and it's all your fault! Instead of working on the project last weekend, I completely lost track of time reading the excellent report that you sent.

Should we assume that the recipient (in Belgium) knew the writer fairly well and realized that he likes to add a clever or humorous twist to his letters? Should we also assume the recipient knows that in U.S.

English an exclamation point at the end of a sentence is often a signal that the comment isn't meant to be taken seriously? I wouldn't assume any of that. I doubt that many, if any, people in other countries truly understand American humor and our love affair with the exclamation point. In fact, most people, upon reading a remark like the one just mentioned, would be terribly distressed that something bad was their fault. Now you know why the title of this chapter is "Say What You Mean— Literally."

Here are some other examples. As you read them, imagine the response of the foreign recipients who have translated each remark literally.

I am so sorry that I forgot to enclose the product brochure with my April 17 letter. I promise to give myself twenty lashes! (*Reader:* Really, you do not have to go *that* far.)

Here is a copy of our orientation handbook, otherwise known as our "company bible." (*Reader:* Ah ha. So it *is* true that Americans worship a material god.)

Let me apologize for such a long letter. I didn't mean to write another *War and Peace.* (*Reader:* Another *what*?)

My sincere apologies for the error in the figures I quoted. My assistant must have been brain dead when he compiled the statistics. (*Reader:* Then shouldn't someone bury him?)

By spring we expect to have a prototype ready, begin testing, maximize our technology, and save our souls! (*Reader:* Hmmmm. Here we save our souls through good deeds.)

I just returned from the shark-infested swamps of Washington, D.C., and have the information you requested. (*Reader:* Strange, the pictures I have seen of Washington did not show any swamp.)

I was so excited about your offer that I went right out and hugged a cactus! (*Reader:* That must have hurt.)

I received your letter about having the disks stolen on your return trip. I can imagine how much you liked that! (*Reader:* Oh, yes, I always enjoy being robbed.)

Forgive my delay in answering your letter of August 9. I must need a brain transplant. (*Reader:* Can they *do* that?)

Thank you for the compliment, but I'm no different from anyone else with two arms, two legs, and a company jet! (*Reader:* I wonder if all Americans are rich and obnoxious or just obnoxious.)

Search your letters for jokes, double meanings, irony, and other remarks that can't or shouldn't be translated literally. Delete those comments and stick to straightforward statements like the rewrite in the following example.

> *Original:* I can't believe I sent you last year's schedule—you must think I can't read. The current schedule is enclosed.
>
> *Rewrite:* Thank you for letting me know that I sent you last year's schedule. I am enclosing the current schedule and apologize for any inconvenience that the delay has caused you.

Acronyms

We have to talk about acronyms—those cute little abbreviations that are pronounced like actual words. They're everywhere. The only things I see more of are weeds in my garden after a spring rain. You've probably noticed that some people can't get through a paragraph without using acronyms. Well, I can hardly get through the morning paper without a dictionary of abbreviations at my side. Businesspeople are among the worst offenders, particularly in technical and scientific areas, and that's a serious problem in international correspondence.

You can safely assume that people in other countries are not familiar with U.S. English abbreviations. Even if the designation is universal, remember that words are often arranged differently in a name in other languages, and hence the English initials may not be clear to a non-English reader. The "International System" of weights and measures (metric system), for example, is the "Système International" in French. Because it is known worldwide according to the French wording, the common abbreviation is *SI*, even though *IS* would seem more logical according to the English wording. The difference in wording is one reason that abbreviations don't work with an international audience. The other reason is that many translators in other countries are lucky to have an up-to-date ordinary English dictionary, let alone a separate dictionary of abbreviations.

If you mention something only two or three times in a letter, spell it out each time or use a short reference such as this:

> *Full name:* Remler Engineering Datafile
> *Shortened reference:* the Remler Datafile, or the Datafile

In both domestic and foreign correspondence, if you have to mention the name over and over in a long letter or other document, such as a report, and believe an acronym would be helpful, spell out the name in full the first time you mention it, and then put the acronym in parentheses immediately after the spelled-out name.

> The Remler Engineering Datafile (RED) is a master computer file of engineering standards in the United States. A printed copy of the RED is available upon request without charge to clients and customers of Remler Engineering. To receive a copy of the RED, write to the following address:

An abbreviation consisting of the initials of key words in a name is called an *initialism: CPU* = central processing unit. Each letter is pronounced separately—*C-P-U.* An abbreviation is called an *acronym* only when it can be pronounced as a word in itself: *CAP* = computer-aided production. The letters spell an actual word that is pronounced as a word. Ordinary abbreviations such as *admin.* for "administration" shouldn't be used at all in any correspondence, domestic or foreign. Also, initialisms such as *apn* for "average peak noise" and weights and measures such as *ml* for "milliliter" should be spelled out in international correspondence. (For more about the metric system, refer to Chapters 3 and 9.)

Here are some abbreviations culled from international letters and enclosures. They should have been, but often weren't, handled as recommended above.

ACDMS	Automated Control of Document Management System
ACMS	Advanced Configuration Management System
ACTI	Advisory Committee on Technology Innovation
ADABAS	Adaptable Data Base System
ADDS	Automatic Direct Distance Dialing System
ADF	Asian Development Fund
ADIS	Automatic Data Interchange System
AFRASEC	Afro-Asian Organization for Economic Cooperation
AID	Agency for International Development
AMF	Arab Monetary Fund
AMPS	Automatic Message Processing System
ANC	African National Congress
ASCII	American Standard Code for Information Interchange

ASEAN	Association of South East Asian Nations
ATLAS	Automatic Tabulating, Listing, and Sorting System
BAA	Bureau of African Affairs
BAM	basic access method
BCU	Bureau of Consular Affairs
BEM	behavior engineering model
BEWT	Bureau of East-West Trade
BFEA	Bureau of Far Eastern Affairs
BIEPR	Bureau of International Economic Policy and Research
BIOA	Bureau of International Organization Affairs
BIZNET	(American) Business Network
CAD	computer-aided design
CAEU	Council of Arab Economic Unity
CAM	computer-aided manufacturing
CAP	computer-aided production
Caricom	Caribbean Community
CCTV	closed-circuit television
CEA	Council of Economic Advisers
CEDR	Committee for Economic Development and Research
CEEC	Council for European Economic Cooperation
CENTO	Central Treaty Organizations
CIOCS	Computer Input/Output Control System
CMEA	Council for Mutual Economic Assistance
COE	Council of Europe
COINS	Computerized Information System
CPU	central processing unit
DART	datagraphic automated retrieval technique
DBMS	Data Base Management System
DES	Data Exchange System
DIS	Dow Industrial Service
DMS	Data Management System
DOC	Department of Commerce
DOD	Department of Defense

DOS	disk operating system; Department of State
DSRS	Data Storage and Retrieval System
EAEC	East African Economic Community; European Atomic Energy Community
EBRD	European Bank for Reconstruction and Development
EC	European Community (Common Market)
ECE	Economic Commission for Europe
ECM	European Common Market
ECME	Economic Commission for the Middle East
ECWA	Economic Commission for Western Asia
EDIS	Engineering Data Information System
EFTA	European Free Trade Association
EXIMBANK	Export-Import Bank
FCIA	Foreign Credit Insurance Association
FETS	Far East Trade Service
FS	Foreign Service
FSI	Foreign Service Institute
GAO	General Accounting Office
GATT	General Agreement on Tariffs and Trade
GECREF	Geographic Reference (System)
GERT	Graphical Evaluation and Review Technique
GIS	Global Information System
GMT	Greenwich mean time
IAL	International Arbitration League
IBRD	International Bank for Reconstruction and Development
ICA	International Communications Agency
IDA	International Development Association
IFC	International Finance Corporation
IMF	International Monetary Fund
INP	International News Photos
INTECOM	International Council for Technical Communication
INTELSAT	International Telecommunications Satellite Organization
IOS	Investors Overseas Services

IRO	International Relief Organization
ISO	International Standards Organization
ITC	International Trade Organization
ITU	International Telecommunications Union
LAC	League of Arab Countries
LACM	Latin America Common Market
LAN	local area network
LAS	League of Arab States
LCD	liquid crystal display
MART	Maintenance Analysis and Review Technique
MCDS	Management Control Data System
METO	Middle East Treaty Organization
MIS	Management Information System
NATO	North Atlantic Treaty Organization
NEATO	Northeast Asian Treaty Organization
NSA	National Standards Association
OAS	Organization of American States
OAU	Organization of African Unity
OCAS	Organization of Central American States
OCR	optical character reader
ODC	Overseas Development Corporation; American Development Council
OECD	Organization for Economic Cooperation and Development
OECS	Organization of East Caribbean States
OEEC	Organization for European Economic Cooperation
OICD	Office of International Cooperation and Development
OPEC	Organization of the Petroleum Exporting Countries
OPIC	Overseas Private Investment Corporation
OTC	Overseas Telecommunications Commission
OWAEC	Organization for West African Economic Cooperation
PAC	Pan American Congress
PATO	Pacific-Asian Treaty Organization

PBX	private branch exchange
PERT	Program Evaluation and Review Technique
PLO	Palestine Liberation Organization
QAR	quality assurance record
R&D	research and development
RAM	random-access memory
ROM	read-only memory
SAM	sequential-access method
SBA	Small Business Administration
SCORE	Service Corps of Retired Executives
SEATO	Southeast Asia Treaty Organization
SEC	Securities Exchange Commission
SYMPAC	Symbolic Program for Automatic Control
TWX	Teletypewriter Exchange (now Telex II)
UN	United Nations
UNCTAD	United Nations Conference on Trade and Development
UNEDA	United Nations Economic Development Association
UNESCO	United Nations Educational, Scientific, and Cultural Organization
UNIDO	United Nations Industrial Development Organization
UPU	Universal Postal Union
USASCII	USA Standard Code for Information Interchange
USGPO	United States Government Printing Office
USIS	United States Information Service
VOA	Voice of America

Oxymorons

Some people have the soul of a poet, which is wonderful when they're writing poetry or other fiction. Then those poignantly contradictory words, such as *bittersweet,* can moisten dry eyes and elicit a pensive sigh from receptive readers. But what will such oxymorons do to your foreign contacts? If they prompt a tear or a sigh, it will probably be out of frustration; the very nature of an oxymoron tends to muddy the communication waters. Most of the time such contradictory expressions will make a translator miserable, and the rest of the time they will make readers question your judgment in employing this technique with a foreign audience.

Believe it or not, I found some oxymorons in my samples of international correspondence. Here's a letter in which the writer managed to fit in two such expressions. A suggested substitution that will be much clearer to the reader appears in brackets after each oxymoron.

> We want to let you know that our company has changed its fiscal year from December 31 to October 30. This will provide *different uniformity* [uniformity] to our accounting procedures, which will improve our response time in issuing both invoices and remittances. It will not, however, change our purchase or sales arrangements with any of our suppliers or customers.

> I know that our representative Mrs. Weiland spoke with you about this by telephone, so we are confident that this *expected surprise* [accounting change] will not disturb the fine relationship we have with your company. But if you have any questions, please call me or Mrs. Weiland. We value your business and want to continue providing the best possible service to you and your firm.

Here are a few more, with suggested substitutions for each expression.

> It has been two months since we corresponded, and we have been concerned with the *loud silence* from across the ocean since writing to you on June 6. [On June 6 we wrote to you to ask if you had any questions about our distribution schedule. We are concerned that we have not had a reply from you and wonder if our letter reached you.]

> I am *proudly humble* [pleased] to accept your offer to revise the terms of our agreement.

> Yes, our market has been contracting for three successive winters. This *normally abnormal* [abnormal *or* unusual] situation has occurred because of changes in our domestic economy.

> Thank you for the kind remarks in your letter of November 2. We, too, are pleased with the *modestly extravagant* [encouraging] increase in sales.

As you can see, not all of the oxymorons were written to sound poetic. Some of them appear to be unintentional. But it doesn't matter—they have to go. To a foreign reader who interprets everything literally, anything remotely contradictory is likely to cause confusion.

Watch for words that sound contradictory, such as the following, and rephrase those expressions in a clear, positive manner.

accepting denial

advancing retraction

adversarial proponent

aggressively mild

agreeably disagreeable

blind vision

boldly fearful

calmly aroused

clearly clouded

conflicting agreement

conservative breadth

curious indifference

descending ascent

destructive restoration

doubtful assurance

doubtful certainty

fresh stagnation

open enclosure

openly confining

plentiful scarcity

restless relaxation

selfish indulgence

similar disparity

slow acceleration

strictly lax

superficial depth

temporary permanence

unalterable flexibility

unfair justice

ungracious hospitality

unrestricted suppression

veiled revelation

vibrantly mellow

virtuous corruption

wisely naive

Common Bloopers

Not only do you have to be very literal with a foreign audience, but you also have to be very accurate. Mistakes in English usage will only complicate matters and thwart your efforts to be precise and clear. Almost everyone makes mistakes in usage, and some of them are repeated more often than others. These common bloopers make life especially difficult for foreign readers and translators.

Misused Modifiers

You would think there's a conspiracy in progress concerning misused modifiers. I wonder why we're so determined to misuse them. They aren't that difficult to understand. A *modifier* is just a word or group of words used to describe or limit (i.e., modify) other words: a *long* letter. *Long* describes the letter, so it's a modifier. When the modifier modifies a noun, such as *letter*, it's an adjective; if it modifies almost anything else, it's an adverb: an *exceptionally* long letter. *Exceptionally* tells you *how* long the letter is. It modifies the adjective *long*, so it's an adverb.

Dangling Modifiers.   Putting modifiers in the wrong place in a sentence can make you sound foolish. It's important to get the modifier as close as possible to the word(s) it modifies. When a modifier is misplaced and doesn't have anything to modify, it is said to be dangling. If you tend to dangle your modifiers, you'd better enclose a package of Tums with each letter you send.

I've seen a lot of dangling modifiers in international correspondence, for example:

> While working on the report, the policy directive was issued.

In that example, the introductory clause "While working on the report" appears to modify "the policy directive" but doesn't. Policy directives don't work on reports. To undangle it, the writer should say something like this.

> While working on the report, *I* received the new policy directive.

Some of the danglers *almost* sound sensible, and those are the ones that are the most common.

> Waiting for my boss to call, the news of more layoffs reached my desk.

Danglers like that fill the letters going out to foreign readers. It's easier to see why they're incorrect after looking at the corrected version. Here's a way to rephrase the previous example:

> Waiting for my boss to call, *I* received the news of more layoffs.

Here's one in which the modifier is too far away from the word it actually modifies, causing misreading.

> Before he arrived, Mr. Smith had left his office to meet Mr. Yamahoto at the airport.

He refers to Mr. Smith as the sentence now reads, suggesting that Mr. Smith had left his office before he had even arrived at it. The introductory words should not modify *Mr. Smith,* so the sentence needs to be reworded.

> Before Mr. Yamahoto arrived, Mr. Smith had left his office to meet him at the airport.

Sometimes a remark with a misplaced clause can sound just plain silly.

> She saw the *package from Malaysia getting into the elevator.*

All by itself? That's the impression a *literal* translation gives. This is how the writer should have arranged the sentence.

> Getting into the elevator, *she* saw the package from Malaysia.

"Getting into the elevator" refers to "she," not the package. This one is similar.

> Mrs. Mason *heard the bad news flying* across the Atlantic.

What did she hear—wings flapping? The literal translation is that the bad news was flying, not Mrs. Mason. This is how it should be stated.

> Flying across the Atlantic, *Mrs. Mason* heard the bad news.

> Here's one that will confuse even an English-literate reader.

> Before he reached Tokyo, his boss decided to change his schedule.

Whose schedule did the boss decide to change? I don't know. So let's add a name and see if that helps.

> Before Mr. Jamison reached Tokyo, his boss decided to change Mr. Jamison's schedule.

> Some misplaced words make a comment sound so ridiculous that it's hard to explain how it happens—but it does.

> I saw a rare bird sitting on the windowsill talking on the telephone.

Rare or not, birds don't use telephones. Obviously, it should read:

> Talking on the telephone, *I* saw a rare bird sitting on the windowsill.

After a while, when you see enough of these examples, you start to think that it doesn't take grammatical genius to correct such errors, just a little common sense. For example:

> The Chinese delegation toured the print shop snacking on cheese and crackers.

I'm sure that none of us knows any print shops that devour cheese and crackers, so to rephrase:

> The Chinese delegation, snacking on cheese and crackers, toured the print shop. *Or:* The Chinese delegation toured the print shop while snacking on cheese and crackers.

Squinting Modifiers.   Squinters aren't discussed as much as danglers, but they'll confuse your foreign contacts just as much. A *squinting modifier* is one placed between two elements without clearly modifying just one of the two.

Mr. Stanley's habit of interrupting *continually* annoyed the others.

Did Mr. Stanley *continually interrupt* the others? Or did his habit of interrupting *continually annoy* the others? We need to unsquint the modifier.

Mr. Stanley's habit of always interrupting annoyed the others.

Here's another example that will make even an English-speaking reader pause a moment.

Our company's plan to open a new store *quickly* excited the employees.

Is the company going to open a new store quickly? Or did the plan quickly excite the employees? The sentence needs rewriting.

The company's plan to open a new store quickly was the cause of excitement among the employees. *Or:* The company's plan to open a new store created sudden excitement among the employees.

Other Misplaced Words.   I found a lot of misplaced single words, too, in my collection of sample letters. It's amazing how one little word in two or three different places changes everything. This type of carelessness is widespread.

We *only* told the staff about the plans.

We told *only* the staff about the plans.

We told the staff *only* about the plans.

In the first example, we only *told* the staff about the plans; we didn't do anything more, for example, give them a printed explanation. In the second example, we told only *the staff,* no one else. In the third example, we told them only about the *plans,* not about anything else. Here's another one-word stumbling block.

My secretary *even* knows how to service the equipment.

Even my secretary knows how to service the equipment.

In the first example, the secretary knows how to *service* the equipment as well as how to do other things with it. In the second example, presumably everyone, even the *secretary,* knows how to service the equipment.

Dangling, squinting, or otherwise misplaced, the misused modifier can bring on a heavy nail-biting session for your foreign contacts. This is one area of correspondence that needs ongoing attention.

Fractured English

If there were a law against the misuse of English, the jails would be even more overcrowded than they are now. The way we fracture the language—and most of us are guilty—really is a crime. Much of this chapter and the next one deal with this problem because it is so serious in international correspondence.

It's interesting that different professions fracture English different-ly. Journalists, for example, have almost created a whole new language, with terms such as *elder statesman* (senile, out-of-work politicians), *spry seniors* (any retired person who isn't in a coma), and *self-made million-aires* (wealthy crooks). Businesspeople do the same thing, using terms such as *consider further* (stall), *realistic agenda* (what we want to do), and *downsize* (avoid bankruptcy).

It's not all bad. Although this chapter extols the virtue of saying what you mean, literally, you don't always want to do that. Even though a difficult client, for example, may have you on the verge of hara-kiri, you'll be in worse shape if you say something insulting. To avoid finger pointing and offending someone by using harsh criticism, we often intentionally *don't* say what we mean.

Most of the time, however, we fracture English unintentionally. Said Rose Mofford when she was governor of Arizona: "I feel now that somewhat it is." She had been asked if Arizona was racist because at one time it didn't observe a Martin Luther King holiday. Here are a few more examples of the unintentional fracture. Some of them may be Freudian slips, but I think most are just a matter of carelessness.

> I'm pleased to report that in my department, more men than women *com-promise* the clerical staff.

> Thank you for your detailed proposal. Before I comment on it, however, my associate and I would like to take time to *analize* it in depth.

> I'm sorry to let you know that from our *vintage point*, the market appears to be too small for us to be able to compete successfully.

> Whereas our competitor's prices have become more and more *exuberant*, ours have remained for years at the same reasonable level.

Finally, here's a one-sentence double fracture.

> We try to keep *a breast* at all times so that our public image will remain a *testicle* to our progressive record in both domestic and foreign affairs.

How would you like it if your foreign contacts translated some of these gems literally? Enough said.

Grammar Gremlins

Have you caught a grammar gremlin lately? *Gremlins* are small gnomes that are responsible for malfunctioning equipment. *Grammar gremlins* are the mistakes responsible for malfunctioning language. Certain errors involving the parts of speech keep appearing in correspondence. As usual, any error becomes more serious in the hands of a foreign reader who often has to struggle even with correct English.

Nouns. A common error is using a subject containing more than one noun for the subject of a sentence and having the verb of the sentence agree with the wrong one. The verb has to agree with the subject in number (singular or plural) and person (*I am, he is, we are, they are,* and so on).

> *Wrong: A package* [singular subject] of documents *were* [plural verb] sent to you yesterday.
>
> *Right: A package* [singular subject] of documents *was* [singular verb] sent to you yesterday.

A sentence may have a parenthetical element between the subject and the verb, but it shouldn't be counted in deciding whether the subject is singular or plural.

> *Wrong: Mr. Hartshorne,* with four of his staff, *are* attending the Stockholm Conference.
>
> *Right: Mr. Hartshorne,* with four of his staff, *is* attending the Stockholm Conference.

Most collective nouns are treated as singular and take a singular verb, but some may be singular or plural, depending on your meaning. A collective idea (two or more parts forming a single idea) is singular.

> The *news is* good.
>
> The *dynamics are* [or *is*] apparent.
>
> *Statistics is* a difficult subject.
>
> The *statistics are* correct.
>
> The *committee is* ready to report.
>
> *Davis and Davis is* a consulting company.
>
> *A good product and a receptive market is* our objective.

To decide if the word *there* takes a singular or plural verb, reword (invert) the sentence.

There *is/are* two calls waiting: Two *calls are* there waiting.

Pronouns.   A pronoun, such as *he, she, him,* and *her,* has to agree with the verb, just as a noun must agree with the verb.

They are ready.

She is ready.

Neither is ready.

Pronouns such as *some* or *all* could be singular or plural, depending on your meaning.

All is not lost.

All of us *are* prepared to work late.

The pronouns *both, few, several,* and *many* are always plural.

Both are writers.

Few are that intelligent.

A pronoun also has to agree with its *antecedent* (the grammatical term for the word in the sentence to which it refers).

Wrong: Everyone has their responsibilities.
Right: Everyone has *his* or *her* responsibilities.

The pronoun *it* is singular when it is used indefinitely, even when it refers to a plural noun.

Wrong: It are the salespeople who know the customer best.
Right: It is the salespeople who know the customer best.

If a relative pronoun, such as *who,* is the subject, you have to find its antecedent to decide if the verb should be singular or plural.

Jack is *the one* [singular antecedent] of the managers *who* [relative pronoun] *is* [singular verb] being transferred.

Jack is one of the *managers* [plural antecedent] *who* [relative pronoun] *are* [plural verb] being transferred.

In case these two sentences seem the same to you, notice that in the first sentence Jack is *the one manager* being transferred; in the second sentence, Jack is just one of *several managers* being transferred. If the distinction still isn't obvious, reword such sentences so that you don't have to worry about them.

> Jack, one of the managers, is being transferred. *Or:* Jack is one of several managers being transferred.

Writers tend to use *which* and *that* interchangeably, but many grammarians prefer that this rule be followed: Use *that* if a clause is critical to a sentence (restrictive clause); use *which* if a clause can be omitted and set any such nonessential clause off with commas (nonrestrictive clause).

> *Restrictive clause:* The program *that is called* A–Z Graphics is no longer available.
>
> *Nonrestrictive clause:* The A–Z Graphics program, *which is one of my favorites,* is no longer available.

Case.   Nouns and pronouns are said to be in the nominative case or objective case, depending on their function in a sentence. A noun or pronoun that is the subject of a sentence is in the nominative case; one that is in the predicate and renames the subject is also in the nominative case. Nouns or pronouns that are objects of a verb or preposition are in the objective case. Examples of pronouns in the nominative case are *I, you, she, he, it, we, they, who;* in the objective case, *we, you, her, him, it, us, them, whom.*

> Mrs. Arnold and *she* [subject: nominative case] were in Germany.
>
> *It* must have been *he* [predicate nominative, renames subject: nominative case].
>
> *Whom* [object of verb *believe:* objective case] do you believe? (You do believe *whom?*)
>
> Mr. Billingsley nominated *him* [object of verb *nominated:* objective case].
>
> The suggestion applies to Adam and *her* [object of preposition *to:* objective case].
>
> Everyone attended but *him* [object of *but,* meaning "except," used as preposition: objective case].

Reflexive pronouns, such as *yourself* and *herself,* should not be used instead of either a nominative-case or an objective-case pronoun.

> *Wrong:* The president asked Mrs. Laxalt and *myself* to represent the company.

Right: The president asked Mrs. Laxalt and *me* to represent the company.

Adjectives and Adverbs. An adjective modifies a noun or pronoun: a *difficult* task. Most of the problems with adjectives arise because of confusion with adverbs, which modify verbs, adjectives, or other adverbs.

Our products are *new* [adjective modifying noun *products*].

Our products are *very* new [adverb modifying adjective *new*].

We feel *bad* [adjective modifying pronoun *we*] about the misunderstanding.

He types *badly* [adverb modifying verb *types*].

She looks *sad* [adjective modifying pronoun *she*].

She looked *sadly* [adverb modifying verb *looked*] at the closed door.

Verbs.   To use verbs correctly, you have to use tenses correctly. Verb tenses are used to tell you when an action takes place, for example, present (I *call*), past (I *called*), and future (I *will call*). Regular verbs usually form the past tense and past participle by adding *d* or *ed* (*called*). Many verbs are irregular, however, and require a completely different spelling in some forms (*eat, ate, eaten*), so you have to rely on memorization in those cases. But the regular verbs follow a familiar spelling pattern for all six main tenses: simple and progressive present, past, future, present perfect, past perfect, and future perfect.

The *simple present tense* indicates that something is currently happening; the *progressive present tense* combines a form of the verb *to be,* such as *am,* with the present participle of the main verb. The *present perfect tense* indicates that something has been completed at the time it is mentioned or is continuing into the present.

Simple present: I *call* the staff each morning.

Progressive present: I *am calling* the staff now.

Present perfect: He *has called* the staff as of now.

The *past tense* indicates that something happened previously. The *past perfect tense* indicates that something happened before a *specific* time in the past.

Past: I *called* the staff yesterday.
Past perfect: I *had called* the staff by noon yesterday.

The *future tense* indicates something pertaining to a future time. The *future perfect tense* indicates something that will have happened before a *specific* time in the future.

Future: I *will call* the staff next week.

Future perfect: I *will have called* the staff by noon next Monday.

Common sense will help you answer many questions about verb usage, particularly in regard to confusing or illogical shifts in tense or in indicating events that happened before a *specific* time in the past or will happen before a *specific* time in the future.

Wrong: After he *wrote* [past tense] to Mrs. Acma on Wednesday, he *had written* [past perfect tense] to his sales representative.
Right: After he *had written* [past perfect tense] to Mrs. Acma on Wednesday, he *wrote* [past tense] to his sales representative.

Wrong: By Friday he *prepared* [past tense] his argument.
Right: By Friday he *had prepared* [past perfect tense] his argument.
Right: On Friday he *prepared* [past tense] his argument.
Right: By next Friday he *will have prepared* [future perfect tense] his argument.

The active and passive voice are important tools in correspondence. Use the *active voice*, which is preferred in most situations, when you want to be direct and straightforward.

This is what Mrs. Reston *did*.

I *recommend* that we accept the proposal.

Use the *passive voice* if you want to avoid assigning blame or responsibility to someone.

This is what *was done*.

It *is recommended* that we accept the proposal.

When a verb is used with an *either-or* conjunction, the second part of the conjunction determines whether the verb should be singular or plural.

Either the cable or the *tools are* in the second box.

Neither Ms. Barnes nor *Mr. Lewis is* in today.

Prepositions.   Most prepositions, such as *to, for, in,* and *off,* don't seem as mysterious as other parts of speech, such as verbs and pronouns, but they are often misused. Sometimes, for example, a preposition is doubled unnecessarily.

> *Wrong:* He picked the book *off of* the floor.
> *Right:* He picked the book *off* the floor.

Sometimes one preposition is incorrectly used following two phrases requiring different prepositions.

> *Wrong:* We have a need and interest *in* job training.
> *Right:* We have a need *for* and interest *in* job training.

Conjunctions.   The conjunctions *as* and *so* confuse many writers. The rule is to use *as . . . as* with positive statements and *so . . . as* with negative remarks.

> She is *as capable as* her predecessor.

> She is not *so capable as* her predecessor.

Use the nominative case for a pronoun that follows the conjunction *than.*

> He types faster than *I* [do type].

> Do not use *like* as a conjunction; it is either a verb or preposition.

> *Wrong:* He thinks *like* [incorrect as conjunction] I do.
> *Right:* He thinks *as* [correct as conjunction] I do.

Sound-Alikes

A serious mistake is using the wrong word in a letter not because you don't know the right word but because the wrong word sounds just like the right word. Sound-alikes with different meanings or spellings are called *homophones.* If you're in a hurry and your mind is wandering to other things, it's easy to write a similar but incorrect word. Computer spell checkers won't help either if the "wrong" word is spelled correctly. Substituting a word that means something entirely different from what you intended can turn a sentence, or even a whole letter, into nonsense. This is especially true in international correspondence, since foreign readers tend to translate everything literally.

The first sound-alike problem that I noticed in a letter seemed so unlikely that I thought it was someone's attempt to be funny.

The computerized program will be introduced in our Far Eastern sales office, *witch* will monitor the effect on order fulfillment during a two-month period.

Witch? It almost reads as though a witch will do the monitoring. Although a foreign reader may know that the company doesn't employ witches, someone who doesn't have a good understanding of English won't quickly or easily guess that *witch* should have been *which*.

You may be thinking that *witch* was a typo or that it was up to the secretary to proofread the letter. That may be true, but the result only underscores the need to be aware of the problem and take steps to avoid it or correct it when it does occur. To the foreign reader, it doesn't matter whose fault it is.

Look at some more sound-alike problems that were discovered in correspondence.

The electrical devices are as yet *unsouled* [unsold].

We *baste* [based] this opinion on our many years of experience in regional development.

You are right that the best *coarse* [course] is to test your product before we develop a long-term distribution agreement.

I understand your reason for the *depravation* [deprivation].

Thank you for your *patients* [patience].

Your remarkable *feet* [feat] in securing the endorsement of your government has contributed greatly to our success.

This *principal* [principle] is widely accepted in our industry.

We will *exorcise* [exercise] our option to renew our agreement for an additional three months.

I hope you will *saver* [savor] this sample of our honey-nut chocolates.

The device *omits* [emits] a high-pitched signal when it is receiving.

I am happy to *except* [accept] your offer to prepare an address list.

The wood base is *overlade* [overlaid] with copper.

We realize that your office will be closed on this *holey* [holy] day.

With your *aide* [aid], we will soon have our office fully staffed.

We appreciated your *meddlesome* [mettlesome] letter suggesting modification in our terms.

We want to *canvas* [canvass] all customers before making a final decision.

When our representative Mr. Boxleitner *eluded* [alluded] to a demonstration, he was referring to your June exhibition in Frankfurt.

I am enclosing a *pear* [pair] of sample containers.

We want to *complement* [compliment] you and your staff on your helpful evaluation.

The results will be worth the *weight* [wait].

Your analysis is *voracious* [veracious] and will be considered carefully by our executive board.

Since you plan to visit an *ant* [aunt] in New York for a week, perhaps we could arrange to meet at your convenience during that time.

The major component in the system is *stationery* [stationary].

According to the *senses* [census], the number of one-and-three-quarter-ton trucks exported has declined in the past decade.

We hope to be *their* [there] before the rainy season.

Mr. Van Neff, who is an American citizen of *Boar* [Boer] descent, knows several members of your organization.

We want to offer you the best *council* [counsel] that we have available.

After we have *caste* [cast] the material, we will send a sample for your inspection.

It's bad enough if such mix-ups create confusion, but what if they create hard feelings as well? The fourth example seems to suggest that the reader is corrupt or perverse. Another example (about midway in the list) accuses the reader of being meddlesome, and a third suggests that the reader is greedy. Although it's hard to imagine someone taking such mistakes seriously, stranger things have happened in international communication. It isn't worth the risk.

The problem of sound-alikes or look-alikes can occur between languages as well as within a language. Sometimes this happens with *cognates*, words related to each other in different languages. It's important not to assume that a familiar-looking or familiar-sounding word in another language has a meaning similar to its English meaning.

You might, for example, see the word *lösen* in a German letter and associate it with the English word *lose* or *loosen*, but *lösen* actually means "solve" in German. Similarly, *Hose* in German isn't the same as *hose* in

English, which refers to a "woman's stockings" or a "flexible tube used to direct water"; in German it means "trousers." *Mentire* in Italian might remind you of the English noun *mentor,* but it's really a verb meaning "to lie." *Toppa* in Italian doesn't mean "top" but rather refers to a "keyhole" or "patch." As you can see, it's always necessary to be wary of words in different languages that appear to sound or look similar.

PROBLEM WORDS AND EXPRESSIONS

Idioms

Of all the language problems in international communication, idiomatic usage ranks almost at the top of the list. *Idioms* are words and expressions peculiar to a language. They often have a meaning that differs from their logical or grammatical meaning and—here's the worst part—can't be translated literally into another language without confusing or losing the meaning. You know what that means, right? *Don't use idioms.*

Someone once told me that idioms were a "gray area" to him. He didn't know it at the time, but he was using an idiom. One reason that most of us don't pay much attention to idioms is that they are so common; in fact, it would be an understatement to say that idioms are plentiful. The other reason we tend not to think about them is that they are generally accepted in domestic usage. Some idiomatic expressions, in fact, such as *see it through,* originated in the ranks of slang and cliches (discussed in the next chapter): "Now that we've started, we expect to *see it through.*"

The following list of idioms is far from complete, but it will give you a source against which to check your letters. If you see any of these words or expressions in your international correspondence, delete them or change them to simple, literal English that your foreign readers can more easily translate. For example:

Original: It *stands to reason* that our prices must be competitive.
Rewrite: We realize that our prices must be competitive. (*Or simply:* Our prices must be competitive.)

aboveboard	all in a day's work
Achilles' heel	as far as
act of God	as regards
aim to prove	at cross-purposes
air one's views	back down
airtight reason	back out of something

back someone up

backlash

bad name

bare bones

be a headache

be in the red

bears and bulls
  (stock market)

behind the scenes

behind the times

bide one's time

black market

blackball

bottle-neck

brace yourself

broaden the mind

brushoff

by the way

by word of mouth

call it a day

call to mind

can't help feeling

captive market

change of heart

change one's mind

clear the air

close at hand

closed mind

corner the market

cutthroat competition

day in, day out

deadend

die hard

down to earth

doubt whether

evenhanded

explore every avenue

face value

falling market

a field day

fifty-fifty

fighting chance

firm footing

firsthand

flesh out

flood the market

foot dragging

free hand

free from

give the benefit of doubt

golden opportunity

gray area

guardian angel

handout

hard-nosed

have in mind

have it both ways

have no time for

head for

head start

heavy-handed

high places

high time

hinge on

hold back

identical with

in a big way

in all conscience

in all good faith

in character

in good taste

in one's element

in search of

in season

in the eyes of the law

in the same vein

in the wake of

kind of

lame excuse

lay down the law

leave a lot to be desired

let's face it

light touch

listen to reason

live up to

loophole in the law

lose face

make headway

make time

make up for lost time

make up one's mind

mark time

mastermind

a matter of time

mental block

moral support

mouthful

no earthly reason

no way

nosedive

a nose for

an off day

offhand

old hand

on its way out

on the face of it

on top

one of these days

open mind

order of the day

out of character

out of one's element

out of place

out of season

out of thin air

over one's head

peace of mind

pet name

to plague

plan to stay

play it safe

play the market

presence of mind

pressed for time

price oneself out of the
market

to prune something

put a new face on it

put heads together

question of the hour

race against time

a rash of

ray of hope

rising market

rough time

rule of thumb

saving grace

secondhand

see daylight

see eye to eye

see in black and white

see it through

sense of proportion

sharp tongue

shelve (defer)

shop around

show one's true colors

skin-deep

slip one's mind

snowed under

split hairs

stands to reason

take heart

take one's time

take time off

time is of the essence

time is running out

to mean business

to table something

troubleshooter

unmindful of

uphill fight

water down

well heeled

white elephant

with an eye toward

within the letter of the law

work around the clock

year in, year out

A different kind of idiom consists of a word followed by a preposition. Although these idioms are perfectly grammatical and acceptable in standard English, prepositional idioms can be troublesome to foreign readers. It's best to reword them when possible. Instead of saying "We *acquiesce in* the proposal," for example, you could restate it as "We *accept* the proposal." The following list contains some prepositional idioms you should avoid.

abhorrence of

accord with

acquiesce in

acquitted of

angry with a person

averse to

blame him for it

capable of doing

comply with

conform to

correspond to

differ with

different from

envious of

independent of

inferior to

oblivious of

superior to

try to

Commonly Confused Words

Here's another serious problem in international correspondence: commonly confused words. By now you must be wondering if any aspect of letter writing is *not* a problem. However, this book focuses on letter-writing problems and how to solve them, so it only *seems* as though everything we do is wrong.

Let's assume that you want to tell your foreign contacts about a signal in one of your products that goes on *uninterrupted* whenever the equipment is operating. Which of the following expressions is correct?

The signal is *continual*.

The signal is *constant*.

The signal is *continuous*.

In one of the sample letters from my collection, the writer mentions a *continuous* signal in one paragraph and a *continual* signal in another paragraph. A *continual* signal usually refers to one that is repeated at close intervals, with a gap or space between the intervals. A *continuous* signal is always uninterrupted, with no gap or interval. A *constant* signal also is unceasing, although more flexibility is accepted in the use of this term.

From this example, it becomes clear how important it is to use the right word in your international correspondence or even in your domestic correspondence for that matter. The reader who interprets or translates your letters literally might reach the wrong conclusion if you confuse terms that seem similar but have different meanings or implications.

This subject of confusable words was described as the most useful chapter in one of my earlier books: *Guide to Better Business Writing* (New Century, 1981). Domestic and international letter writers alike called and wrote to say that it had saved them from making many erroneous and, in some cases, potentially costly statements. In response to the crucial importance of this topic in international correspondence, the next list is a dictionary of confusable terms, updated and expanded from the original list that I prepared more than a decade ago. Unless stated to the contrary, these words are not terms that you should avoid, like slang or cliches, but are acceptable English words that are simply often confused with one another. Although many overlap in meaning and are used interchangeably, it is best to take even subtle differences into account in international correspondence.

a while, awhile. *A while*, a noun phrase, refers to a period or interval. (If you can wait for a while longer, the information will be ready by Friday, March l.) *Awhile*, an adverb, means "for a short period or interval." (The director wanted to work awhile before leaving.) Do not use *for* with *awhile* (*not* for awhile) since *for* is implied.

ability, capacity. *Ability* means "the physical or mental power to do something." (The new computer has the ability to solve complex problems.) *Capacity* tends to mean "a physical measure of content" (capacity of one hundred cubic feet) or "the power to absorb or learn something." (He has the mental capacity to negotiate the contract.)

about, around, round. *About* means "in the area" (about here), "nearly or approximately" (about one week), or "almost" (about finished). Do not use *at* with *about* (*not* at about the end of the week). Also, do not use *about* unnecessarily (*not* about one to two weeks). *Around* is often used in place of *about* (stop around noon), although grammatical authorities discourage this habit. It is used informally to mean "here and there" (drive around, wait around) but should not be used in that sense in international correspondence. *Round* is a colloquial substitute for *about*. (I'll see you round one o'clock.) It, too, should be avoided in international correspondence.

abridged, unabridged. *Abridged* means "reduced; shortened" (an abridged version of the regulations). *Unabridged* means the opposite of *abridged:* "not reduced or shortened; complete" (the unabridged, original document).

accept, except. *Accept* means "to receive, to take; to agree with, to say yes." (We are happy to accept your offer.) *Except,* as a verb, means "to make an exception of; to omit or exclude." (He was excepted from the list of candidates.) As a preposition, it means "other than." (Everyone agreed except my boss.)

accidentally, accidently. *Accidentally* means "by chance; without design." (He cut off the long-distance call accidentally.) *Accidently* is a misspelling of *accidentally.*

acknowledge, admit. *Acknowledge* means "to concede; to grant; to say that something is true." (The client acknowledged the problem.) *Admit* also means "to concede or to say something is true" (she admitted her mistake) but is used more often to suggest the involvement of force, pressure, or fault.

adapt, adept, adopt. *Adapt* means "to change something for one's own purpose; to adjust." (I adapted the meter to our console.) *Adept* means "proficient, skilled." (She is adept in foreign languages.) *Adopt* means "to accept something without changing it." (They adopted the resolutions.)

adverse, averse. *Adverse* means "opposed; strongly disinclined." (The company had an adverse response to the government's action.) *Averse* means "reluctant; having a distaste for." (She is averse to learning French.)

advice, advise. *Advice,* a noun, means "a recommendation or suggestion." (My advice is to place your order while the parts are in stock.) *Advise,* a verb, means "to counsel, to give advice." (The president advises all employees to observe the new regulations.) *Advise* is often misused in business correspondence for *tell* or *say.*

affect, effect. *Affect,* a verb, means "to influence." (How will the policy affect our schedule?) *Effect,* as a noun, means "a result." (What effect did the announcement have on our foreign contacts?) As a verb, it means "to bring about." (The new policy will effect better international relations.)

afflict, inflict. *Afflict* means "to distress; to trouble; to injure." (Chronic fatigue afflicts many executives in stressful positions.) *Inflict* means "to impose; to cause to be endured." (He inflicted his tyrannical attitude on the staff.)

aid, assist, help. *Aid* means "to provide relief or assistance" and suggests incapacity or helplessness on the part of the recipient. (The government aided the refugees.) *Assist* means "to support or aid" and suggests a secondary role. (Her staff will assist in the presentation.) *Help* means "to assist; to promote; to relieve; to benefit," and suggests steps toward some end. (He helped them prepare the machine for overseas shipment.)

all ready, already. *All ready,* an adjectival phrase, means "completely ready." (The presentation will begin when they are all ready.) *Already,* an adverb, means "previously." (The station was already closed when we arrived.)

all right, alright. *All right* means "safe; acceptable; yes." (The proposal looks all right to me.) *Alright* is a nonstandard and misspelled version of *all right.*

all together, altogether. *All together* refers to everyone in the same place. (The staff was all together for the arriving dignitaries.) *Altogether* means "wholly; completely; all told." (Altogether, he accomplished a great deal.) *Completely* is preferred by some authorities instead of *wholly.*

alter, change. *Alter* means "to make different without changing into something else." (She altered the report before mailing it.) *Change* also means "to make different" but is not restricted in the sense that *alter* is. (He changed his clothes for the international reception.)

although, though. *Although* means "regardless; even though." It is preferred over *though* at the beginning of a sentence. (Although the plan failed, we learned a lot from the experience.) *Though* means the same thing but is also used as a substitute for *however* and *nevertheless* in the middle of a sentence. (It is true, though, that prices are too high.)

amend, emend. *Amend* means "to improve; to make right." (The president wants to amend the contract.) *Emend* means "to correct; to alter." (The manager will likely emend the report's introduction.)

among, between. *Among* refers to the relationship of more than two things. (The exchange of opinions among the foreign participants was hostile.) *Between* refers to the relationship of two things or more than two things if each one is individually related to the others. (Relationships between the five members of the committee had become very strained.)

anxious, eager. *Anxious* refers to uneasiness or worry. (I am anxious to know their response to our proposal.) *Eager* suggests earnest desire or anticipation. (I am eager to undertake the new project.)

anybody, anyone. *Anybody* means "one person" and takes a singular verb. It is spelled as two words only in reference to an actual body. (They could not find any body in the collapsed building.) *Anyone* means the same thing as *anybody*. (Anyone is welcome.) Authorities frequently recommend using *anyone* instead of *anybody*.

appraise, apprise. *Appraise* means "to estimate." (He appraised the property and recommended a sales price.) *Apprise* means "to inform." (We apprised them of our progress.)

apt, liable, likely. *Apt* means "fit" (apt in international marketing) or "inclined to do something" (apt to exceed his quota). *Liable* means "obligated by law; responsible." (The company is liable if an accident occurs on the property.) *Likely* means "probable." (An economic recession is likely.) Although these words are used interchangeably in informal domestic correspondence, the distinctions should be observed in international correspondence.

as, since. *As* is a weaker conjunction than *since*, but it has other uses in the English language: preposition, adverb, and pronoun. *Since* (or *because, when*) is more effective and is preferred. (Since the report is late, we will have to reschedule the next meeting.)

as . . . as, so . . . as. *As . . . as* is preferred for positive expressions. (The next series of negotiations should be as successful as the last one.) *So . . . as* is often preferred, but not essential, for negative expressions. (The revised copy is not so good as the original version.)

as if, as though, like. *As if* is less formal than *as though*. (She hesitated to begin the project, as if she were afraid it would fail.) *As though* is used in the same sense and, like *as if*, is followed by a verb in the subjunctive mood. (He angrily rejected the suggestion, as though it were a personal affront.) *Like* is widely used and misused in informal writing and conversation (like I said), but since authorities still classify it as a preposition, not a conjunction, it should be used with a noun or pronoun that is *not* followed by a verb. (The manager acts like a dictator.)

assure, ensure, insure. *Assure* means "to guarantee." Only *assure* is used in reference to persons. (I assure you that we expect to complete the work on time.) *Ensure,* a less common variation of *insure* in the United States (but favored in Britain), means "to make certain." (This long-range policy will ensure our continuing success.) The principal meaning of *insure* is "to guard against risk or loss." (This policy will insure your company's possessions.)

balance, remainder. *Balance* refers to equality of totals (we want to balance the budget) or to bookkeeping (please double-check the balance in our account). *Remainder* should be used in all other instances to mean "what is left over." (One of the letters was mailed this morning, and the remainder are almost ready for mailing now.)

barely, hardly, scarcely. *Barely* means "meagerly; narrowly." (The equipment could barely fit into the small carton.) *Hardly* has connotations of difficulty. (The pilot could hardly control the plane in the driving wind and rain.) *Scarcely* means "by a narrow margin" and suggests something hard to believe. (He could scarcely believe his idea was rejected.) Do not use a negative with any of these terms, since each already has a negative quality (*not* not barely, not hardly, not scarcely). Although the words are used interchangeably in domestic correspondence, the distinctions should be observed in international correspondence.

because, due to, owing to. *Because* should be used with nonlinking verbs. (They were exhausted because of overwork.) *Due to* means "caused by" and may follow a linking verb. (Their exhaustion was due to overwork.) *Due to* is often used by careless business writers as a wordy substitute for *since* or *because. Owing to* is primarily used as a compound preposition. (The strategy succeeded owing to his excellent leadership.)

begin, commence. *Begin* means "to start; to cause something to come into being." (Let us begin.) *Commence* means the same thing but should be reserved for legal or other formal writing. *Begin* is preferred in most business communication.

beside, besides. *Beside,* a preposition, means "next to." (He parked the truck beside the shipping entrance.) *Besides,* most commonly used as an adverb, means "in addition to" (we have another report besides this one to get out) or "moreover." (Besides, I have more pressing matters to handle.) *Besides* should be avoided in international correspondence.

bilateral, unilateral. *Bilateral* means "affecting two sides." (The bilateral agreement imposed new restrictions on both importers and exporters.) *Unilateral* means "affecting one side; undertaken by one party." (The chairman's unilateral decision met strong resistance.)

brochure, leaflet, pamphlet. *Brochure* refers to a small booklet or pamphlet. *Leaflet* refers to a folded or unfolded, single printed sheet, not stitched or trimmed at the fold. *Pamphlet* refers to an unbound, printed publication with a paper cover or no cover. The three terms are often used loosely and interchangeably in the business world, without agreement on exact meanings. Regardless of accepted definition, consistency in use is essential.

can, may. *Can* refers to ability. (He can sell anything.) *May* refers to permission. (You may begin negotiations any time.)

candid, frank. *Candid* means "open; straightforward." (Her remarks were candid.) *Frank* means the same thing but suggests an outspoken, possibly less tactful remark. (He was very frank in expressing his disagreement.)

canvas, canvass. *Canvas,* a noun, means "a closely woven cloth." (The top was made of canvas.) *Canvass,* a verb, means "to solicit votes or opinions." (The company wanted to canvass prospective customers.)

capital, capitol. *Capital* means "a stock or value of goods." (The company needed more capital to expand.) It also means "the city that is the seat of government." (*Taipei* is the capital of Taiwan.) In the United States, *capitol* refers to a state building. It is always capitalized in reference to the seat of the U.S. Congress. (The Capitol in Washington, D.C., was recently enlarged.)

censor, censure. *Censor* means "to examine for possible deletions." (The editor censors all documents.) *Censure* means "to condemn; to blame." (The committee censured the derogatory report.)

client, customer, patron. *Client* refers to someone who consults a professional person. (We met our client at the airport.) *Customer* refers to someone who purchases a commodity or service. (The letter helped our customer decide what to do.) *Patron* has the same meaning as *customer* but also refers to someone who supports someone or something. (The chairman of the board is well known in Europe as a patron of the arts.)

close, near. *Close* means "very near" (close race) or "intimate" (close friend). Near means "closely related" or "within a short distance" (near neighbors). Avoid the phrase "a near victory." The two words are often used interchangeably in informal domestic correspondence, but with *close* indicating less separation than *near.*

close, shut. *Close* means "to prevent passage to or from." (Close the door.) *Shut,* which has the same meaning as *close,* is more emphatic.

common, mutual. *Common* refers to the sharing of something. (They have a common purpose.) *Mutual* refers to something directed and received in equal amount. (The two competitors had a mutual respect for each other.)

comparatively, relatively. *Comparatively* refers to a degree of comparison (the competition was comparatively mild) but is often used incorrectly when no comparison with another factor is involved. *Relatively* refers to the state of something in relation to something else. (This new software is relatively easy to learn.) *Relatively* is overused by many business writers.

compare, contrast. *Compare* means "to examine for similarity or difference." *Compare* is followed by *with* when it refers to examining two like things to discern similarities and differences. (We compared our record with theirs.) But in describing similarities between otherwise unlike things, *compare* is followed by *to*. (He compared the electric typewriter to a dinosaur.) *Contrast* means "to show only differences." The noun form of *contrast* is often followed by *to*. (The new electronic typewriters, in contrast to the old models, have features that rival those of a computer.) But the verb *contrast* is usually followed by *with*. (His present position contrasts markedly with his old one.)

complement, compliment. *Complement* means "to complete." (The new study complements the previous report.) *Compliment* means "to flatter or praise." (His employer complimented him on his achievements.)

complementary, supplementary. *Complementary* means "completing to make up the whole." (The parking and shipping operations are complementary.) *Supplementary* means "added to something." (The catastrophic rider is supplementary to his basic policy.)

compose, comprise. *Compose* means "to make up by combining." (Three rooms compose the suite. Or: The suite is composed of three rooms.) A general rule is that the parts (three rooms) compose the whole (the suite). *Comprise* means "to include." (The company comprises four thousand employees.) A general rule is that the whole (the company) comprises the parts (the employees).

concept, idea, notion. *Concept* refers to a general idea derived from specifics. (He formulated his concept of cost budgeting.) *Idea* refers to a plan, a thought, or a representation. (This is not my idea of a smooth operation.) *Notion* suggests an inconclusive or vague thought. (She had some notion that the shop might be closed.) *Notion* should be avoided in international correspondence.

connotation, denotation. *Connotation* is the suggested meaning of words beyond the dictionary definition. For example, *home* has the connotation of comfort and security. *Denotation* is the primary dictionary meaning of words. *Home,* according to the dictionary, has the denotation of "a place where one lives; a residence."

consistently, constantly. *Consistently* means "with uniformity or regularity; with steady continuity." (He consistently pursued the same theme in all of his letters.) *Constantly* means "with steadfast resolution or faithfulness" (England has constantly been an ally), or "without interruption." (The machines ran constantly.)

continual/continuous. *Continual* means "repeated over and over at close intervals" and sometimes implies a rapid succession. (The roar of the engines was continual.) *Continuous* means "connected; unbroken; going on without interruption." (The computer operates continuously.)

continue, resume. *Continue* means "to keep on without interruption." (She continued working through the night.) *Resume* means "to start again after interruptions." (They resumed operations after the equipment was repaired.)

convince, persuade. *Convince* means "to lead someone to understand, agree, or believe." (Using charts and graphs to document her findings, she convinced her employer that funding was inadequate.) *Persuade* means "to win someone over; to succeed in getting someone to do something." (I persuaded him to consider our services.) Only *persuade* may be followed by an infinitive.

covert, overt. *Covert* means "hidden." (The agency was conducting covert operations.) *Overt* means "open to view." (The committee's work was always overt.)

credible, creditable. *Credible* means "believable; reasonable." (His reason for failing to appear is credible.) *Creditable* means "deserving credit; worthy of praise." (Her suggestion was creditable.)

currently, presently, momentarily. *Currently* means "during the time now passing; in the present time." (The company is currently expanding its overseas division.) *Presently* means "shortly or before long." (Mr. Zhao will arrive presently.) *Momentarily* means for an instant; very soon." (He was only momentarily troubled by the news.)

customary, usual. *Customary* means "according to usual practice." (It is customary in our company for all employees to take their vacation at the same time.) *Usual* means "common, normal, or ordinary." (He left for work at the usual time.)

decisive, incisive. *Decisive* means "conclusive; final." (The merger was a decisive victory for management.) *Incisive* means "direct; cutting; clear-cut." (His decisions are always incisive.)

deduction, induction. *Deduction* refers to reasoning by moving from the general to the particular. (All computers accept some form of symbolic data; by deduction, therefore, our T60 should accept symbolic input.) *Induction* refers to reasoning by moving from the particular to the general. (Having read thousands of international business letters, most of which have one or more grammatical errors, I used the process of induction to conclude that most businesspeople need further education in basic English composition.)

degree, extent. *Degree* refers to a step or stage. (By degrees, we are moving closer to agreement.) *Extent* refers to the range or scope of something. (The extent of his authority was sharply curtailed by the governing board.) Both *degree* and *extent* are overused in business writing (to the extent that, to the degree that, to some extent/degree) and should be avoided in international correspondence.

deny, refute. *Deny* means "to disclaim; to refuse." (He denied ever seeing the visitors at the site.) *Refute* means "to prove wrong." (She cleverly refuted the customer's contention.)

depositary, depository. *Depositary* means "a person or group entrusted with something." (The trustees of the organization are the depositaries.) *Depository* means "a place used for safekeeping something." (The bank vault will serve as a depository for the documents.)

different from, different than, different to. *Different from* is preferred by careful business writers when it is not followed by a clause with a verb. (My objective is different from yours.) *Different than*, however, is preferred when followed by a clause with a verb. (The results were different than he had expected they would be.) *Different to* is a form of British usage.

disability, inability. *Disability* suggests a mental or physical impairment. (Both applicants had the same disability.) *Inability* suggests a lack of power or capacity. (She failed the entrance exam because of her inability to understand data processing.)

disinterested, uninterested. *Disinterested* means "objective, free from selfish motive; unbiased." (The researchers tried to remain disinterested while making their survey.) *Uninterested* means "indifferent, not interested." (He was uninterested in the new offices.)

disorganized, unorganized. *Disorganized* means "lack of an orderly system; lack of coherence." (A disorganized person would never succeed in this position.) *Unorganized* means "not characterized by an orderly whole." (Before the emergence of a union, the disgruntled employees were unorganized.)

displace, misplace. *Displace* means "to move something from its usual place." (A collision displaced the sign at the entrance.) *Misplace* means "to put in a wrong place." (I misplaced the Kuwaiti file.)

disqualified, unqualified. *Disqualified* means "made ineligible; deprived of." (He was disqualified from participating in the project.) *Unqualified* means "not having the required qualifications; not fit." (She was unqualified for the position.)

disregardless, irregardless, regardless. *Disregardless* and *irregardless* are both improper versions of *regardless*. *Regardless* means "despite everything." (I am going ahead with our plan regardless.)

dissatisfied, unsatisfied. *Dissatisfied* means "unhappy; upset; displeased." (She is dissatisfied with her new position.) *Unsatisfied* means "not content, not pleased; wanting something more or better to be done." (The president was unsatisfied with the outcome.)

doubt if, doubt that, doubt whether. *Doubt if* should be avoided in business writing. *Doubt that* is the preferred expression in negative or interrogative sentences when little doubt exists. (I doubted that we could meet the deadline.) *Doubt whether* is usually limited to situations involving strong uncertainty. (I doubt whether anything will come of it.)

each other, one another. *Each other* is used when referring to two persons or objects. (The two representatives consulted each other before taking action.) *One another* is used when referring to three or more persons or objects. (The four attendees were debating the issue with one another before the meeting.)

elicit, illicit, licit. *Elicit* means "to bring out." (The questionnaire attempted to elicit a favorable response.) *Illicit* means "unlawful." (The organization was a front for illicit smuggling.) *Licit* means "permissible." (The promoter engaged in strictly licit activities.)

emigrate, immigrate. *Emigrate* means "to leave one country or region to settle in another." (Feldman emigrated from Israel last year.) *Immigrate* means "to enter and settle in a country of which one is not a native." (Yoshida immigrated to the United States this spring.)

eminent, imminent. *Eminent* means "distinguished; conspicuous" (the eminent statesman). *Imminent* means "impending" (an imminent disaster).

endless, innumerable. *Endless* means "boundless; interminable." (The opportunities in foreign trade are endless.) *Innumerable* means "countless; too many to count." (The export regulations are innumerable.)

especial, special. *Especial* means "of great importance; highly distinctive." (The company's extensive benefits are of especial importance to the employees.) *Especially* means "mainly; notably." (The benefits were well received, especially the insurance coverage.) *Special* means "having some particular quality or some distinctive identity." (This is a special lubricant for typewriter elements.)

essential, necessary. *Essential* means "basic; indispensable; necessary," and suggests a sense of urgency. (It is essential that we meet our deadline.) *Necessary* also means "indispensable" but usually sounds less urgent than *essential*. (Your presence is necessary to show our support.)

essentially, substantially. *Essentially* is used most often to mean "basically." (The new copier is essentially the same as the old one.) The word *essential* (see above) implies something indispensable. (Insurance is essential.) *Substantially* is used in the same way to mean "basically," but the adjective *substantial* suggests a significant size or quantity. (The company showed a substantial net gain.)

everybody, everyone. *Everybody* means "every person" and takes a singular verb. (Everybody is there.) *Everyone* means "everybody" and is the preferred choice of many business writers. When spelled as two words, it refers to each person. (Every one of them is in agreement with this plan.)

example, instance, sample. *Example* means "a particular item that represents a group or type." (The labels are an example of our addressing and mailing supplies.) It also means "pattern; model." (The technique is an example worth following.) *Instance* means "a situation that is used to illustrate something." (In this instance, the strategy failed.) *Sample* means "a part; a specimen." (Here is a sample from our new line of merchandise.)

explicit, implicit. *Explicit* means "clear; fully developed." (The branch manager presented an explicit statement of his objectives.) *Implicit* means "understood but not revealed or expressed." (The company's faith in the market was implicit in its actions.) It also means "without doubt or reservation." (He has implicit faith in the new computer system.)

extended, extensive. *Extended* means "spread out; prolonged." (The extended session lasted another hour.) *Extend* is overused by many business writers in its sense of "offer" or "send." *Extensive* means "having a wide range or extent; broad." (She has extensive knowledge in that scientific field.)

farther, further. *Farther* refers to physical distance or spatial measurement. (Salespeople travel farther today as a result of increasing global contacts.) *Further* refers to quantity or degree. (This roll of film will go further than I expected.) As a verb, it means "to promote." (He hopes to further his career.) Some business writers have stopped using both *farther* and *further* and are using only one of them (usually *further*) for all situations.

fashion, manner, mode. *Fashion* usually means "a particular style at a particular time." (His business suit is the latest fashion.) *Manner* describes behavior or social conduct. (The director's manners were exemplary.) *Mode* means "a particular form of something." (His mode of governing is straightforward and open.)

feasible, possible. *Feasible* means "capable of being done." (The suggestion sounds feasible to me.) *Possible* means "within realistic limits; likely to occur." (An economic upturn next quarter is possible.)

fewer, less. *Fewer* is used to describe numbers. (Fewer people attended the meeting this week.) *Less* is used to describe amounts or quantities. (Production was less than usual this month because of the weather.)

first, firstly. *First* is the preferred form of this adverb and is used to stress points. (First, we have to examine the effect.) Business writers should remember to be consistent in making points: first, second, third (*not* first, secondly, thirdly). *Firstly, secondly,* and so on all add *-ly* unnecessarily.

frequent, recurring. *Frequent* means "habitual; persistent; occurring at short intervals." (He is a frequent customer.) *Recurring* means "occurring again and again; occurring repeatedly." (The recurring problem suggests a weakness in the system.)

gloomy, pessimistic. *Gloomy* implies darkness or depression. (She was gloomy after losing an important sale.) *Pessimistic* means "an inclination to expect the worst; an inclination to emphasize the negative or adverse aspect." (He was pessimistic about the outcome of the campaign.)

good, well. *Good*, as an adjective, means "praiseworthy; useful; beneficial; free from problems." (She did a good job.) *Well*, as an adjective, means "in good health." (She feels well.) As an adverb, it means "in a proper manner; with skill." (He handled the situation very well.) *Good* should not be used for *well* in response to the greeting "How are you?" (Very well, thank you.)

grammar, usage, syntax. *Grammar* means "the study of words and their relationships; the system of inflections and syntax in a language." *Usage* refers to the rules that apply to written and spoken language. *Syntax* refers to the way words are used together to form phrases, clauses, and sentences.

guarantee, guaranty. *Guarantee,* as a noun, means "an assurance that some condition will be met." (The product had a one-year guarantee.) As a verb, it means "to assure that some debt or obligation will be fulfilled." (The company guaranteed its work.) *Guaranty,* as a noun, is used most often in today's business world to mean "the fact of giving security" (contract of guaranty; act of guaranty). As a verb, *guarantee* is preferred over *guaranty.*

handle, manage. *Handle* means "to control or manage; to deal with," and is preferred over *manage* when physical action is involved. (He handled the equipment like a pro.) *Manage* also means "to control or handle; to deal with," and is preferred over *handle* when nonphysical action is involved. (She managed the department efficiently.)

happen, occur, transpire. *Happen* and *occur* mean "to take place." (The accident happened yesterday. The computer breakdown occurred before closing.) The use of *transpire* to mean "happen" or "occur" should be avoided.

if, whether. *If* is used to introduce one condition and often suggests doubt. (I'll meet you at the airport if the weather permits.) *Whether* is used to introduce more than one condition. (Her client asked whether he should continue shipments or wait for further instructions.)

imagine, suppose. *Imagine* means "to form a mental image of something." (I like to imagine myself establishing a global empire.) *Suppose* means "to assume or suspect something." (I suppose you have the contract already prepared.)

imply, infer. *Imply* means "to suggest by inference or association." (The report implies that research was inadequate.) *Infer* means "to reach a conclusion from facts or circumstances." (The manager inferred from the report that research was inadequate.)

impracticable, impractical. *Impracticable* means "not capable of being used or accomplished." (The plan is impracticable.) *Impractical* means "not capable of dealing sensibly or practically with something." (Her approach is impractical.)

incidentally, incidently. *Incidentally* means "as a subordinate matter" or "parenthetically." (Incidentally, I have the latest figures on that.) *Incidently* is a misspelling of *incidentally.*

ineffective, ineffectual. *Ineffective* means "not producing the intended effect; not effective," but often also suggests incompetence in some particular area. (He is ineffective as a salesperson.) *Ineffectual* also means "not producing the intended effect; not effective," but often also suggests a general lack of competence. (He is an ineffectual leader.)

ingenious, ingenuous. *Ingenious* means "resourceful; inventive; clever." (Let me compliment you on your ingenious approach.) *Ingenuous* means "innocent; childlike; candid." (The new employees are ingenuous.)

irony, sarcasm, satire. *Irony* is the use of words or statements to express something other than their literal meaning. ("Nice vase," she said, pointing to the broken pieces on the floor.) *Sarcasm* is a sharp, critical, derisive, often bitter and cruel form of wit. (I see that you made one sale this week—that's twice as many as you made last week, isn't it?) *Satire* is a combination of wit and irony, usually directed toward vice or folly. (The play is a satire about American values.) Do not use any of these devices in international correspondence.

irreversible, irrevocable. *Irreversible* means "not capable of being changed or reversed" and usually refers to some pattern or course of action. (The trend is irreversible.) *Irrevocable* means "not capable of being revoked or repealed" and usually refers to a specific action or statement. (His decision to resign was irrevocable.)

judicial, judicious. *Judicial* means "of or relating to justice or the judiciary." (He wanted to hear the judicial proceedings.) *Judicious* means "having or exercising sound or wise judgment." (She was judicious in the way she used the information.)

know, realize. *Know* means "to perceive; to understand." (I know a better way to handle this situation.) *Realize* means "to accomplish; to grasp fully," and implies a more thorough understanding than *know*. (I realize the implications of our company's policy.)

lack, need, want. *Lack,* as a noun, means "a deficiency or an absence." (The program suffers from a lack of money.) *Need,* as a noun, refers to a lack of something desirable or useful and is often used in an emotional context. (The need was for security.) *Want,* as a noun, refers to a lack of something needed or desired. (Many people in the Third World countries live in want.) As verbs, *lack* suggests a deficiency; *need,* a necessity; and *want,* a desire.

lawful, legal. *Lawful* means "being in harmony with some form of law; rightful, ethical." (The directors believed their action was lawful.) *Legal* means "founded on the law; established by law." (Such demonstrations are legal in democracies.)

libel, slander. *Libel* means "printed or written defamation causing injury to someone's reputation." (The newspaper account of the scandal constitutes libel.) *Slander* means "oral defamation causing injury to someone's reputation." (The remarks he was overheard making about his ex-employer could be considered slander.)

locality, location. *Locality* means "a specific place" and usually refers to a particular geographic area. (The species is native to that locality.) *Location* means "a place of occupancy; a place designated for a special purpose." (Bonn would be a good location for our international sales office.)

luxuriant, luxurious. *Luxuriant* refers to abundant growth. (The plant life is luxuriant here.) *Luxurious* means "characterized by self-indulgence or luxury." (The executive suite is luxurious.)

maintain, repair, service. *Maintain* means "to preserve; to keep in existing condition." (The company doesn't maintain its equipment properly.) *Repair* means "to restore; to fix." (They need to repair the copier.) *Service* also means "to keep in existing condition" and implies inspection as well as repair and maintenance. (The company services all brands of electronic typewriters.)

majority, minority, plurality. *Majority* means "a number greater than one-half of the total." *Minority* means "a number less than one-half of the total." *Plurality* means "the number of votes in excess of those cast for the closest contender when there are two or more candidates." (Abel received 25,000 votes, Baker received 20,000 votes, and Carson received 4,000 votes; thus Abel had a plurality of 5,000 votes.)

meticulous, scrupulous. *Meticulous* refers to extreme care in attending to details. (Her work is meticulous.) *Scrupulous* refers to high principles and conscientious regard. (He is scrupulous in dealings with foreign representatives.)

mysterious, mystical, mythical. *Mysterious* refers to something inexplicable or puzzling. (The chemical's mysterious action produced unpredicted results.) *Mystical* refers to something having a spiritual or unapparent significance. (The ritual has mystical overtones.) *Mythical* refers to something imaginary; something involving a myth. (The mythical story about the giant amused the foreign audience.)

official, officious. *Official* means "relating to an office or position of authority or trust." (Her official duties start tomorrow.) *Officious* means "meddlesome." (His actions struck the other employees as officious.)

omission, oversight. *Omission* means "something left out; something undone or neglected." (The omission was unintentional.) *Oversight* means "an inadvertent omission or error." (Her name was not on the program because of an oversight.)

one's self, oneself. *One's self* is used less often than *oneself*, except when the emphasis is on the *self*. (Psychologists say one's self is an amazing entity to be explored endlessly.) *Oneself* is the preferred spelling in most general usage. (One has to discipline oneself when corresponding with foreign contacts.)

oral, verbal. *Oral* means "spoken; by mouth." (They had an oral agreement but nothing in writing.) *Verbal* means "consisting of words, written or spoken." (The verbal instructions are unclear.) To be more precise, use *written* instead of *verbal.*

part, portion, share. *Part* means "a subdivision of the whole." (This is one part of the proposal.) *Portion* means "a part or share of something usually intended for a specific purpose." (This portion of the program is reserved for questions and answers.) *Share* means "the part or portion of something belonging to or given by someone." (His share of the profits is assigned to his capital account.)

persons, people. *Persons* is often preferred in references to a few individuals or when specific individuals are being discussed. (The president and the treasurer were the only persons there from the board.) *People* is often preferred in references to large groups or indefinite numbers. (People from other cultures sometimes find it difficult to adjust to new ways.)

point of view, standpoint, viewpoint. *Point of view, standpoint,* and *viewpoint* are used (often overused) interchangeably by business writers. They refer to an attitude or opinion. (From his point of view, the contract was already null and void.) Avoid all of them in international correspondence and recast sentences using expressions such as "We believe that . . ."

practical, practicable. *Practical* means "sensible; useful; realistic." (He used a practical approach to the problem.) *Practicable* means "usable; workable." (That idea is simply not practicable.)

prescribe, proscribe. *Prescribe* means "to lay down as a guide; to order." (She will prescribe a thorough review.) *Proscribe* means "to condemn; to outlaw." (The government will proscribe all Western literature.)

presumably, supposedly. *Presumably* refers to something that is taken for granted or reasonably assumed to be true. (Presumably, he is correct, since he ran all of the required tests.) *Supposedly* refers to something that is believed or imagined, sometimes mistakenly, to be true. (The order to halt production supposedly came from someone in the executive offices.) Both of these terms should be avoided in international correspondence.

principal, principle. *Principal,* as a noun, means "chief participant or head" (the principal in the contract) or "a sum of money." (The loan payment included principal and interest.) As an adjective, it means "most important or consequential" (the principal reason). *Principle,* a noun, refers to "a rule, doctrine, or assumption" (the principle of universal sovereignty).

proved, proven. *Proved* is the past tense and past participle of *prove*. (They proved their contention.) *Proven* is an adjective (the proven method) and also a past participle. (The volunteers have proven their loyalty.) *Proved*, however, is the preferred past participle. (The volunteers have proved their loyalty.)

qualitative, quantitative. *Qualitative* refers to quality or essential character. (Their qualitative analysis of the photographs included criteria for clarity and perspective.) *Quantitative* refers to quantity or a measurement. (Their quantitative analysis of the containers included measurements of size and volume.)

raise, rear. *Raise*, as a verb, means "to arouse; to elevate." (Raise the platform.) As a noun, it commonly means "an increase in pay." (She got a raise last month.) *Rear*, as a verb, means "to raise upright" (The animal reared its legs) or "to bring up a child." (She reared four children.) Colloquially, one also *raises* children.

reaction, reply, response. *Reaction* means "a response to stimuli." (The injection caused a violent reaction.) It should not be used to mean a response that is an "attitude, viewpoint, or feeling." *Reply* means "a response in words." (She faxed her reply.) *Response* is "a reply; a reaction; an answer." (The client's response was positive.)

redundant, superfluous. *Redundant* means "more than necessary; repetitive," and usually refers to wordiness in oral and written communication. (That paragraph is redundant.) *Superfluous* means "exceeding what is needed," but the emphasis is on something useless or unnecessary rather than repetitive. (Many of his suggestions are superfluous.)

reported, reputed. *Reported* means "made known." (They reported the error immediately.) *Reputed* means "considered; believed; supposed." (The company is reputed to be a leader in the industry.)

shall, will. *Shall*, traditionally, is used in the first person to express future time. (I shall be happy to go.) Some authorities believe *shall* sounds stuffy and snobbish and prefer to use *will*. *Will*, traditionally, is used in the second or third person to express future time. (He will be happy to go.) Contemporary usage shows an increasing preference for *will* in all instances (I will, you will, he will, she will, they will).

stationary, stationery. *Stationary*, an adjective, means "fixed, immobile." (The computer system is stationary.) *Stationery*, a noun, means "writing paper and related office supplies." (It is time to order new stationery.)

strain, stress. *Strain,* as a verb, means "to misuse; to filter; to stretch beyond belief; to overexert." (He strained the business relationship by being too demanding.) As a noun, it means "excessive exertion or tension." (No strain on his heart was evident.) *Stress,* as a verb, means "to accent; to emphasize." (He stressed the danger involved.) As a noun, it means "pressure; tension." (She suffered great stress during the competition.)

subconscious, unconscious. *Subconscious* refers to mental activities of which one is not conscious or aware. (They wondered what subconscious motive he had for provoking his employer.) *Unconscious* refers to loss of consciousness or awareness. (She was unconscious for an hour after the accident.)

systematize, systemize. *Systematize,* the more familiar verb, means "to arrange systematically; to put in order." (The committee needs to systematize its work.) *Systemize,* although used less often, means the same as *systematize.* Both terms are forms of business jargon that should be avoided in nonbusiness writing and in international correspondence.

that, which. *That* refers to persons, animals, or things and should be used to introduce restrictive clauses—clauses that are essential to explain the preceding information. (The group that won last year came in first again.) The clause "that won last year" provides essential information that defines *which* group. It should *not* be set off with commas. *Which* refers to animals and things and should be used to introduce nonrestrictive clauses—clauses that are not essential for the reader to understand the meaning of the other information in the sentence. (The new contract, which is the most complex contract I have ever seen, is ready for signing.) The clause "which is the most complex contract I have ever seen" is not essential for the reader to understand that the contract is ready to be signed. It *should* be set off with commas.

toward, towards. *Toward* is the shorter, and thus preferred, version of the word meaning "in the direction of; approaching" (moving toward our goal). *Towards* is a variation of *toward.*

trace, vestige. *Trace* means "evidence of something that has passed." (She could find no trace of the file.) *Vestige* means "a visible sign or an actual mark of something that has passed." (The ruins are the last vestige of the ancient city.)

varied, various. *Varied* means "diverse; with numerous forms." (The logos on business letterheads are varied.) *Various* means "dissimilar; separate; different." (The memo was sent to various divisions in the company.)

viable, workable. *Viable,* an often overused and misused term, means "capable of existence." (The new company is a viable entity.) *Workable* means "practicable; feasible; capable of working or succeeding." (The plan seems workable to me.)

want, wish. *Want* suggests a need or longing. (I really want that contract.) *Wish* is used more often to suggest hope as well as desire. (I wish I had about ten more clients.)

who, whom. *Whom* is the objective form of *who. Who* is always in the subjective case. In the sentence "The man who is in charge will be here shortly," *who* is the subject of *is.* In the sentence "The man whom he left in charge will be here shortly," *whom* is the object of *left.*

Antagonistic Words

There is a point where instructors back off from their insistence that you always be precise and clear. That happens when they start worrying that someone will do what foreign readers do and interpret those instructions literally, so literally that other considerations, such as tact, are tossed aside. So now we need to add a couple more ingredients to the mix: common sense and diplomacy. It may be precise and clear, for example, to state that you have "nothing but contempt" for your contact's position on a trade issue and consider his view to be "outrageously unreasonable." However accurate that may be, if you say it you'll probably have to look for a new customer.

Using precise language that irritates someone is just as bad as using vague or unfamiliar expressions—worse, in fact. Some words that are used in a certain context or that enforce a certain tone create the impression of an outright assault. Writers often refer to such words as "loaded" because they can provoke a potentially explosive response.

> *Loaded:* Thank you for the material. I am afraid, however, that it is inadequate. We require further information on last year's sales by consumer age group.

> *Neutral:* Thank you for the material, which will be very useful in our market study. It would be helpful if we could also have additional information on last year's sales by consumer age group.

> *Loaded:* Although your warning that the market is short-term may prove to be correct, we believe that view is generally shortsighted and have decided to proceed anyway.

> *Neutral:* We appreciated your valuable caution that the market is short-term. After receiving your suggestion, our marketing staff thoroughly studied this possibility and agreed that the risk exists. For other reasons, however, they have decided to proceed.

Some words, used with the wrong tone, imply that the reader is dumb, careless, dishonest, or unimportant. If you call yourself stupid, that's one thing (even if questionable); if you imply that your contact is stupid, that's something else. Here's a list of words that either should not be used or should be used only in sentences crafted with great care and sensitivity.

abolish	dense	inadequate
absurd	deny	incompetent
abuse	deplore	insist
admonish	deprive	intolerable
afraid	desert	invalid
allege	despise	irritate
ambiguous	destroy	liable
apparently	dictate	lie
argue	disaster	ludicrous
assume	dismal	meager
bad	dispute	meddle
banal	dominate	mediocre
beware	dumb	menial
biased	exaggerate	misinform
blame	extravagant	misrepresent
bleak	fail	mistake
cancel	false	mundane
careless	fault	must
censure	fiasco	naive
cheap	flagrant	negligence
claim	flimsy	obligated
commonplace	foul	obstinate
complain	hamper	obstruct
contempt	hapless	opinionated
contend	harass	overbearing
control	hate	perhaps
damage	hinder	pessimist
deceive	hurt	precipitate
defy	ignorant	prejudice
demand	impede	premature

pretentious	shirk	tamper
quibble	shortsighted	tardy
radical	slow	timid
repulsive	squander	troublesome
rude	stagnant	ugly
ruin	stubborn	unfair
ruthless	stupid	unsuccessful
sarcastic	superficial	useless
senseless	superfluous	wasteful
shameful	tainted	weak
		wrong

Vague Words

With this section, we've come full circle in this chapter. Notwithstanding the need to be tactful and sensitive at all times, the greatest problem in international correspondence is still the failure to be adequately precise and clear for a foreign reader who translates everything literally. Without question, it's important to avoid untranslatable or difficult-to-translate expressions, such as neologisms, trendy words, humor, acronyms, oxymorons, idioms, grammatical errors, incorrect (confusable) terms, and loaded words. But even if you use language that avoids all of those problems, is it truly precise and clear?

Some words may not be offensive or trendy and a foreign reader may be able to find them in his or her English dictionary. But are the words *specific* enough for your contact to know exactly what to do and when to do it or what to expect you to do and when you will do it? Being specific means using exact dates, not *soon* or *at your convenience* or *this winter.* It means replacing generic words, such as *distribute,* with a more precise term, such as *mail,* when the generic term doesn't tell the reader enough about what to expect or do.

Vague: I will telephone you sometime in the next week or two.

Specific: I will telephone you Tuesday morning, Frankfurt time, February 17, 19—.

Vague: I will let you know our decision in the near future.

Specific: I will let you know our decision by September 1, 19—.

Vague: You suggested recently that we meet on your next trip to the United States.

Specific: You suggested in your June 11 letter that we meet on your next trip to the United States.

Vague (and negative): We won't be able to ship the merchandise until our stock is replenished.

Specific (and positive): The denim trousers you ordered are temporarily out of stock. However, we expect to ship this merchandise to you on Monday, August 15, 19—.

You're thinking that you might not want to commit yourself to a specific date. Fine.

We expect to receive a new supply of this merchandise in August. We will notify you as soon as we know the exact date the goods will be shipped to you.

An important objective is to give the reader *some* specifics, even if no more than a guarantee that you will write again as soon as you can be more definite. Usually, though, it doesn't hurt to mention a date when you will write again.

I will write to you again by August 1 to let you know if the material has arrived in our shipping department.

Often, it is even safe to give an approximate date of shipment, if you are reasonably certain about it, since you can always write back and say that this or that happened and you deeply regret that your shipping date has been moved ahead to so and so. Most readers anywhere, here or in other countries, appreciate knowing if something is going to happen in about two weeks or two months or two years. It's nearly always possible to narrow the possibilities to that extent.

As mentioned earlier, you might want to be vague to avoid offending someone. Such a situation is an exception to the rule about being specific. It may also be necessary to be vague to avoid revealing some critical information about your company, and it is definitely better to be vague in regard to mentioning names or assigning blame when a mistake is involved. There are other ways to point out an error.

Specific: We noticed the error *you* made in your October 6 letter. *Or:* We believe *your* figure of $1,432.42 is incorrect.

Vague: We wonder if the amount of $1,432.42 quoted in your October 6 letter was intended to be $11,432.42.

Admittedly, pointing out errors is a touchy business, but it isn't necessary to go to the extreme of ignoring an error—unless it's unimportant or nonessential to your business transactions. In that case, why bring it up? But if it's important to request a correction, go ahead and mention the error without referring to the person who made it.

In all other situations, when there is no need to avoid assigning blame, pick a specific term over a generic term if it will answer questions the reader has or will help the reader understand what you want to convey. Here are some generic terms that don't mean much to the person reading them. Unless you have a good reason not to reveal anything specific about your business, avoid these wishy-washy, muddled expressions or make your terms clear by explaining them in your letters. An example of a specific substitute follows each vague term in the next list.

activity:	fund raising
affair:	seminar
building:	warehouse
capacity:	2 tons
change:	delete paragraph 2
concerns:	questions about . . .
conditions:	(1) . . . , (2) . . .
design:	drawing of . . .
distribute:	mail
economics:	financial losses
effect:	reduction in sales
emotion:	anger
enlighten:	persuade to . . .
facilities:	staff offices
function:	annual meeting
good:	accurate
great:	wide
misfortune:	fire
neat:	orderly
nice:	polite
obligation:	debt
operations:	manufacturing
properties:	shopping malls
procedures:	(1) . . . , (2) . . .
sometime:	July 2, 19—
soon:	in one week
system:	method for . . .
vehicle:	car
work:	programming

CHECKUP

Now that we're all experts on being precise and literal, and since we decided in Chapters 1 to 3 not to do other questionable things that would offend or confuse foreign readers, let's test ourselves. No, this isn't a quiz. It's a check to see if the suggestions thus far in the book will work.

Here are a few poorly written letters from my collection of sample letters, along with suggested rewrites. Don't feel that the revised versions are the only correct alternatives. You may have a much better idea, or at least you may have suggestions that would make the letters more suitable for your clients or customers and your relationship with them.

It would be foolish to try to provide model letters that are suitable for every businessperson in every country of the world. A letter written to someone in Japan, for example, might not be suitable for someone in Saudi Arabia. Countries have vastly different business, social, and religious customs that could affect what you say and how you say it (more about country differences in Chapters 8 and 9). So the following examples are generalized models. They're provided here primarily for us to see how easy it is to locate and correct the so-called taboos of international correspondence, such as humor, contractions, too much familiarity, and vagueness. The first letter in each of the examples is the bad example; the second one is the revised version.

Keeping in mind that readers in other countries usually interpret everything they read literally, notice some of the problems in the first of the two letters to Mr. Pushkarov, including slang and cliches, such as "Is my face ever red!" "I don't know how on earth . . ." "The express company will . . . get them out of your hair." The writing overall, in fact, lacks the preciseness and clarity that letters to non–English-speaking recipients need ("I think that will take care of it"). Also, did you notice the incorrect spelling, *accidently,* and several contractions, such as *don't* and *I've*? Finally, the closing "Regards" is too familiar for an international audience.

The first of the two letters to Mr. Katsumi has similar problems. For example, it uses contractions and the abbreviation *TMI* rather than the full company name. The noun *principle* is incorrectly used for the adjective *principal,* and the vague word *recent* is used instead of a specific date. The letter also refers to *you,* rather than *your company,* which many Japanese readers would find inappropriate. The concluding sentence, "We're looking forward to your prompt reply," is questionable. Many foreign readers might think they were being rushed or pushed. In addition, the request being made would be much easier to understand if it was presented more clearly and simply as a list of specific items. In this letter, too, the closing "With best wishes" is much too familiar for the first contact with a Japanese reader.

The first of the two letters to Mr. Tinoco also uses unfamiliar English, with new words such as "New Age," cliches and slang such as "A-1" and "green light," idioms such as "as regards," and vague terms such as "your line." These expressions are likely to puzzle most foreign readers and create a translation nightmare. Like the closing in the other letters, the closing in this letter ("Cordially") is too familiar for a foreign audience.

WORLDWIDE VIDEO AIDS, INC.
1301 FOURTH STREET
COLUMBIA, SC 29201
U.S.A.

phone 803-555-1601 / fax 803-555-1602

April 9, 1994

Your order BAS-2237

Mr. Ognyan Pushkarov
Bulgarska Academy
430 Stamboliski Boulevard
Sofia, Bulgaria

Dear Mr. Pushkarov:

Is my face ever red! I don't know how on earth that box of standard cassettes accidently found its way into your order for videocassettes. Please forgive us for the confusion and inconvenience.

I've instructed our Shipping Department to air express a box of videocassettes to you today. The express company will also pick up the box of standard cassettes and get them out of your hair.

I think that will take care of it, but if there's any further problem, don't hesitate to let me know. We appreciate your business and will do our utmost to satisfy your needs.

Thanks for your patience.

Regards,

John R. Simmons
Manager

jct

WORLDWIDE VIDEO AIDS, INC.
1301 FOURTH STREET
COLUMBIA, SC 29201
U.S.A.

phone 803-555-1601 / fax 803-555-1602

April 9, 1994

Your order BAS-2237

Mr. Ognyan Pushkarov
Bulgarska Academy
430 Stamboliski Boulevard
Sofia, Bulgaria

Dear Mr. Pushkarov:

We sincerely regret the confusion about your order of March 16, 1994. You had asked for twelve cartons of our English-language videocassettes. Our Shipping Department accidentally included one box of standard cassettes.

The Shipping Department is sending you another carton of videocassettes by Western Air Express today. We have also asked the express company to return the standard cassettes to us.

We are sorry for the inconvenience this error has caused. Thank you for your cooperation and understanding. We appreciate your business.

Sincerely,

John R. Simmons
Manager

jct

TRANSMASTER INNOVATIONS, INC.
18 WEST AVENUE
ORLANDO, FL 32808

phone 407-555-8312 / fax 407-555-8313

September 16, 1994

Mr. H. O. Katsumi
Katsumi Electronics Ltd.
10 Ichiban-cho
Tokyo 102, Japan

Dear Mr. Katsumi:

We're very much interested in an ad of yours
that ran in a recent issue of <u>New Electronics</u>.

TMI is always looking for good electronic
products and accessories to keep our old customers
happy and to attract new ones. Would you please
tell us more about your principle products? Also,
please send your wholesale prices, your terms, and
ordering instructions.

Thanks for your help. We're looking forward
to your prompt reply.

With best wishes,

Arnold G. Baerwald
General Manager

gf

TRANSMASTER INNOVATIONS, INC.
18 WEST AVENUE
ORLANDO, FL 32808

phone 407-555-8312 / fax 407-555-8313

September 16, 1994

Mr. H. O. Katsumi
Katsumi Electronics Ltd.
10 Ichiban-cho
Tokyo 102, Japan

Dear Mr. Katsumi:

We have read with interest your company's advertisement of Katsumi electronic accessories. This information appeared in the March 1994 issue of New Electronics.

TransMaster Innovations wants to provide a wide selection of electronic products and accessories for its customers. We would like to know more about your company's products and accessories. Please send us the following information:

- Wholesale price list
- Payment terms
- Instructions for placing orders

Thank you.

Sincerely yours,

Arnold G. Baerwald
General Manager

gf

THE WOODHILL GALLERY
606 LAKESIDE BOULEVARD
CHICAGO, IL 60650
U.S.A.

phone 312-555-0900 / fax 312-555-0901

June 23, 1994

Your reference MAZCR

Mr. Jean-Pierre Tinoco
CAR Artifacts
12 Avenue President Dacko
Bangui, Central African Republic

Dear Mr. Tinoco:

    Thanks for sending the four sample figures to our sales office for our review and consideration in regard to including your figures in our quarterly home decor catalog.

    The figures were really A-1 quality and would appeal to both our traditional buyers and the new age crowd. As regards your products, our president is very much interested in carrying them, but first our marketing people need to take a look at the figures. After I get a green light from them, I'll let you know one way or another what we'd like to do.

    Let's hope it works out that we can carry your line. I know I was very impressed, and everyone else had the same favorable reaction. Thanks much for thinking of us.

        Cordially,

        (Mrs.) Madeline C. Kalck
        Marketing Division

sr

THE WOODHILL GALLERY
606 LAKESIDE BOULEVARD
CHICAGO, IL 60650
U.S.A.

phone 312-555-0900 / fax 312-555-0901

June 23, 1994

Your reference MAZCR

Mr. Jean-Pierre Tinoco
CAR Artifacts
12 Avenue President Dacko
Bangui, Central African Republic

Dear Mr. Tinoco:

Thank you for sending us the four sample carved figures. I have sent them to our Nationwide Home and Decor sales office for evaluation.

We were pleased with the quality of the hand-carved figures. Our president would like to consider them for inclusion in our October 1994 catalog. First, our Marketing Review Committee will evaluate the figures and the price schedule on July 26, 1994. We expect to have the committee's report within a week after the review. I will then write to you with our decision on August 2.

We appreciate your interest in using our catalog to sell your products.

Sincerely yours,

(Mrs.) Madeline C. Kalck
Marketing Division

sr

5

The Language Demons Among Us

A LOT OF PEOPLE are worried about sloppy language and the television and trade-press reports that it's costing corporate America millions of dollars every year. We all get very nervous when something starts costing us money. Although language problems have always existed, they have worsened in the past several decades.

Something happened in the 1950s. Before that, both management and the academic community still insisted on clear, precise, practical language, without frills or distortions. Since then, U.S. English has been invaded by a frightening array of imprecise, sometimes senseless words and expressions. New words are created almost every day, whether or not they're needed, and they're no longer the clear, specific terms that everyone, here and in other countries, can recognize and understand.

The experts disagree about why this erosion has occurred. Is it unconscious, or is sloppy language a deliberate attempt to disguise sloppy thinking? Right or wrong, most people believe that the deterioration of our language is the fault of the academic community, which they claim is graduating more and more people who can barely read or write. Those who support this position argue that it's no wonder recent generations are picking up street language or the fuzzy jargon that resounds through millions of offices across the country; these people never learned anything better and were never taught the serious consequences of using sloppy language.

Suddenly, in this global society of the 1990s, alarms are sounding everywhere. If even Ameri-

118

cans are becoming distressed by today's fuzzy, unfamiliar language, what do people in other countries think? Miscommunication is more than an annoyance—ask anyone who has experienced one of the mishaps mentioned in this book. It's a very real threat to everyone engaged in international trade.

Enough about the problem. What about the solution? What can we do? One thing we can and must do is get rid of those destructive language demons, such as slang, jargon, and cliches, that have infiltrated our language. Expecting a foreign reader to cope with a renegade vocabulary is simply asking too much.

SPECIALIZED LANGUAGE

Jargon

How would you define *jargon*? To give you an idea of how fuzzy specialized language can be, even the term *jargon* means different things to different people. To some, it refers to the specialized language of a particular business or profession, such as the term *rollover* (reinvestment) in the financial community. To others, it means any confusing language, such as *systematize* (to order or arrange according to a plan). To some, it refers to any simplified language or language "shorthand," such as *output* (something produced). The one common aspect of all the definitions is that jargon in any form isn't intelligible to everyone. In this book we're concerned about words and expressions that aren't intelligible to a foreign audience, and jargon is a perfect example of such language.

The owner of a small firm that provides various business services to clients in African and European countries strongly endorses the view that specialized language can ruin an international relationship. Yet in one of our conversations I noticed that his speech was heavily laced with jargon and wondered if the same was true of his letters. A few of the expressions that I quickly jotted down after one visit were *game plan, optimize, smart money, empowerment, consumer confidence, bottom line, mobility, free ride, back burner, hedge, end user, stonewall,* and *benchmark.* But I don't think this person realized that he was using some form of jargon in every other sentence.

If you believe, as I do, that we're all slaves to our habits, good or bad, it's reasonable to suspect that jargon is so widely used that it appears not only in our domestic correspondence but also in our international correspondence. I know that I found it in the sample letters I have in my collection. Here are a few examples.

Budgetwise, we should be able to complete our study in time.

Lack of time was the *causative factor* in that case.

Our *frame of reference* is that the shipments were accidentally rerouted.

The *operative* word is "agreement."

We need to *optimize* sales in Japan before expanding our *base.*

We already know that jargon is a specialized language, which means it isn't understood by everyone. But sometimes it isn't intelligible or comprehensible to anyone. That's why there are terms such as *shop talk, buzzword,* and *gobbledygook.*

If you think of *jargon* as specialized language used in a trade or profession, you might consider *shop talk* to be *super*specialized jargon, something that (so far) isn't generally used outside the particular area of business or the profession where it originated, for example: *hoofer* (dancer), *lettuce* (paper money), *splash* (major news story), *bulge* (rise in stock prices or shares).

Anyone who reads a daily paper or listens to television newscasts sees or hears buzzwords. *Buzzwords* are important-sounding, often imprecise substitutes for clear terms and expressions, usually created and used to impress laypeople, for example: *candy-store problem* (a problem for which a wide variety of choices exists), *mouse-milking* (investing a large effort for only a small result), *haircut* (neat trimming of expenditures that leaves the main item intact), and *gridlock* (inaction caused by the inability of opposing sides to agree or compromise). Sometimes buzzwords and other forms of jargon are used intentionally to avoid giving away information about a confidential or sensitive subject. John J. Tarrant, commenting in *Savvy* on the need to say what you mean, said that business writing should always be "clear, precise, and direct," except when you want it to be "cloudy, inflated, and meandering."

Gobbledygook is the vaguest, most abstract form of jargon that exists. When you read something so obtuse or convoluted that it's completely meaningless, you're reading *gobbledygook.* Here's one example from my collection of letters that I had no trouble assigning to this category.

> We have extended our operations into the lateral areas of market opportunity within which dual parameters are instrumental in effecting acceptable aggregation or return. Notwithstanding the capacities of functional distribution sequences, I project relative economies in our systematic procedural practices. We will, of course, utilize the customary channels in effecting equitable relations to support mutual benefits pursuant to successful activities prior to initiation.

Do you know what that means? I have no idea, and I've read it about a dozen times. I wonder if the writer himself knows? That one gets my "Stupid-of-the-Month" gobbledygook award.

Let's give this next example—from a letter by a different businessperson—the gobbledygook runner-up award.

> To inaugurate the hypothetical equivalency representation, I am enclosing a compendium of arbitrary properties for your perusal and corresponding propagandizement. Although the proclamation of acquiescence in commercialization may be a common misrepresentation, we propose to prioritize this condition by delineating and extricating any such impracticable comparisons.

Again, do you know what that means? Again, I don't. In fact, it makes me dizzy to read it—not as dizzy as the writer must have been, however.

You can see how widely jargon varies, from slightly hard to understand and unclear to completely nonsensical and meaningless. If an English-speaking American of moderate intelligence can't make sense of something, how can a non–English-speaking foreign reader possibly understand it?

If you suddenly fear that you may be using jargon and not even be aware of it, check your letters for terms and expressions such as those in the next list. If you find any such expressions, substitute a specific term that will be more familiar to a foreign reader. Common definitions follow each example. Keep in mind that for an international audience, the objective is not to use as few words as possible but to express something as clearly as possible so that the foreign reader will understand it. Don't be puzzled if something that you thought was a cliche or slang expression is listed here as jargon. Certain words and expressions may fit into more than one category.

abort: discontinue.

advance planning: planning.

access: enter, retrieve.

across the board: in each office, department, etc.

after market: after something has been sold or purchased.

angel: someone who backs or invests in something.

at liberty: out of work.

ax: end, stop before completion.

back burner: a position of little importance.

back to back: consecutive.

bag: get, successfully acquire something.

balloon payment: lump sum payable at the end of a loan period.

ballpark figure: estimate.

bear: someone who believes stock prices will fall.

bottom line: actual cost or price.

bounce around: consider.

budgetwise: in regard to the budget.

bull: someone who believes stock prices will rise.

cap: set a limit to.

causative factor: cause.

change agent: someone who takes steps to change things.

comeback: successful return.

contact: telephone, write, etc.

cover up: hide the truth.

credibility gap: inability to believe something.

crossover: activity in more than one area.

deadend: having no exit or opportunity.

debug: find and correct errors.

down time: idle period created through an error.

downsize: reduce in size.

E-mail: computer mail, facsimile, etc.

eta: estimated time of arrival.

expertise: special knowledge.

eyes only: confidential.

fallout: consequences.

fast track: quick route to advancement.

fax: facsimile.

finalize: end, finish.

flap: disturbance.

frame of reference: viewpoint, theory.

flipflop: change views to opposite position.

flop: failure.

free ride: benefit acquired without paying or contributing.

freeze: stop and hold something at its present position.

game plan: plan, approach.

graveyard shift: shift from midnight to early morning.

gut feeling: instinctive belief.

hammer out: prepare, write, etc.

hardball: tough approach.

hardware: equipment.

high tech: advanced technology.

hype: promote through exaggerated claims.

inaugurate: begin.

infrastructure: underlying foundation or basic framework.

in-house: within the company.

input: ideas, comments, information provided to a person or machine.

interface: connection, meeting.

interpersonal: personal, human.

kick around: discuss.

kill: terminate, end, stop.

knockout: something exceptionally appealing.

know the ropes: to know the procedure.

long haul: long-term, until completion.

man-hours: hours worked.

markup: increase in price.

Mickey Mouse: petty, unnecessary.

moot point: debatable point.

muzzle: keep quiet, stop from commenting.

network: establish a link.

nitpick: focus on minor points.

off the record: confidentially.

off-line: relating to a computer not controlled by a central machine.

on-line: relating to a computer controlling operations and peripherals.

on the fence: unable to decide.

operative: defining, determining, important.

optimize: enhance, improve, increase.

optimum: most.

option: right to, alternative.

output: what is produced.

overkill: too much.

paradigm: archetype, model, outline, pattern.

parameter: boundary, constraint, guideline.

phase: part, stage.

prior to: before.

prioritize: list in order of importance.

rap: blame.

red ink: financial loss.

rep: representative.

responsive: sensitive, responding.

rollback: a return to lower prices.

rollover: reinvestment.

sacred cow: something too important to change.

scenario: estimate, event, situation.

smart money: those who know best.

stonewall: be inflexible, adamant.

systematize: arrange according to a plan, put in order.

time frame: time.

top of the line: leading product, best product.

turnover: change in personnel or products, with new ones coming in and previous ones going out.

update: bring up to date.

user-friendly: easy to learn and use.

viable: capable of working or developing.

window: opening in idea, attitude, etc.; opportunity.

workup: routine diagnostic procedures.

zap: strike, shock.

Euphemisms

You could develop an argument in favor of using euphemisms, which are inoffensive substitutes for potentially offensive expressions. (For example, *intoxicated* is a euphemism for *drunk*.) After all, who wants to offend someone? This book, in fact, advocates being especially sensitive when corresponding with people in other countries. So doesn't it logically follow that we should use euphemisms whenever possible in our international correspondence? At the moment, you may believe the answer should be yes. But by the end of this discussion, you will probably change your mind, at least in regard to most situations.

A disturbing problem with euphemisms is that they tend to distort the actual meaning of something, making it seem better or worse than it really is. If you call a garbage collector a "sanitation engineer," for example, it appears to elevate the status of garbage collectors to that of civil, electrical, mechanical, and other engineers whose job requirements include holding a bachelor's degree or completing other higher education. The garbage collector, meanwhile, may not even need a high school diploma. Both types of "engineering" positions involve honest, reputable work, but both types of workers are not *engineers* in the traditional sense of the word. In this context *engineer* is a euphemism intended to be more pleasing to everyone.

It could just as easily work the other way. The euphemism might diminish rather than elevate. When you refer to someone as "departed" instead of "dead," you may think it softens the impact. But it's very misleading. If you write to your foreign contact that Ms. Rogers, the president of your company, "has departed" and won't be able to meet the person next month as planned, what will the reader think? To someone unfamiliar with the details or recent events, it might suggest that Ms. Rogers inconsiderately left for a vacation or decided to meet another customer somewhere else. Although you know where she *really* went, the reader doesn't have a crystal ball. So euphemisms, although well intentioned, can cause misunderstanding.

Since the pros and cons of using euphemisms are debatable, try applying common sense to individual cases in deciding whether or not you should use one. If the euphemism could be misinterpreted or might confuse your foreign contact, find a better word. If all other words are simply too offensive, too sexist, or too inappropriate in some other way that would make you appear crude and unprofessional, use the euphemism. The euphemism *firefighter,* for instance, is preferred over the traditional term *fireman,* which is now considered sexist. In most of the following examples, though, the actual expression would be more specific and clearer to a foreign reader than the euphemism.

> **abdomen:** stomach, belly.
> **act of God:** disaster.
> **altogether:** nudity.
> **amenity center:** public toilet.
> **appropriate:** take.
> **archivist:** library clerk, museum clerk.
> **assault:** rape.
> **au naturel:** naked.
> **benign neglect:** neglect.
> **birthday suit:** nakedness.

bite the dust: die.

blessed event: birth.

bosom: breasts.

brainwash: change someone's beliefs.

buy the farm: die.

capital punishment: death penalty.

casket: coffin.

casualty: victim.

comfort station: public toilet.

confidential source: informer.

confrontation: fight, heated argument.

correctional facility: prison.

cover story: lie.

custodial engineer: janitor.

custodian: janitor.

deceased: dead, dead person.

deep-six: destroy.

demise: death.

departed: dead.

direct mail: unsolicited mail.

disadvantaged: poor.

embroider the truth: lie.

erotica: pornography.

exceptional child: retarded, disabled, handicapped child.

expecting: pregnant.

experienced tires: recaps, retreads.

expire: die.

explosive device: bomb.

facilities: toilet.

food preparation center: kitchen.

free enterprise: private enterprise.

furlough: layoff from work.

game management: hunting.

golden years: old age.

hairpiece: toupee, wig.

halitosis: bad breath.

happy hour: time for enjoying cocktails and relaxation.
hard of hearing: deaf.
head: toilet.
high: drunk.
hit: murder.
indigent: poor.
indisposed: ill, nauseated, sick.
interment: burial.
intoxicated: drunk.
job action: strike or slowdown.
john: toilet; customer of prostitute.
kickback: bribe.
landfill: garbage dump.
lay to rest: bury.
love child: illegitimate child.
loved one: dead person.
low-income: poor.
marketing representative: salesperson.
minority: black, Hispanic, Asian, etc.
mortality rate: death rate.
motion discomfort: motion sickness, nausea.
not doing well: dying.
nude: naked.
obituary: death notice.
pass away: die.
paying guest: boarder.
plant: bury.
police action: war.
powder room: toilet.
preowned car: secondhand, used car.
prevaricate: lie.
private parts: genitals.
procedure: operation (medical).
put down: kill, put to death.
put to sleep: kill, put to death.
quaint: small.

quarantine: blockade.

recession: small depression.

recycle: reuse.

relieve from job: fire.

remains: corpse, dead body.

remuneration: pay, wages, etc.

respect: fear.

restroom: public toilet.

rotund: fat.

salvage: steal.

sanitary engineer: garbage collector.

scenario: plan, sequence of actions.

senior citizens: old people.

social disease: gonorrhea, syphilis, etc.

speculate: gamble.

stable growth: slow growth.

stretch the truth: lie.

take under advisement: defer action.

terminate: end.

tissue: toilet paper.

traffic expediter: shipping clerk.

underachiever: someone who isn't doing as well as possible.

underdeveloped: poor, backward.

underprivileged: destitute, poor.

unmentionables: underwear.

verbalize: talk.

washroom: toilet.

white lie: lie.

Provincialisms

The use of *provincialisms*, expressions peculiar to a particular region, doesn't cause as many misunderstandings today as in the past. Watching television and being part of a very mobile society have helped us to become familiar with every part of the country. The greatest differences today from one region to another are in pronunciation rather than vocabulary. But anyone who writes letters to people in other countries needs to be aware that provincialisms may inadvertently creep in and confuse a foreign reader. To prevent that, guard against casual references such as *chuck* (throw), *tote* (carry), and *piece* (distance). Provincialisms like these that have spread across the country may today be part of the American colloquial vocabulary, but they are not always part of standard English.

You've probably noticed that in some parts of the United States, the residents still pronounce certain words as if letters had been added to them. If you live in northern New England, particularly near Boston, you'll be familiar with the added *r: i-de-er* (idea). It's important to prevent such local speech patterns from affecting your writing. Therefore, even if you add an *r* to the word in speech, spell it as *idea*. This rule should apply to other expressions, such as *anywheres* (anywhere) that you may have picked up in your youth or acquired after living somewhere for a long time. Regardless of pronunciation, spell out all words in international correspondence according to nationally accepted standard English.

In other parts of the world, such as some of the poorer African nations, the population is less mobile and modern communications media such as television aren't widely available to unite the population culturally and bring regional variations together into one language. In such cases, regional distinctions remain firmly entrenched. Just as a foreign reader would have trouble translating our provincialisms, we could have trouble translating regional expressions in another country. Let's hope our foreign contacts will weed out their provincialisms too.

Slang

An essay in *Time* magazine more than a decade ago ("If Slang Is Not a Sin") suggested that slang isn't fun anymore (that is, if it's not a sin). Good. That may eliminate some of the temptation to use it in letters and other writing. It's such a menace to international understanding that I'm always disturbed when I read a letter with slang expressions. I've talked to managers, too, who said that it would be fine with them if slang were suddenly to vanish from the vocabularies of all their employees. They're talking about arbitrarily coined, sometimes crude or outrageous expressions.

One college professor called *slang* "disreputable, abused English." It's that and more. Slang is a new, specialized language created by a particular person or group, often *not* to define something new but rather to make a statement about or to ridicule something that already exists. Many slang expressions are coined by young, school-age children who want to have their own language, something that will express their rebellious nature and set them apart from their parents and teachers. But they're not the only ones coining new words; during the past decade the drug culture has contributed numerous slang expressions. Computer users, however, may soon be the largest group of language abusers. As you probably know, a computer that isn't working is *down* or has *crashed;* ornamental characters, such as bullets, are *dingbats;* and a brief, usually large increase in voltage is a *spike.* One computer writer has cheerfully admitted that simple, clear English is too old-fashioned and boring for his taste; it doesn't fit the snappy, clever, ultramodern image he wants to portray.

One nice thing about slang is that it usually doesn't last too long. Slang depends on novelty and distinctiveness (or shock value) to qualify for adoption. Those qualities are supposed to be a major part of its appeal. So a slang expression either dies a natural death over time by losing its freshness through repetition, or it stays around so long that it ceases to be slang and just becomes another tired cliche or a part of the regular language. In any case, it disappears from current slang vocabularies.

Many slang expressions are part of the informal language used in everyday life. Others are too obscene or too ridiculous to be usable in the working world. Foreign readers with strict religious customs and strong moral values won't appreciate expressions that to them are distasteful, crude, or immoral. Can you imagine saying to a very religious Arab or a conservative Japanese client, "Let's get naked," which is slang for "let's have a good time"?

Along with such completely unacceptable expressions are many generally inoffensive ones that will nevertheless be just as misleading to foreign readers. If you write that a project report is "on the shelf," the reader will interpret it as "resting on a shelf," such as a bookshelf. You, of course, would have meant that the report is inactive or not currently being considered.

What to do? Use the same procedure as recommended for other specialized language. Edit out the slang expressions that you write out of habit and replace them with standard English words that a foreign reader can translate more easily. The following list has some slang expressions taken from my letter collection, with suggested rewrites.

Slang: We will *give it our best shot.*
Rewrite: We will do the best job we can.

Slang: At this point, we will be happy simply *to get out from under* it.
Rewrite: We will be satisfied if we can avoid further expense.

Slang: The contract is *cut and dried,* but let us know if you have any questions.
Rewrite: The contract contains our regular provisions, but let us know if you have any questions.

Slang: I will *follow up* on April 30.
Rewrite: I will write again on April 30.

Slang: We will *stay on top of* the problem.
Rewrite: We will control the problem.

Slang: We have decided *to scrap* the original plan and *start from scratch.*
Rewrite: We have decided to abandon the original plan and develop a new plan.

Slang: One thing is *for sure*—we must pack our shipments more carefully.
Rewrite: We must pack our shipments more carefully.

Slang: I believe we can *work this out.*
Rewrite: I believe we can find a solution.

Slang: I will be *on the road* the first week in July.
Rewrite: I will be traveling the first week in July.

It's obvious to most people that you shouldn't use expressions that are obscene; expressions that refer to God, Allah, or other deities in a sacrilegious way; expressions with sexual connotations; or expressions that irreverently refer to a part of the body. Most people in business evidently understand how far they can go, because my collection of letters includes only a few coarse expressions. But I found plenty of the milder variety.

Those of you who can't seem to get rid of the habit of using slang in everyday conversation, BEWARE. Check your international correspondence against the following list and try to develop a new habit of rephrasing slang expressions into something literally translatable. (For more about nonstandard English expressions, refer to the list of cliches later in this chapter.)

ace: someone with unusual skills.

ace in the hole: a hidden advantage.

ahead of the game: in a winning or advantageous position.

all the way: completely, until the end.

and how: yes.

as per usual: as usual.

ask for it: provoke.

asleep at the switch: inattentive.

ax: dismiss.

baby-sit: attend to, care for.

back down: surrender, retreat.

back off: moderate one's stand.

back out: cancel, renege.

back to square one: back to the beginning.

backup: in reserve.

bad-mouth: denigrate.

Band-Aid: temporary solution, short-term relief.

bank on: rely on.

bargaining chip: something offered in negotiations.

big league: important.

blockbuster: great success.

bogus: phony.

bomb: fail.

boxed in: in a tight, awkward position.

bracket creep: movement into higher tax bracket because of inflation.

buck: dollar.

bump: dismiss, fire.

burnout: incapacitating exhaustion.

buy into: accept.

by the book: according to the correct procedure.

call it quits: stop.

canned: standard, stock.

carry the load: be responsible for.

cash in: withdraw.

ceiling: upper limit.

check out: examine.

clean: innocent, not illegal.

click: succeed.

clout: power.

cold turkey: abruptly, without warning.

connect: get along with.

cutthroat: harsh.

deadbeat: one who doesn't pay debts.

do homework: prepare.

double whammy: two-part difficulty.

down: defeated.

dump: shabby place.

dynamite: excellent.

eat one's words: retract.

even out: restore balance, equality.

eyeball: look at.

eye-opener: something that informs.

fallout: result of something.

fancy footwork: skillful evasion.

fast buck: money made quickly.

Fed: federal government.

fed up: tired.

feedback: response.

fool around: pass time idly.

for real: as good or bad as it appears.

fouled up: confused.

freewheeling: acting independently.

from the word go: from the beginning.

front-runner: leader.

garbage: nonsense.

get going: begin.

get it together: arrange properly.

get off the ground: start successfully.

get on the ball: improve performance.

get-together: meeting, party.

go haywire: fail, break down.

going-over: examination.

had it: be tired of something.

hang on: persist.

hang-up: mental block.

hard-nosed: stubborn.

have a thing about: be concerned with.

have hands full: be fully occupied.

have-not: poor person.

have someone's number: know the truth about someone.

have the inside track: have a strong advantage.

hit: something popular or successful.

hit the fan: cause trouble.

hot air: nonsense.

hot property: something valuable.

hustle: hurry.

ID: identification.

idiot box: television.

in hock: in debt.

in nothing flat: quickly.

itchy: restless.

jam: trouble.

jive: tease.

junk: worthless things.

kaput: broken.

kick around: discuss.

kiss-off: dismissal.

knee-jerk: reflex.

knock out: produce.

know the score: understand what matters.

laid back: relaxed.

lay on the line: be candid.

lean on: pressure.

let's face it: let us accept the truth.

long shot: one not likely to win.

low blow: unfair tactic.

lowdown: facts.

macho: aggressively masculine.

make a big production: overreact.

make it: succeed.

make waves: cause trouble.

media hype: intense, favorable publicity.

mess up: create a problem, get in trouble.

mileage: advantage, profit.

miss the boat: lose opportunity.

mop up: defeat.

name: important person.

no way: absolutely not.

nobody: unimportant person.

no-go: not proceeding properly.

not carved in stone: not permanent; not irrevocable.

no-win: impossible to win.

number cruncher: person or machine that processes numbers.

nuts and bolts: fundamental components.

off the top of one's head: without further thought.

old hat: old-fashioned.

on a roll: having continued success.

on the ball: alert.

on the spot: expected to respond at once.

once-over: scrutiny.

out of luck: with no chance of success.

pack it in: stop, give up.

palm off: provide something inferior as though it were acceptable.

paper tiger: a threat that lacks force.

pay up: settle an account.

penny-pincher: one who is stingy.

peter out: exhaust.

piece of cake: something easy.

pink slip: notice of dismissal, discharge.

played out: exhausted.

plum: prized.

polish off: finish, consume.

pony up: pay.

pro: professional.

psyched up: excited, prepared.

punch up: improve.

pushover: one easily defeated.

put away: dispose of.

put-on: act meant to deceive.

rat race: stressful, competitive situation or way of life.

read like a book: understand thoroughly.

red-faced: embarrassed.

right on: exclamation of approval.

ring a bell: sound familiar.

runaround: evasive treatment.

sack: discharge.

schmaltzy: sentimental.

score: succeed.

security blanket: something or someone representing safety or comfort.

shakeup: reorganization.

shoo-in: easy winner.

sling mud: defame.

small fry: unimportant people or things.

snafu: confused situation.

snow job: strong persuasion or deception.

straight face: face showing no emotion.

stuffed shirt: pompous person.

suck up: flatter.

tab: bill.

take care: be careful.

take it easy: be calm.

talk turkey: speak candidly.

tout: advocate.

track record: performance record.

trial balloon: something to test reaction.

turn off: lose interest.

turn on: arouse interest.

two-bit: cheap, tacky.

up: optimistic.

upbeat: encouraging.

waffle: be evasive.

wangle: get something by being clever or using unorthodox methods.

washout: failure.

whole hog: completely, without reservation.

wild about: enthusiastic about.

wild card: something unpredictable.

world-class: outstanding.

wrinkle: defect.

X-rated: pornographic, obscene.

yen: craving.

zap: disable.

EXCLUSIVE LANGUAGE

Any language that excludes certain people or groups from the same consideration and treatment given to other people or groups is discriminatory. Although the discrimination may be unintentional, the consequences are the same. Someone is usually offended, and the person doing the offending is seen as biased and insensitive.

We're doing better all the time, however. American businesspeople have been paying more and more attention to this problem. It hasn't been solved, though, and a lot of people are still insensitive or indifferent to the discomfort of others. How does discrimination affect international correspondence? It should be a major concern, but I'm not sure it is. Someone once responded to a chapter that I wrote on nondiscriminatory communication by saying that discrimination isn't a "big deal" in international communication. He noted that in many parts of the world, women are practically slaves or, at best, servants, and most of the international business in those countries is conducted by men. So he reasoned that no man there would even think about whether his behavior might be sexist. I hope that's a minority opinion.

Here's the other side. First, sexism is only one piece of the discrimination pie. Racism and bias toward the disabled are huge problems too. Second, it is *very* risky to assume that a foreign contact isn't sensitive to prejudice because his or her country has customs that are more traditional than those in the United States. In many countries, in fact, people have customs that honor the individual above all else, and they expect others to avoid any hint of criticism or unkindness (more about this in Chapters 8 and 9). Third, why would anyone want to practice part-time sensitivity, developing the habit of using nondiscriminatory communication at home and using discriminatory communication abroad? Wouldn't it make more sense to use nondiscriminatory communication all the time, everywhere?

A sensitive, thoughtful, unbiased person is always going to command more respect than an insensitive, thoughtless, biased person. Regardless of where they live, people will not likely appreciate or trust Americans who use stereotypes, ethnic cliches, offensive connotations, sexism, racism, demeaning humor, put-downs, exploitation, and conde-scension. Such a person wouldn't warm your heart and, even more important, wouldn't be someone with whom you would want to do business.

Sexism

A lot of attention has been paid to the use of titles in the United States, and in the business and professional world the title *Ms.* is now regularly used for all women except those who ask to be addressed as *Mrs.* The title *Miss* has virtually disappeared. In other countries, however, *Miss* is still common, and *Ms.* is virtually unknown. For more information about proper address forms in other countries, refer to the discussions of forms of address, salutations, and the inside address in Chapter 2.

Nondiscriminatory writing involves a lot more than correct use of titles. You have to think "equality." If you're writing to a foreign contact, for example, and refer to a man and a woman in your letter, don't respectfully use the title *Mr.* for the man and then address the woman by only her first name as though she were a child.

> *Wrong:* My associate *Mr. Reuben Towne* and my secretary *Marge* will accompany me when I visit your company in August.
>
> *Right:* My associate *Mr. Reuben Towne* and my secretary *Mrs. Marjorie Symons* will accompany me when I visit your company in August.

> *Wrong:* My associate Mr. Reuben Towne and my secretary Mrs. Marjorie Symons will accompany me when I visit your company in August. *Mr. Towne* and *Marge* will return to the United States on August 27.
>
> *Right:* My associate Mr. Reuben Towne and my secretary Mrs. Marjorie Symons will accompany me when I visit your company in August. *Mr. Towne* and *Mrs. Symons* will return to the United States on August 27.

The American vocabulary is gradually changing to replace sexist references (*authoress*) with nonsexist substitutes (*author*), and people are learning that a reference to skills and abilities (*capable*), not physical features (*pretty* or *handsome*), is what counts for both men and women in business. A few holdouts are still fussing about the need to do all this, but for most of us, using nonsexist references has become a habit that we don't even pause to consider.

> *Sexist:* This accessory will revolutionize the way in which *mankind* will benefit from the computer.
>
> *Nonsexist:* This accessory will revolutionize the way in which *people* [or *humankind*] will benefit from the computer.

Sexist: We spent more than one thousand *man-hours* on this project.

Nonsexist: We spent more than one thousand *hours of labor* on this project.

Sexist: Our *salesmen* have studied the recent changes in the market.

Nonsexist: Our *salespeople* have studied the recent changes in the market.

Sexist: Stephen Paletto and his *attractive* assistant Edna Webster will be in charge of the travel arrangements.

Nonsexist: Stephen Paletto and his *capable* assistant Edna Webster will be in charge of the travel arrangements.

Sexist: The *men and girls* in my department want to thank you for the interesting and useful book you sent.

Nonsexist: The *men and women* [or *staff*] in my department want to thank you for the interesting and useful book you sent.

Sexist: The *woman speaker* will discuss export regulations in the 1990s.

Nonsexist: The *speaker* will discuss export regulations in the 1990s.

Sexist: The guests and their *wives* will stay at the Hilton.

Nonsexist: The guests and their *spouses* will stay at the Hilton.

Sexist: Each person must make *his* own arrangements.

Nonsexist: Each person must make *his or her* own arrangements. *Or: People* must make *their* own arrangements.

Racism

An importer told me that unintentional racial and ethnic bias is like an open fly or an open blouse. By the time you realize that you left it open, it's too late; you've probably already embarrassed or offended someone, and you've definitely embarrassed yourself. That's what a racial or ethnic misstatement will do—embarrass or offend your foreign contact before you have time to think about what you said.

You may be corresponding with people in other countries who represent the very culture in the United States that you're inadvertently stereotyping. If you write to an Asian customer, for example, and enclose a brochure with pictures of employees at work in your company that shows Asians in low-level positions, what does that tell your contact? Your language can do the same damage—reveal racial and ethnic bias that you and your company may not even realize exists.

The most important rule in nondiscriminatory communication is never to call attention to someone's heritage (or color) if it has nothing to do with the matter you're discussing.

Wrong: Frank Morales, our *Hispanic traffic coordinator,* will let you know the date of shipment.

Right: Frank Morales, our *traffic coordinator,* will let you know the date of shipment.

Take special care not to link compliments with race or color. The combination of flattery and race usually backfires, because it may unintentionally imply that someone of a particular race or color is usually the opposite of what your compliment says.

Wrong: D. Harold Joseph is an *intelligent and industrious black* [or *African-American*] sales manager.

Right: D. Harold Joseph is an *intelligent and industrious* sales manager.

Stereotypes abound in this country, and subtle biases perpetuate the problem. The tendency to divide the world into white and nonwhite is especially offensive. Those of us who do this need to remember that people are proud of their heritage and don't like being classed simply as white or nonwhite.

Wrong: Our company has a special orientation program for new *nonwhite* citizens.

Right: Our company has a special orientation program for new *Hispanic, Asian, and African-American* citizens.

Other taboos include trite cultural references. An example of a trite reference is asking African-Americans about their soul food or asking Asian guests about their abilities in kung fu. Color references are deadly too. Even though Russia is struggling toward democracy, its Communist past isn't that far away, so you should avoid unnecessary use of the word *red.* If you were referring to a car with *red* paint, that would be fine, but if you used *red* to refer to anger (*seeing red*), that might not be so fine. The same would be true if you were corresponding with businesspeople in Taiwan and called an unscrupulous competitor *yellow;* your contact might incorrectly think that you were linking skin color (*their* skin color) with unscrupulous behavior. Who knows what someone will think? The safest practice is to avoid color in association with feelings or character labels.

It's very easy to make some of these mistakes, and it doesn't help that the terminology keeps changing. Some people think *black* is beautiful, but others dislike all colorizing and prefer terms such as *African-American.* The adjective *oriental* is too general or too imprecise in many contexts, and you may need a slightly more specific term, such as *Asian,* or a much more specific term, such as *Japanese* or *Vietnamese.* The same is true of *Hispanic*. If you want to be more specific, you need to identify a group by country of origin, such as *Spanish* or *Brazilian*.

In addition to trying to keep up with the latest terminology, we have to worry about our own prejudicial views. Many people have a hard time shedding their inner prejudices and overcoming the stereotypes that they learned at an early age. As Thomas à Kempis said more than five hundred years ago: "Olde custom is harde to breke." Yes, it is. But in a global society, in which we deal with people from many different heritages and cultures, "breke" it we must.

Disabilities Bias

Some of the people who receive your international letters may have a disability, and if they do, you may be sure that they'll notice anything you say that seems to reflect insensitivity or indifference toward their condition. You may not often have occasion to say anything pertaining to disabilities, but it only takes one misstatement to sour a relationship.

Since *disability* isn't a synonym for *inability*, there is rarely a need to focus on someone's condition. In most cases, the focus should be on the person's abilities.

> *Wrong:* Annette P. Rogers is an outstanding *deaf market strategist* at Overseas Industries.
>
> *Right:* Annette P. Rogers is an outstanding *market strategist* at Overseas Industries.

If it serves a *necessary* purpose to mention a person's disability, avoid describing it in terms that might be offensive.

> *Wrong:* Annette P. Rogers, who is *deaf and dumb,* will teach a course in business sign language.
>
> *Right:* Annette P. Rogers, who is *speech and hearing impaired,* will teach a course in business sign language.

Avoid making the person and the disability inseparable. If you *must* refer to a disability, word your remarks so that you refer to a person who *happens* to have a certain condition.

> *Wrong:* The *epileptic Henry Sawyer* is preparing a report on environmental hazards that affect employees with disabilities.
>
> *Right:* Henry Sawyer, *who has epilepsy,* is preparing a report on environmental hazards that affect employees with disabilities.

Do you ever hear words such as *crippled* (disabled) or *fit* (seizure) used in your company? Not everyone is aware that certain terminology reflects insensitivity toward the disabled. Sometimes, though, people go to the other extreme and pretend a problem doesn't exist at all or that it doesn't amount to much more than a hangnail ("your little problem"). Such remarks actually magnify the situation and embarrass everyone.

If your company doesn't have training materials available about discriminatory behavior, check your local library and bookstore for films and books on sexual, racial, and disabilities bias. The more you know, the more sensitive you'll be, and the better your chances will be of avoiding a serious gaffe. A good start is realizing that nondiscriminatory writing is a necessity in *both* domestic and international communication.

TIRED LANGUAGE

A student once asked me why I referred to cliches and other trite expressions as "tired language" when other words in the English language, such as *table, person,* and *work,* had been around just as long and were used just as often. Obviously, more is involved than the number of times a word or expression has been used. Also, a language must have basic, standard words that are used over and over or people would have to communicate in sign language.

Some expressions, however, depart from basic, standard terminology. They represent an attempt to express something with humor or color or an effort to summarize wisdom in a few words. There's nothing wrong with that, and in the beginning these expressions probably succeeded in enriching the language. But when *overused,* they lose their freshness and interest. Eventually, they become annoying. I once listened to someone who used the expression "that's the way the ball bounces" so often during a meeting that the rest of us were ready to bounce something off his head. It was maddening.

Cliches and other trite expressions are not only "tired" language; they're tiresome to those who have to listen to them used relentlessly. Hearing a cliche once or twice doesn't bother most people, and sometimes these expressions are used cleverly by writers and speakers at just the right time in just the right way. But when they make us lazy and we become repetitious, our speech and writing lose their sparkle. Our language starts to sound banal, dull, and—yes—tired.

Cliches

"All things being equal," I'll "bet my bottom dollar" that you think I'm "beating a dead horse" when I go "on the warpath" against language demons, such as cliches, and insist that those who use them in international correspondence are "skating on thin ice." Or am I "barking up the wrong tree"?

Everyone who uses cliches, stand up. Is anyone still sitting? I'm not. I admit that it's hard to carry on a conversation without using an occasional cliche. I do, however, try to keep them out of my domestic letters and *never* to use them in international correspondence.

Remember the principal message in Chapter 4? People in other countries usually translate what you say literally. So the fact that cliches are overused, tired, unimaginative expressions isn't the worst part. We need to be more concerned about the fact that they often seem absurd when you translate them literally, as your foreign contacts will do. Just imagine how they might interpret them.

I don't want to *upset the apple cart*. (*Reader:* Not to worry. We do not even have an apple cart.)

After I went home and thought about it further, I decided to *seize the bull by the horns*. (*Reader:* How daring! The most I have ever done is seize a dog by the tail.)

After all, we don't want to *put all our eggs in one basket*. (*Reader:* Why? Is the basket too small?)

I believe this assignment will *separate the men from the boys*. (*Reader:* Is this another form of segregation in the United States?)

I hope that the comments in my last letter didn't offend you. I apparently had a bad case of *foot-in-mouth disease* that day. (*Reader:* How disgusting.)

I've had my *nose to the grindstone* all week. (*Reader:* Your job sounds very dangerous.)

We'd like to *hammer out* an agreement by July 1. (*Reader:* I thought the United States of all places would be using pencils and paper by now.)

If I could *blow my own horn* a moment, I believe our product is far superior to our competitor's product. (*Reader:* I play the violin. Perhaps we could play a duet the next time we meet.)

Their response was a real *shot in the arm*. (*Reader:* Oh, no, I am so sorry. Has your arm healed yet?)

I see no need to *beat a dead horse*. (*Reader:* Good. Violence is senseless anyway.)

Although you can see why cliches don't work in international correspondence, it isn't fair to give the impression that all familiar expressions are ridiculous. Many cliches were proverbs that represented many years of wisdom. People in other countries also use proverbs and other sayings to summarize a situation. We might, incidentally, have as much trouble translating such remarks from other languages as our counterparts have in translating our sayings from English.

About 70 percent of the letters in my collection contain cliches; in some cases several appear in a single letter. Considering the heavy usage, people probably don't realize they're using cliches or how much trouble cliches cause in international correspondence. Either way, it's time to launch a major campaign to get this particular demon out of our international writing. To help your foreign contacts translate your letters accurately and sensibly, review the following list so that you can edit out all such cliches and substitute clear, precise, standard English.

> **actions speak louder than words:** what you do is more important than what you say.
> **add insult to injury:** be unkind to someone who has already been hurt.
> **all Greek to me:** incomprehensible.
> **all in the same boat:** all sharing some experience.
> **all thumbs:** awkward.
> **all wet:** wrong.
> **alpha and omega:** beginning and end.
> **and I don't mean maybe:** I'm serious.
> **apple of one's eye:** something or someone who is cherished.
> **as fate would have it:** as it happened.
> **as the crow flies:** by the shortest route, without regard to roads.
> **at arm's length:** intentionally kept at a distance.
> **at one's fingertips:** readily available.
> **at this point in time:** now.
> **ax to grind:** special concern for something.
> **babe in the woods:** innocent.
> **backhanded compliment:** a compliment that seems to be a criticism.
> **bag of tricks:** all available resources.
> **bark up the wrong tree:** pursue the wrong thing.
> **be all things to all people:** try to please everyone.
> **be buffaloed:** be puzzled, thwarted.
> **bear the brunt:** assume the burden or responsibility.
> **beat a dead horse:** belabor an issue that is no longer of interest.
> **beat around the bush:** be indirect.

bed of roses: soft, desirable situation.

beg the question: accept as fact something not yet proven.

bend someone's ear: tell someone something.

benefit of the doubt: favorable decision even though the evidence may not support it.

beside the point: irrelevant.

better late than never: excuse for being late.

better safe than sorry: excuse for caution.

betwixt and between: neither one thing nor another.

bide one's time: wait for an opportunity.

big shot: someone who is important.

bird in the hand is worth two in the bush: what you already have is worth more than the prospect of more later.

bird's-eye view: broad view.

bite off more than one can chew: undertake more than one can handle.

bite the bullet: prepare for a difficult task.

blaze a trail: lead the way in a new venture.

blessing in disguise: misfortune that turns out to be beneficial.

blow hot and cold: be inconsistent.

bolt from the blue: a surprise.

bone of contention: matter of dispute.

bottom line: net result.

break the ice: overcome awkward silence.

bright and early: early, ahead of time.

bum's rush: undignified ejection or rejection.

burden of proof: need to prove an assertion.

burn the candle at both ends: overwork.

bury the hatchet: settle a dispute.

butter up: flatter.

by and large: overall, on the whole.

by leaps and bounds: quickly.

call in question: challenge.

call someone's bluff: challenge someone to prove something.

can't make heads or tails out of it: can't make sense out of it.

can't see beyond the end of one's nose: can't see beyond the immediate problem.

captain of industry: leader in business community.

cast aspersions: make a damaging charge.

cast the first stone: be the first to criticize.

catch more flies with honey than vinegar: accomplish more by being nice than by being unpleasant.

change of heart: reversal of opinion.

checkered career: record of successes and failure.

chicken out: lose one's nerve.

child's play: very easy.

chips are down: situation is unfavorable.

clean as a whistle: neat, clean, pure.

clear the air: be candid, remove complications.

close shave: narrow escape.

cold feet: fearful, doubtful.

conventional wisdom: generally accepted ideas.

cool as a cucumber: calm.

cream of the crop: the best of a group.

cross that bridge when you come to it: deal with a problem later.

cut and dried: routine.

cut and run: leave quickly.

dead letter: something or someone that no longer is important.

dead to rights: certain, without possibility of error.

deep-six: discard.

die is cast: decision has been made.

dog eat dog: ruthless.

dot the i's and cross the t's: be thorough.

draw the line at: refuse to cross a boundary.

dyed in the wool: ingrained.

eagle eye: sharp watch or examination.

egg on one's face: embarrassment.

eleventh hour: latest possible time.

entertain high hopes: have high expectations.

every man has his price: there is a limit to everyone's principles.

face the music: confront something unpleasant.

fair shake: fair treatment.

fall by the wayside: drop or lose.

fat cat: wealthy person.

feel the pinch: suffer from adverse conditions.

few and far between: infrequent.

fight tooth and nail: fight or work hard.

finishing touch: final details or work.

fly in the ointment: obstacle.

with flying colors: with success.

food for thought: something to consider.

foot-in-mouth disease: habit of saying the wrong thing.

for the birds: worthless.

force to be reckoned with: something or someone of significance that must be taken into account.

from A to Z: from beginning to end.

from the word go: from the beginning.

get a handle on: find a way to cope with.

get down to brass tacks: deal with the essentials of something.

get to the bottom of: find the underlying reason.

go back to the drawing board: return to redesign something.

go for broke: risk everything.

going in circles: not accomplishing anything.

half the battle: a significant accomplishment.

handwriting on the wall: something bad about to happen.

hang in the balance: be undecided.

hard and fast: rigid.

have a bone to pick: have an issue to discuss or argue.

have both feet on the ground: be practical.

have one's back to the wall: be in a desperate position.

hell to pay: severe consequences.

hit the nail on the head: reach the right conclusion.

hold forth: discuss at length.

holding the bag: being left with the responsibility.

hue and cry: uproar.

if worst comes to worst: if things get really bad.

in a nutshell: briefly.

in a word: briefly.

in hot water: in trouble.

in the long run: over a long period.

jaundiced eye: prejudiced view.

John Hancock: signature.

keep one's head above water: stay solvent.

keep the ball rolling: sustain something.

know the ropes: know how to do something.

lay one's cards on the table: be candid.

leave no stone unturned: be thorough.

leave out in the cold: exclude.

let sleeping dogs lie: don't stir up trouble.

let the chips fall where they may: don't worry about the consequences.

letter-perfect: perfect.

lock, stock, and barrel: everything.

long shot: something with little chance of success.

lost cause: hopeless effort.

make no bones about it: be direct.

make or break: succeed or fail.

month of Sundays: long time.

more than one bargained for: beyond what one expected.

muddy the waters: confuse things.

neither rhyme nor reason: no reason.

net result: outcome.

no skin off my nose: no concern of mine.

nose to the grindstone: hard at work.

off and running: on the way.

off the beaten track: isolated, inaccessible.

on the fence: neutral, undecided.

on the go: busy, moving quickly.

on the tip of one's tongue: on the verge of remembering.

open and aboveboard: fair.

open question: undecided issue.

out on a limb: in a dangerous position.

over a barrel: at a disadvantage.

pack it in: quit.

paper over: conceal.

pave the way: prepare for.

peter out: fade away.

plain as day: obvious.

play one's cards right: make good decisions.

play with fire: invite trouble.

point of no return: point when it is too late to change something.

pull it off: succeed.

put a good face on it: make a bad situation seem better.

put all one's eggs in one basket: rely on one thing.

put one's best foot forward: show one's best image.

put the cart before the horse: take steps in illogical order.

put on the back burner: postpone.

rack one's brain: strain to think of something.

rank and file: ordinary people.

read between the lines: determine what is really meant by what is written.

read something into it: assume something more than was said or done.

red-letter day: important day.

rings a bell: sounds familiar.

roll with the punches: adjust.

rubber check: a check returned for insufficient funds.

rule of thumb: general guide.

run its course: go to completion.

run of the mill: ordinary, usual.

save face: avoid embarrassment.

second to none: the best.

see eye to eye: agree.

see red: become angry.

seize the bull by the horns: take bold action under difficult circumstances.

separate the men from the boys: reveal who is tough and mature.

ship of state: nation.

short end of the stick: worst side of unequal deal.

shot in the dark: conjecture.

sight unseen: without inspection.

sit tight: wait.

skate on thin ice: risk danger.

soft soap: flattery.

sound as a dollar: reliable.

split hairs: argue over fine points.

stem the tide: stop or change something.

string along: deceive.

take by storm: gain sudden acceptance.

take with a grain of salt: be skeptical.

talk it up: promote.

that's the way the ball bounces: that is fate.

thorn in one's side: continuing annoyance.

throw light on: clarify.

tip of the iceberg: only a small part of something.

too good to be true: not likely.

turn the tide: change things.

up to snuff: equal to a certain level of quality.

wave of the future: significant trend.

whole ball of wax: entire situation.

whole new ball game: a new or different situation.

whys and wherefores: questions and answers.

word of mouth: spoken communication.

wreak havoc: destroy.

Trite Expressions

How old are you? If you're too young to be wearing bifocals, you won't recall the way letters looked in the first half of this century or even a few decades ago. Some expressions considered trite today were fashionable then. But in recent decades the stiffness and formality that previously characterized letters has given way to conversational informality. Although this book cautions against conversational language and too much informality in international correspondence, some formal expressions are too far out of date and too stiff even for a foreign audience.

Occasionally, I see some of the following oldies, which (unintentionally, I'm sure) reveal the writer's age. As you'll notice, many of these expressions are imprecise and meaningless, and a foreign reader would find them difficult to translate.

Trite: In answer to your question of March 11, I *beg to inform you* that we expect to mail the report on May 5, 19—.

Better: In reply to your question of March 11, we expect to mail the report on May 5, 19—. *Or:* Thank you for asking about our report. We expect to mail it on May 5, 19—.

Trite: Enclosed please find a questionnaire for you to use in evaluating our company's service.

Better: We are enclosing a questionnaire for you to use in evaluating our company's service.

Trite: I have before me your letter of August 5, 19—, and in response propose the following terms:

Better: In reply to your letter of August 5, 19—, we propose the following terms:

Trite: We appreciate your *valued* suggestion.

Better: We appreciate your helpful suggestion. *Or:* We appreciate your suggestion.

Trite: Thanking you in advance for any information you can send about the Far East Shipping Lines, I remain, Yours faithfully,

Better: I will appreciate any information that you can send about the Far East Shipping Lines. Sincerely yours, *Or:* Please send us information about the Far East Shipping Lines. Sincerely,

Trite: We wish to acknowledge receipt of your letter of April 13, 19—.

Better: Thank you for your letter of April 13, 19—.

Trite: Your letter of the 9th received and *contents carefully noted.*

Better: We are enclosing the brochure you requested in your letter of April 9, 19—.

Trite: A copy of the regulations has been sent *under separate cover.*

Better: A copy of the regulations was sent by airmail (par avion) today.

Trite: Thank you for your telex of *recent date.*

Better: Thank you for your telex of December 2, 19—.

Trite: As per your recommendation, we will review Section 4.

Better: As you recommended, we will review Section 4.

Trite: Your order has been *duly* forwarded to our factory in Richmond, Virginia.

Better: We have sent your order to our factory in Richmond, Virginia.

Trite: We are enclosing *herewith* [*or* attaching *hereto*] a description of our T-123 Processor.

Better: We are enclosing [*or* attaching] a description of our T-123 Processor.

Trite: We take pleasure in sending you this photograph of your president and our board of directors.

Better: We are happy to send you this photograph of your president and our board of directors.

Trite: Please return one signed copy of the agreement *at your convenience.*

Better: Please return one signed copy of the agreement by February 3, 19—.

Trite: Please let us know your decision *at an early date.*

Better: Please let us know your decision by November 26, 19—.

Trite: Thank you for your *esteemed favor* of the 23rd.

Better: Thank you for your letter of June 23, 19—.

Trite: The *undersigned* will send you our service agreement as soon as we receive your authorization.

Better: I will send you our service agreement as soon as we receive your authorization.

Trite: Pursuant to your request, we are sending four copies of the dealer contract.

Better: As you requested, we are sending four copies of the dealer contract.

Trite: We wish to bring to your attention the fact that our agreement will expire on April 30, 19—.

Better: We want to remind you that our agreement will expire on April 30, 19—. *Or:* Our agreement will expire on April 30, 19—.

Trite: Please be advised that your order will be shipped on July 17, 19—.

Better: Your order will be shipped on July 17, 19—.

CHECKUP

It's time to look at more letters from my sample collection. These letters contain some of the language demons that this chapter has exposed. Like the models in Chapter 4, the letters that follow are generic examples provided both to illustrate language that won't work in international correspondence and to demonstrate how to replace it with language that is effective. The first letter in each of the examples is the poorly written example; the second one is a revised version.

Notice that the first of the two letters to Mr. Andreani opens with the trite and wordy phrase "Enclosed herewith please find." Poor word choice is evident in the second paragraph, in which the furniture is described as "cheap" rather than inexpensive or low-cost. In addition to using slang ("in nothing flat"), the letter oozes with jargon and gobbledygook ("to effect functional stations that will privatize operation activities," "to optimize functions"). Finally, the complimentary close is too familiar for a foreign audience.

The first of the two letters to Mrs. Chung starts with the antagonistic and provocative phrase "your letter *claiming*." The trite and wordy "We wish to advise" opens the second paragraph, which also includes slang and cliches ("without a hitch," "get to the bottom of it.") The last paragraph resorts to another trite expression, "valued order," and the letter concludes with the too-familiar closing "Regards."

The first of the two letters to Mr. Lopez is overly enthusiastic ("waiting and eager") and talks down to the reader as if he's a child ("brand new account"). It uses needless, trite expressions such as "attached hereto" and "Until then, I remain." It also contains jargon ("access it," "rep") and cliches ("as time moves on"). Referring to the man as "Mr. Arnold H. Redmond" and the woman as just "Carol" is sexist—both should have titles. Finally, the closing "Faithfully yours" is out of date.

GLOBAL FURNITURE WAREHOUSE
1800 PIONEER ROAD SOUTH
ST. PAUL, MN 55101

phone 612-555-3000 / fax 612-555-3001

March 11, 1994

Your reference OAI-R1

Mr. Giulio Andreani
Attolico, Inc.
Via Veneto 114/A
Rome, Italy

Dear Mr. Andreani:

Enclosed herewith please find additional information on our Reflections of Success Workstations.

As the brochure explains, this cheap furniture system consists of components that can be combined in nothing flat. Different combinations can be used to effect functional stations that will privatize operational activities. Surface heights are adjustable to optimize functions.

We hope you'll find this information enlightening as you consider the applicability of this system. Please contact us if you have any questions. We appreciate your interest.

Cordially yours,

Raymond D. Fisk
Sales Manager

akm

March 11, 1994

Your Reference OAI-R1

Mr. Giulio Andreani
Attolico, Inc.
Via Veneto 114/A
Rome, Italy

Dear Mr. Andreani:

Thank you for requesting additional information about our Reflections of Success Workstations.

A brochure that explains how the system works is enclosed. This low-cost furniture system consists of desk, cabinet, and bookshelf components. These components can be combined quickly and easily in different patterns. Individual work areas can be designed to match each person's needs. Also, the height of all work surfaces is adjustable for different types of work.

We hope the enclosed information will help you to evaluate our Reflections system, Mr. Andreani. Please let us know if you have any questions. We appreciate your interest.

Sincerely,

Raymond D. Fisk
Sales Manager

akm

THE COMPUTER PUBLISHER
1300 SUNSHINE STREET
P.O. BOX 2000
ANAHEIM, CA 92808

phone 714-555-9208 / fax 714-555-9209

August 16, 1994

Mrs. Chung Minwen
Beijing Technical Institute
Xiu Shui Bei Jie 7
Beijing, China

Dear Mrs. Chung:

I have before me your letter claiming that our NewFont sample diskette and Guidebook never reached you.

We wish to advise you that these items were recently sent by overseas express, and you should have received them by now. Usually, our shipments get through without a hitch, but this time the package was apparently lost. In any case, you may be sure we'll get to the bottom of it.

Since you need the material by August 28, we'll express another shipment as soon as possible.

Please accept our apologies for this delay. We appreciate your valued order.

Regards,

(Ms.) Bette Hann
Shipping Supervisor

rdf

THE COMPUTER PUBLISHER
1300 SUNSHINE STREET
P.O. BOX 2000
ANAHEIM, CA 92808

phone 714-555-9208 / fax 714-555-9209

August 16, 1994

Mrs. Chung Minwen
Beijing Technical Institute
Xiu Shui Bei Jie 7
Beijing, China

Dear Mrs. Chung:

We were sorry to learn that our NewFont sample diskettes and guidebooks never reached you.

Four diskettes and guidebooks were mailed in one package on July 30, 1994, by Oceanwide Air Express. The material was scheduled to reach you on August 5.

The express company is now searching for the lost package. Since you need the materials by August 28, we are sending replacements today by air express. They are expected to reach you on August 24.

Please accept our apologies for this delay, Mrs. Chung. We appreciate your order and hope you will enjoy the NewFont diskette and guidebook.

Sincerely yours,

(Ms.) Bette Hann
Shipping Supervisor

rdf

SOUTHWESTERN MILLS, INC.
19 DESERT PALMS ROAD
PHOENIX, AZ 85308

phone 602-555-7465 / fax 602-555-7466

November 7, 1994

Mr. Carlos Fernando Lopez
Ensenada Tapestries
Insurgentes Sur 201
Col. del Valle
03100 Mexico D.F., Mexico

Dear Mr. Lopez:

Congratulations! We have opened a brand new
account for you and are waiting and eager to help
you access it.

Attached hereto is a small booklet outlining
the terms and conditions of your account. Don't
hesitate to contact us if you have any questions
or concerns that we can lay to rest.

We realize that as time moves on, your needs
may change. If they do, you can reach Mr. Arnold
H. Redmond or his assistant, Carol, at the
letterhead address. He is our Latin American rep
and is looking forward to working with you.

Until then, I remain,

Faithfully yours,

William C. Worth
Manager, New Accounts

hg

SOUTHWESTERN MILLS, INC.
19 DESERT PALMS ROAD
PHOENIX, AZ 85308

phone 602-555-7465 / fax 602-555-7466

November 7, 1994

Mr. Carlos Fernando Lopez
Ensenada Tapestries
Insurgentes Sur 201
Col. del Valle
03100 Mexico D.F., Mexico

Dear Mr. Lopez:

Congratulations, Mr. Lopez. Your company's application for credit has been approved. A new account has been opened in the name of Ensenada Tapestries.

A small booklet is enclosed stating the terms and conditions that apply to this account. Please let me know if you have any questions about this information. I will be happy to clarify the details by telephone or letter.

If you have other credit needs or if you want to discuss your orders, please write or telephone us. Our Latin American representative is Mr. Arnold H. Redmond. His assistant is Mrs. Carol Sholas. You may reach them at the address printed on this letter. I know that both Mr. Redmond and Mrs. Sholas will be happy to help you.

We appreciate your interest in our fabrics. Thank you for choosing Southwestern Mills as your supplier.

Sincerely,

William C. Worth
Manager, New Accounts

hg

6

Why Short Is Beautiful

BIGGER IS NOT ALWAYS BETTER. Many people think that a big word or a long sentence is impressive and shows that the writer is highly intelligent. Not true. In international correspondence, in fact, complexity can cause translation difficulties as well as confusion and misunderstanding.

Put yourself in the position of your foreign contacts. Which would you rather translate—a letter with short, simple words and sentences or one with long, complex words and lengthy, rambling sentences? I'm sure you'll agree that to someone who uses English only as a second or third language, short must be very beautiful.

SIMPLIFIED LANGUAGE

Short Words

One point made earlier in this book can't be over-emphasized: The important thing is to use short, simple words, sentences, and paragraphs, *not* simple concepts. You should continue to think and respond like an adult at your own level of education and training.

One businessperson told me that he had spent his entire life trying to develop a large vocabulary. In recommending simplified language for foreign readers, was I suggesting that he reduce it to the limited vocabulary of a four-year-old? Hardly. A large vocabulary is a great asset in discussing a wide variety of topics and is essential in avoiding the monotony of bland repetition. But other factors are involved in communicating with a foreign audience, and the players in international communication use different rules, topped by this important stricture:

> Whenever possible, choose a short word over a long, complex, unfamiliar, abstract word.

People who work in a technical business or profession with a specialized vocabulary often use unnecessarily complex language. (Chapter 5 describes the pitfalls of using specialized language.) Sometimes, though, writers use long, complex words and sentences to cover up their ignorance or uncertainty. That's worse. But foreign readers don't care *why* you choose complex, cumbersome language. Their only concern is how to translate and understand it.

Sometimes we can just look at a word and decide by the number of letters whether it's unnecessarily long, for example, *terminate* (end) or *endeavor* (try). However, not all long words are more complex than short words. *Congratulate* has twelve letters, whereas *felicitate* has only ten. In any case, who cares about a couple more letters? You can see from this example that you have to consider more than actual word length in judging whether a word is simple or complex.

Affixes. One way to shorten unnecessarily long words is to use fewer affixes (parts added to the beginning or end of a word, such as a prefix or suffix). Notice how the following basic words are made longer and more complex by adding to them.

act: act*ive,* act*ed,* act*ing,* act*or*

advance: advance*ment, re*advance

cancel: cancel*lation,* cancel*ed,* cancel*ing*

circle: *semi*circle, circl*ed,* circl*ing*

confident: *over*confident, *under*confident, confident*ly*

conservative: conservative*ly, ultra*conservative

continue: continu*ed,* continu*ing,* continu*ation*

depend: depend*able,* depend*ent,* depend*ed,* depend*ing,* depend*ence*

destruct: destruct*ible,* destruct*ing, self-*destruct

distant: *equi*distant, distant*ly*

eminent: *pre*eminent, eminent*ly*

examine: *pre*examine, examin*ed,* examin*ing*

exist: *co*exist, exist*ed,* exist*ing*

nation: nation*al,* nation*wide, trans*national

rate: *over*rate, *under*rate, rate*d*, rat*ing*
reverse: revers*ible*, *ir*revers*ible*, reverse*d*, revers*ing*
satisfy: *dis*satisfy, satis*fied*, satis*fying*
structure: *infra*structure, structure*d*, structur*ing*
trust: trust*worthy*, *un*trust*worthy*, trust*ing*, trust*ed*

See what I mean? But this doesn't mean that you should *never* use a word with an affix. That would be impossible. It does mean that you should not use words with affixes unnecessarily or use too many of them in your letters. Reading studies have shown that the more affixes your writing contains, the more complex it is to read, translate, and understand. Often, by slightly restating a sentence you can convert a term lengthened by an affix back to the original word.

With affix: We want to provide *management* for this project.
Without affix: We want to *manage* the project.

Contractions.   We use contractions in all domestic writing except in very formal situations. That's fine, but most such shortcuts are unfamiliar to foreign readers. So the rule in this case is to use the full, longer version instead of the shorter version.

Contractions shouldn't pose much of a problem. They can easily be changed. Simply go through the rough drafts of your letters and substitute the original words for any words that have omitted letters. Look for words with apostrophes, such as those in the list that follows.

aren't: are not	**it's:** it is
can't: cannot	**there's:** there is
don't: do not	**they're:** they are
hasn't: has not	**we've:** we have
he's: he is	**you're:** you are

Also look for short forms of longer words that have become standardized in American writing. In most cases, treat this form of shorthand as an aberration that might not be in a foreign reader's dictionary and might therefore be difficult to translate.

ad: advertisement	**memo:** memorandum
auto, car: automobile	**paper:** newspaper
bike: bicycle or motorcycle	**phone:** telephone
fax: facsimile	**plane:** airplane

Pretentious Language

You may have heard pretentious language called *pompous, formal, stylish, genteel,* or *inflated* language. All of those terms mean the same thing: words that are unnecessarily long, unfamiliar, complex, boastful, ostentatious, exaggerated, excessive, presumptuous, or showy—sometimes all of the above.

Most writers use this type of language to try to impress others, even though it's directly counter to the widely accepted rule to choose a short, simple, familiar, concrete term whenever that choice is available. Pretentious writing usually doesn't work well even with a domestic audience, since the writer tends to sound like a show-off. The consequences are more serious with a foreign audience, since language complexity increases reading, translation, and comprehension difficulties.

Look at the following examples of pretentious language, and if you find yourself using any in your letters, substitute the simple, basic terms. Don't worry if you use more words in your substitution. More is better when it contributes to easier and faster comprehension and lessens the chances of miscommunication. But use common sense in deciding whether a word really is pretentious. Not all of the following words are pretentious all of the time. If you're going to mail a letter to someone today, for example, you'll *send* it, not *forward* it. But if you're having mail that arrives at one address sent on to a new address, someone will *forward* it to you at the new address.

abate: cut down, decrease, drop

abbreviate: shorten

adumbrate: outline

aggregation: total

ameliorate: improve

amorphous: shapeless

approximately: about

ascertain: find out

assist(ance): aid, help

attempting: trying

bear: carry

behest: urgent request

bodeful: ominous

bona fide: genuine

bosom: breast

cast: throw

catarrh: cold

cease: stop

chef d'oeuvre: masterpiece

chemotherapeutic agent: drug

close: shut

cognizant: aware

commence: begin, start

commendation: praise

commercialization: commerce

conceal: hide

concept: idea

conceptualize: conceive, think of

concerning: about

conjecture: guess

construct: make

consummate: complete

customary channels: usual way

deem: judge

deficit: shortage

delineate: describe, draw

demonstrate: show

depressed socioeconomic area: slum

desire: want

desist: stop

dialogue: conversation

dispatch: send

disseminate: circulate, send out

domicile: home

donate: give

dubiety: doubt

duplicate: copy

dwell: live

edifice: building

effect, effectuate: make, do

endeavor(ing): try(ing)

enlighten: tell

envisage: foresee

equivalent: equal

evince: show

expedite: hasten

extend: give

facilitate: ease, help

feasible: possible

feedback: comments, information

felicitate: congratulate

finalize: finish, complete

forward: send

functionalization: use

furnish: provide, send, give

germane: relevant

hiatus: gap, interval

impair: damage, hurt, weaken

in toto: altogether, in all

inaugurate: begin, start

indicate: tell, say, show

initiate: begin, start

implement: carry out

input: advice

inquire: ask

instantaneously: now, quickly

instrumentalities: means, ways

integrate: combine

interface with: meet with

involving: about

ipso facto: by that very fact

lethal: deadly, fatal

locate: find

maintenance: upkeep

maximize: increase

milieu: surroundings, environment

modus operandi: method

multitudinous: many

nadir: low point

obfuscate: confuse

obtain: get

obviate: prevent, do away with

optimum: best

palpable: clear, obvious, visible

parameters: boundaries, limits

partake: share

per annum: a year, each year

per diem: a day, each day

per se: as such
perchance: perhaps
peruse: read
prioritize: order
procedural practices: what to do and how to do it
proceed: go
procure: get
promulgate: circulate, send out
purchase: buy
raison d'être: reason or justification for existing
receive: get
remove: take away
remuneration: pay
render: offer
repast: meal
reside: live
retire: go to bed, go to sleep

salient: important
seek: try, look for
sine qua non: essential element
slumber: sleep
succumbed: died
sufficient: enough
summon: send for
sustain: suffer
terminate: end
transmit: send
utilize, utilization: use
valiant: brave
veritable: true
vessel: ship
vicissitude: change
visualize: foresee
wherewithal: means

Wordiness

One of my first English teachers in college hated wordiness more than any other language flaw and taught her students to attack excess verbiage ruthlessly. That wasn't the only lesson I had to unlearn later in writing to people in other countries. In international correspondence, wordiness can be either an asset or a liability depending on how it is used.

As you analyze each letter you write, consider whether the filler words are just cluttering your sentences or whether they make it easier for the reader to understand the crucial words in the letter. The words that are superfluous or redundant and merely clutter the page should be taken out and the sentences recast if necessary. The italicized words in these examples, taken from actual letters in my collection, don't contribute to further understanding. They just take up space and give a foreign reader more to translate.

After March 1 our two sales offices in Singapore will be combined *into one*.

My *own* secretary will accompany me to Mexico City.

Our firm has *three different kinds of* credit plans.

The *end* result was an error in the June statement.

Please refer *back* to the first article in the contract.

There are some containers *that* have additional brochures.

It is our belief [We believe] that the plan should be revised.

First *and foremost,* our mail order division must be told about the new policy.

Exports increased during the June-to-July period *of time.*

Needless to say, the cancellation disappointed our production staff. [*Or:* The cancellation, as expected, disappointed our production staff.]

I will repeat the instructions *again* when I visit your assembly plant.

In *the majority of* [most] cases, readers respond within two days. [*Or:* Most readers respond within two days.]

At this point in time, we have not [yet] made a decision.

May I ask that you [Please] return one signed copy of the agreement by August 17, 19—.

We need *something along the lines of* a foreign liaison.

The report is *of a confidential nature* [confidential].

I *would* suggest that we begin immediately.

In compliance with your request [At your request], we have deleted the second paragraph.

Here is a summary of the project's *current* status.

The conditions are few *in number.*

The cost of the two binders *amounts to* [is] $27.98.

Keep all words that contribute to readability of a sentence, as well as those that help to describe more fully what you're saying. Adjectives, for example, are often essential for a comment to be explicit and to make sense. All of the italicized words in the following example will help a reader understand your comments better and should therefore be retained.

Distribution trends show that changes have occurred in merchandising techniques throughout the retail market. The *rapid* increase in *modern* merchandising techniques, *however,* is *most* evident in *efficient self-service stores.*

SIMPLIFIED CONSTRUCTIONS

If you want to say something that makes sense to others, you have to organize your words in sentences. In a letter, those sentences are in turn organized in paragraphs. That's the way civilized people communicate. But the sentences and paragraphs themselves may differ greatly, depending on the subject matter and the writer's style.

Short Sentences

You can apply the same principle to sentences as applied to words:

> Short, simple sentences are easier to read, translate, and understand than long, complex constructions.

Also, just as you can count letters in a word, you can count words in a sentence to help you decide whether it is too long. For example, this sentence, taken from a letter in my files commenting on a government market report, has thirty-four words:

> Although the United States, with direct imports and those from European-based subsidiaries, dominates this market with close to an 80 percent market share, U.S. direct imports account for 46 percent of total imports.

Here's a general rule worth remembering:

> Any sentence that has more than twenty words is difficult to understand.

Comprehension, however, also depends on a reader's educational level, native language, and other factors. Nevertheless, according to this general measure, the sentence just stated is too long for easy comprehension by a foreign reader who uses English only as a second or third language. So you need to break it up into smaller units, preferably of no more than ten to fifteen words. Here's one way to rewrite the long sentence in three shorter sentences. The first sentence has thirteen words; the second, eleven words; and the third, twelve words.

> The United States has both direct imports and imports from European-based subsidiaries. It dominates this market with almost an 80 percent market share. U.S. direct imports, however, account for only 46 percent of total imports.

Without judging the sense of this comment, since it's taken out of context, and without knowing the reader's familiarity with the subject, the difference in complexity is still obvious. The shorter sentences are less cumbersome and should be more easily understood by a non–English-speaking reader.

If you want to carry this type of yardstick approach even further, you can count syllables. A sentence with a dozen one-syllable words, such as *count*, will seem shorter than a sentence with six one-syllable words and six words with more than one syllable, such as *accountable.*

You may have noticed that a lot of short sentences make for choppy, abrupt reading. This is why writing instructors tell us to vary sentence length and to use lots of transition words, such as *however.* But choppiness isn't the main concern in international correspondence. A translated message isn't read the same way that a domestic message is read. The very act of translation into another language changes the flow of words; a smooth flow in the original may become choppy after translation anyway. If necessary, occasional transition words, such as *however* or *therefore,* can be used if the choppiness seems to distract from the meaning. Usually, it doesn't. In general, though, you can be certain that your foreign contacts will appreciate a series of short, simple sentences more than a single long, albeit smooth, sentence.

Variety is another concern of many writers. To make a message more interesting, they vary the length of their sentences with a pleasing combination of short, medium, and long constructions. But in international correspondence, this result can be achieved only at the risk of creating more difficult translations for the reader. Most people dealing in global communications will tell you that it's not worth the prospect of miscommunication.

Sentence Fragments.   If you want to send your foreign contacts home with a migraine, sprinkle some sentence fragments throughout your letters. That will do it. Although *occasional* sentence fragments are often used effectively in domestic letters, they don't belong in international correspondence. Notice the fragment following the first full sentence in the next examples. Delete such sentence fragments or rewrite them as complete sentences.

Fragment: When no shipping method is stated, merchandise is sent by ship. Now for specific information. Here are the charges for shipments of 1 to 150 pounds.

Rewrite: When no shipping method is stated, merchandise is sent by ship. Here are the specific charges for shipments of 1 to 150 pounds.

Fragment: The suggestions for content and organization are standard. Most of them, anyway.

Rewrite: Most of the suggestions for content and organization are standard.

Short Paragraphs

To help foreign readers translate your letters accurately, you should do your best to use not only short words and sentences but also short paragraphs. In fact, don't hesitate to use one-sentence opening and closing paragraphs or one-sentence introductions to lists and other illustrated or displayed matter. In addition, try to focus on only one key point in each paragraph; in a complex discussion, summarize often. Don't worry about being repetitive. Repetition is more often a virtue than a vice in international communication. Finally, use lists, block quotations, tables, drawings, or anything else that will make the details of your message clearer to a foreign reader.

Consider how this long, fairly complex paragraph, originally written for a domestic audience, could be simplified and improved for a foreign audience. Assume that the reader has an understanding of the technical nature of the discussion but no understanding of the English language. The reader will therefore have to translate the material into his or her own language.

Original: With the exception of a strong domestic supply of air and gas cleaning equipment, most demands for instruments, components, water treatment, recycling, and solid waste equipment are met by imports. Most imported pollution-control equipment is handled by a handful of local importers and distributors or through sales subsidiaries of foreign principals. Pollution-control products with the best sales potential are scrubbers for sulfur dioxide removal in the metal and pulp industries, equipment handling sludge problems, flow-monitoring instruments, instruments for analyzing metal particle content, optical turbidity instruments, and sorting and recycling equipment.

Rewrite: Most orders for pollution-control equipment and accessories are filled through imports. The orders are for these items:

- Instruments
- Components
- Water-treatment equipment
- Recycling equipment
- Solid-waste equipment

Most orders for imported pollution-control equipment are filled by one of the following sources:

1. U.S. importers and distributors

2. Sales subsidiaries of foreign companies

Air-cleaning and gas-cleaning equipment is manufactured in the United States. Orders are filled by U.S. suppliers.

These pollution-control products have the best sales potential:

- Scrubbers for sulfur dioxide removal in metal and pulp industries
- Equipment for sludge problems
- Flow-monitoring equipment
- Instruments for analyzing metal particle content
- Optical turbidity instruments
- Sorting and recycling equipment

Simplifying a complex discussion by dividing the text into additional paragraphs and converting numerous items into displayed lists may lengthen the message. Sometimes more words are used, and the use of itemized lists may add more lines, increasing the number of pages in a letter. If the cost of postage or electronic message transmission is a crucial factor, you'll have to weigh that cost against the potential cost of any confusion or lack of understanding that might occur if you don't simplify the presentation. Usually, that cost is much higher than any added postage or transmission cost.

CHECKUP

Here are more letters from my collection of samples. Like those in Chapters 4 and 5, the following have been rewritten as generic examples for you to use in testing your skill at improving international messages. The first letter in each of the examples contains language or constructions that could present a problem to a foreign reader. The second one is a revised version.

The first of the two letters to Dr. Singhvi has many problems, including an exceptionally long first paragraph; complex, overlong sentences; and unnecessarily long words, such as "commercialization." The complete letter needs a thorough rewrite to simplify the construction and introduce short words, sentences, and paragraphs. At the same time, contractions should be eliminated and the abbreviation *U.S.* spelled out. Expressions unfamiliar to a foreign reader, such as "for all practical purposes," "a sad fact of life," and "take a look at" should be eliminated. Finally, the closing "Best regards" is too familiar.

The first of the two letters to Mrs. Eliasson has similar problems. Notice that the first paragraph has two extralong sentences, and the second paragraph has just one lengthy sentence. Numerous words, such as "simplification," are unusually long; other word choices, such as "critical objectives and order fulfillment," are also questionable. The entire letter could be simplified and greatly improved by listing or numbering series of items. Finally, the contraction "you'll" should be eliminated, and the closing changed to something less familiar.

In the first of the two letters to Mr. Thoolen, the construction is needlessly complicated. The very long first paragraph should be divided into two or three shorter paragraphs, and each long sentence needs to be rewritten as two or more shorter sentences. Listing the items in the second sentence of the letter would also help the reader. General simplification is needed overall. It isn't necessary, for example, to say "preliminary information." The word *information* alone would be sufficient. The closing in this letter also is too familiar.

March 13, 1994

Dr. T. H. Singhvi
Shanti Path
Chanakyapuri
New Delhi 110021, India

Dear Dr. Singhvi:

Enclosed is the information ("Patent Protection") you recently requested concerning the protection of your invention, with strategies for using patent protection to increase the odds of successful commercialization. As the enclosed pamphlet explains, in some cases, it isn't essential to successful commercialization: "You do not always need patent protection to market a product successfully." There is reason to believe, however, that this option, for all practical purposes, is limited to entrepreneurs. It's a sad fact of life, but the prospects for licensing unpatented devices are slim to none. Many manufacturers, in the U.S. at least, won't even take a look at unpatented concepts and inventions.

Once you've determined that patent protection is suitable in your circumstances, your next step should be to phone or write a registered patent attorney or agent--in your own country or in the U.S.--for counsel on how to proceed. I'm enclosing a list of U.S. attorneys and agents should you want to contact anyone here.

Good luck in protecting your invention.

Best regards,

Adam Steiner
Director

rb

LAW BOOK PUBLICATIONS CENTER
906 DAVIS AVENUE
AUGUSTA, GA 31520

phone 706-555-2185 / fax 706-555-2186

March 13, 1994

Dr. T. H. Singhvi
Shanti Path
Chanakyapuri
New Delhi 110021, India

Dear Dr. Singhvi:

Here is the information you requested about how to protect your invention. The enclosed report, "Patent Protection," also explains how to sell your product.

The report states: "You do not always need patent protection to market a product successfully." Marketing without a patent, however, is usually done only by business owners.

The prospects for licensing a product without a patent are poor. Many U.S. manufacturers will not consider an idea or invention that is not patented.

If you decide to apply for a patent, you should first seek legal help. Telephone or write to a registered patent attorney or agent. Attorneys and agents are available in your country or in the United States. A list of U.S. attorneys and agents is enclosed.

We wish you success in obtaining a patent for your invention. Please let us know if we can offer additional help.

Sincerely yours,

Adam Steiner
Director

rb

BENSON & BENSON, INC.
21 NORTH STREET
PHILADELPHIA, PA 19140

phone 215-555-8787 / fax 215-555-8788

January 2, 1994

Mrs. G. G. Eliasson
Nordraak Ltd.
Thomas Heftyesgate 12
0245 Oslo 2, Norway

Dear Mrs. Eliasson:

Thanks for your communication requesting information on the Benson Action Plan, an effective decision-making tool for small businesses engaged in problem resolution and seeking established management strategies. A brochure is enclosed detailing the critical objectives of increasing the percentage of orders filled correctly, a reduction in the period of time it takes to process an order, and the simplification and streamlining of the order-fulfillment process.

The most acceptable solution to any problem is one that achieves the objectives mentioned above and in which the project manager determines that the key factors in the action plan are met, including schedules, reports, tasks, and communication.

We hope you'll find the enclosed suggestions useful. Please let us know if we can be helpful in any other way.

Cordially,

David Lewis Schurter
Marketing Manager

upm

BENSON & BENSON, INC.
21 NORTH STREET
PHILADELPHIA, PA 19140

phone 215-555-8787 / fax 215-555-8788

January 2, 1994

Mrs. G. G. Eliasson
Nordraak Ltd.
Thomas Heftyesgate 12
0245 Oslo 2, Norway

Dear Mrs. Eliasson:

Thank you for asking about the Benson Action Plan. This plan shows small business owners how to make good decisions. It also tells them how to solve problems and manage their business successfully.

A brochure that describes the plan is enclosed. It explains these important objectives:

1. Increase the number of orders filled correctly
2. Reduce the time needed to fill orders
3. Simplify the process of filling orders

The best solution to any problem achieves those three objectives.

The person who manages this plan is responsible for the following: (1) schedules, (2) reports, (3) tasks, and (4) communication.

We hope that the suggestions in the enclosed brochure will help you, Mrs. Eliasson. Please write or telephone us if you have any questions.

Sincerely,

David Lewis Schurter
Marketing Manager

upm

GENERAL OVERSEAS OUTLETS
2100 4TH STREET
NEW YORK, NY 10003

phone 212-555-7770 / fax 212-555-7771

April 28, 1994

Mr. A. M. Thoolen
Jakarta Development Bank
321 Jalan Kramat Raya
Jakarta 10450, Indonesia

Dear Mr. Thoolen:

We understand that your office has
information for U.S. citizens on site location in
your country for U.S. companies, such as my
company, General Overseas Outlets, which
warehouses U.S. products destined for distribution
in other countries such as yours. We'd like to
have some preliminary information about the
availability of transportation, labor, utilities,
housing, and schools, as well as details on rates
for labor, transportation, and utilities.

Anything you can send will be appreciated.
Thanks in advance for your help.

Regards,

(Ms.) Patricia Weymouth
International Sales

tvl

April 28, 1994

Mr. A. M. Thoolen
Jakarta Development Bank
321 Jalan Kramat Raya
Jakarta 10450, Indonesia

Dear Mr. Thoolen:

Please send us information about choosing a site in your country for our business.

General Overseas Outlets wants to find a location for a distribution center. The company would purchase or lease a building. It would be used to store U.S. products waiting for distribution in your country. Details about building size and number of employees needed are enclosed.

We must first evaluate the location. We need to know if the following requirements are available and their costs or rates:

- Ground and air transportation
- Buildings to store and ship products
- Local labor
- Utilities: sewer, water, electricity, gas
- Houses for employees
- Schools for employee children

We would appreciate receiving this information by June 1, 1994. Thank you for your help.

Sincerely,

(Ms.) Patricia Weymouth
International Sales

tvl

7

Creating a Punctuation Roadmap

MOST OF US don't think much about punctuation. It's something we automatically use a lot or very little, depending on our writing style. So whenever I try to explain how important punctuation is, people inevitably give me a "Who cares?" look: "Isn't she pathetic? How could she be so desperate for something to talk about that she's now extolling the virtues of punctuation?"

Before you decide to skip this chapter, however, I should point out that I'm in good company with my views on punctuation. Some of our foremost communication authorities have been appalled by the lack of appreciation for this aspect of writing. Nearly fifty years ago, in fact, Rudolf Flesch (*The Art of Plain Talk,* Harper & Row, 1946) was already referring to punctuation as the "most important single device for making things easier to read." So there!

Punctuation is important in all types of writing, but it's mandatory in international correspondence. It's as necessary as a roadmap when you're traveling in a strange land. Without the map, your chances of getting lost increase dramatically. Without punctuation, the likelihood of your foreign contact getting lost in your letters also increases dramatically.

To keep this from happening, you have to *over*punctuate your international letters, even though the trend in domestic correspondence is to *under*punctuate. This trend has been encouraged in part because less punctuation means fewer keystrokes in production and hence faster preparation. But it's not always a timesaver in international correspondence, particularly if a misunderstood message has to be clarified later.

PUNCTUATION POINTERS

Important Marks of Punctuation

The key marks of punctuation are the apostrophe, brackets, colon, comma, dash, ellipsis points, exclamation point, hyphen, parentheses, period, question mark, quotation marks, semicolon, and virgule. All of these marks were described in Chapter 3, in which it was also explained that some marks used in a certain context are less familiar to foreign readers.

Punctuation to Avoid

Some marks of punctuation, such as the comma and period, are used in most languages; others, such as the exclamation point or ellipsis points, are less common. Using an exclamation point to indicate that a remark isn't meant to be taken seriously, for instance, won't work with most foreign readers. They'll interpret the statement literally anyway.

> If I ever make that mistake again, I'll kill myself!

Using ellipsis points to mean that your thoughts are trailing off will only confuse a foreign reader.

> The figures may be correct. I wonder . . .

Use a simple period instead, and rephrase to eliminate sentence fragments. Using the virgule to separate nouns of equal weight or to indicate time ranges will also confuse some readers.

> owner/operator
> 1993/1994

Use a hyphen instead.

> owner-operator
> 1993–1994

Unless you're quoting from a copyrighted source and therefore have to repeat the original writer's punctuation, avoid using punctuation in a way that might not be clear to your foreign contacts.

OVERPUNCTUATION

Fix this simple rule firmly in your mind, even though it may mean unlearning many things you were taught in school and ignoring the latest trends in domestic writing.

Always *over*punctuate your international correspondence.

Dangers in Overpunctuation

Now that I've talked you into overpunctuating your foreign letters (I hope), I should mention the dark side. The danger in overpunctuating your letters is that it's easy to stick some commas or other common punctuation marks in the wrong place in one's zeal to overpunctuate a message. We need to keep reminding ourselves of the real objective of using punctuation—to *help,* not hinder, foreign readers. Misplaced punctuation will be just as confusing as too little punctuation. Notice from the following examples what can happen if you add punctuation just for the sake of adding punctuation, without regard to clarity.

> *Wrong:* The use of the metric system, of weights and measures, though preferable, is not compulsory.
> *Right:* The use of the metric system of weights and measures, though preferable, is not compulsory.

In the wrong example, the extra comma added between *system* and *of* changes the meaning. That comma means it should be read as (1) the use of the metric system and (2) the use of weights and measures. But that isn't what the writer meant. The writer was referring to one "system of weights and measures." The next example also adds a comma incorrectly.

> *Wrong:* A revised Convention for the Avoidance of Double Taxation Between the United States and Germany, was adopted on January 6, 19—.
> *Right:* A revised Convention for the Avoidance of Double Taxation Between the United States and Germany was adopted on January 6, 19—.

In the wrong example, the comma between *Germany* and *was* incorrectly separates the subject from the verb. It would be the same as saying:

> John and I, went to the meeting.

The misplaced comma between the subject and the verb creates a pause in reading and makes the reader think that some words must be missing from the sentence, for example:

> John and I, *against our employer's wishes,* went to the meeting.

Misplaced punctuation always raises questions in the reader's mind and often causes the reader to reach the wrong conclusion.

Guide to Interpretation

Although some punctuation is strictly conventional, such as a colon after a salutation (*Dear Mr. Lopez:*), most punctuation is used for clarity—to help readers avoid misreading a statement and to make the meaning of a statement very specific instead of subject to various interpretations.

When you speak, you help listeners understand what you're saying by your inflection, emphasizing certain words, and by pausing in certain places. Sometimes you may add facial expressions or hand gestures to help your listeners know exactly what you mean. In writing, punctuation has to do all of this work, because the reader can't "hear" your emphasis or "see" your gestures. That's a tall order, and it's easiest to fill if you think of punctuation as a necessary roadmap, not some ornamental signs along the highway. For example:

> *Wrong:* In any type of return or refund on a charge sale credit slips are given to the customer.

> *Right:* In any type of return or refund on a charge sale, credit slips are given to the customer.

Pretend you're the foreign recipient of the wrong statement. You're wondering if the writer means this:

> In any type of return or refund, on a charge-sale credit slips, are given to the customer.

No, that does not make sense.

> In any type of return, or refund on a charge-sale credit slips, are given to the customer.

No, that is just as bad.

> In any type of return or refund on a charge sale, credit slips are given to the customer.

Hmmmm. Yes, that sounds better.

Eventually, a foreign reader may be able to insert missing punctuation in the right place so that the sentence makes sense. But how many times will the reader have to repeat the exercise before deciding where to put it? If the reader doesn't know English, what may seem obvious to you won't be obvious at all to the reader. Here's another example that is certain to waste a reader's time.

> To reach our sales manager, Mr. Wyatt Blumenthal, by telephone call before 11 a.m. (U.S. eastern standard time), Monday to Thursday; on Friday, anytime from 9 a.m. to 5 p.m.

The reader will again mentally insert the missing comma *somewhere*.

> To reach our sales manager, Mr. Wyatt Blumenthal, by telephone call, before 11 a.m. (U.S. eastern standard time), Monday to Thursday; on Friday, anytime from 9 a.m. to 5 p.m.

No, perhaps this way:

> To reach our sales manager, Mr. Wyatt Blumenthal, by telephone, call before 11 a.m. (U.S. eastern standard time), [from] Monday to Thursday; on Friday, [call] anytime from 9 a.m. to 5 p.m.

Yes, that must be it.

In the best of cases, the reader *may* realize where the missing punctuation goes after two or more readings. But what if the reader reaches the wrong conclusion, as could happen in this example.

> The price of the instrument has increased $5.00 to $31.95.

Will the reader think that the price has increased *from* $5.00 *to* $31.95? Or will the reader know that the price has increased *by* $5.00 from $26.95 to $31.95? I wouldn't assume that a foreign reader who doesn't know English would understand. A comma after *$5.00* is essential.

> The price of the instrument has increased $5.00, to $31.95.

Rephrasing the sentence would be the best alternative to ensure that the recipient doesn't misread the statement.

> The price of the instrument has increased by $5.00, from $26.95 to $31.95.

The next example has a similar problem.

> When the report is in the committee will make a decision.

Without a comma, the sentence could at first appear to mean "When the report *is in the committee* . . ." A foreign reader might mentally insert not only a comma but a word that appears to be missing.

> When the report is in the committee, [we] will make a decision.

But this is what the writer really meant:

> When the report is in, the committee will make a decision.

The sentence could be recast to make it even clearer, although punctuation is still necessary.

> When the report is ready [*or* finished], the committee will make a decision.

One more example:

> Most European and U.S. suppliers sell in Japan through distributors, sales subsidiaries are also used.

In this case, using a comma instead of a semicolon throws the reader off track. Again, the reader has to guess where to insert what. This might be the first try:

> Most European and U.S. suppliers sell; in Japan, through distributors' sales, subsidiaries are also used.

Or is it:

> Most European and U.S. suppliers sell in Japan; through distributors' sales, subsidiaries are also used.

Or perhaps the reader will decide that *through* is a typographical error for *though*.

> Most European and U.S. suppliers sell in Japan, though distributors' sales subsidiaries are also used.

By now the reader is completely off course and may never see what, to you, is so obvious.

> Most European and U.S. suppliers sell in Japan through distributors; sales subsidiaries are also used.

All that work, just because a comma was incorrectly used in place of a semicolon. Or should the sentence have been rephrased to make it clearer? Try this:

> Most European and U.S. suppliers sell in Japan through distributors *or use* sales subsidiaries.

Often, when a sentence might be misread because of missing or misplaced punctuation, it's a sign that it should be rephrased.

CHECKUP

Here are more generic letters, like those in Chapters 4, 5, and 6, based on actual letters in my collection. They're provided here for you to test your skill at spotting and correcting problems in international correspondence discussed in this book. Especially, look for missing or misplaced punctuation. In the examples, a problem letter appears first, followed by an improved version.

In the first of the two letters to Mr. Monnier, a punctuation error appears in the first line: The year should be enclosed in commas, and "telephone-fax numbers" should be written as two individual items separated by commas. In the second paragraph, a comma is needed after the first and second use of "Newell" and the second use of "Ross," although there are two errors in the second sentence of that paragraph: Ross is still connected with the new firm, and the word *be* should be deleted. The third paragraph should be rewritten to eliminate language that would be unfamiliar to a foreign reader, such as the idiom "In all other respects" and the cliche "business as usual." Finally, the old-fashioned, trite closing "I remain, Yours truly," should be changed.

In the first of the two letters to Mrs. Hohenfellner, the trite phrase "please find enclosed" should be changed. The second sentence should be rewritten in a less confusing way as a list of items. The last sentence of the first paragraph has a comma missing after "succeeded" and could be made simpler and clearer. The entire first paragraph, in fact, is too long. The last paragraph has two contractions, and the closing "Cordially" is too familiar.

In the first of the two letters to Mr. Mizutani, the awkward writing of the overlong first paragraph needs to be improved. As it is, the comma before "therefore" should be a semicolon. In the second long sentence, a comma is missing after "ad" (which should be spelled out), between the two independent clauses, and after "blades." The remark "Thanks in advance" is trite and inappropriate. In this letter, too, the closing is too familiar for a foreign audience.

JUSTIN-HILL-ROSS & ASSOCIATES
ONE WILSON ROAD, SUITE 7
SAN ANTONIO, TX 78207

phone 210-555-1633 / fax 210-555-1634

July 5, 1994

Mr. Jean-Bernard Monnier
Banque de Paris
24 rue Linois
75740 Paris, France

Dear Mr. Monnier:

This is to advise you that on July 1, 1994 the name of our firm was changed to Justin-Hill-Ross & Associates. The address and telephone-fax numbers have remained the same.

Justin and Hill recently bought out the firms of Bagwell, Newell and Ross & Associates. The former owners, Laurence Bagwell, Anne Newell and Timothy Ross are no longer be connected to our firm.

In all other respects, it is business as usual with all former services continuing. Our office at the address on this letter will provide the same full range of services.

We appreciated the opportunity to serve you in the past and hope our past relationship will continue into the future.

I remain,

Yours truly,

Evan Justin III
President

cmr

July 5, 1994

Mr. Jean-Bernard Monnier
Banque de Paris
24 rue Linois
75740 Paris, France

Dear Mr. Monnier:

On July 1, 1994, the name of our firm was changed to Justin-Hill-Ross & Associates. The address, telephone number, and facsimile number are the same.

Justin and Hill recently bought the firms of Bagwell, Newell, and Ross & Associates. Two former owners in those firms—Laurence Bagwell and Anne Newell—are no longer associated with our new firm.

Our office, at the address printed on this letter, will operate as usual. We expect to offer the same full range of services to our clients.

We appreciated the opportunity to serve you in the past. We hope this fine relationship will continue in the future. Justin-Hill-Ross & Associates will always work hard to provide the best service possible to you and your company.

Sincerely,

Evan Justin III
President

cmr

WORLDWIDE TRAINING CONSULTANTS
186 SOUTH END AVENUE
KNOXVILLE, TN 37930

phone 615-555-0022 / fax 615-555-0023

January 6, 1994

Mrs. Helga Hohenfellner
Stuttgart Metalurgie
Beethovenstrasse 17
2104 Stuttgart 10, Germany

Dear Mrs. Hohenfellner:

   Thanks for your letter requesting information
about techniques for improving worker
productivity. Please find enclosed a booklet that
explains how resistance, resentment, skepticism,
job classification, work habits, all these
obstacles were overcome as a work unit was
organized, trained, and took its place on the
plant floor. As the quality of work life program
succeeded the company, responding to the success,
adopted variations of the concept at other plants.

   We hope you'll find this booklet helpful.
Don't hesitate to let us know if we can be of
further assistance.

                    Cordially,

                    James Prindle
                    Director, Training

ak

January 6, 1994

Mrs. Helga Hohenfellner
Stuttgart Metalurgie
Beethovenstrasse 17
2104 Stuttgart 10, Germany

Dear Mrs. Hohenfellner:

Thank you for asking about techniques for improving worker productivity.

I am enclosing a booklet about ways to improve the quality of work life. It explains how these obstacles were overcome in one company:

- Worker resistance
- Worker resentment
- Worker skepticism
- Inaccurate job classifications
- Ineffective work habits

These obstacles were overcome by reorganizing and retraining the company's work units. The modified units were then ready to begin work in the plant.

After the quality of work life had improved, the company used the same work-unit procedure in other plants. The idea of reorganizing and retraining the units was adjusted as needed for each plant.

We hope this information will help you improve productivity in your company. Please write or telephone if we can provide further information.

Sincerely,

James Prindle
Director, Training

ak

LANGLEY DESIGN, INC.
100 COURTYARD PLAZA
OMAHA, NE 68131

phone 402-555-9000 / fax 402-555-9001

March 16, 1994

Mr. Mizutani Masuro
Osaka Home Products Ltd
2-33, Namba 4-chome
Chuo-ku
Osaka 544, Japan

Dear Mr. Mizutani:

Our company wants to modernize all of it's offices with some type of air-comfort system, therefore, we'd like to know more about your electronic air-comfort system, an ad of which appeared recently in <u>Exclusive Electronics</u>. According to your ad you have a circulating system that is unusually quiet at 150 rpm-1500 rpm and inlet cones focus air on blades automatically compensating for changes in temperature winter or summer.

Thanks in advance for the information.

Regards,

(Ms.) Mary Coster-Rome
Purchasing Manager

sjt

LANGLEY DESIGN, INC.
100 COURTYARD PLAZA
OMAHA, NE 68131

phone 402-555-9000 / fax 402-555-9001

March 16, 1994

Mr. Mizutani Masuro
Osaka Home Products
2-33, Namba 4-chome
Chuo-ku
Osaka 544, Japan

Dear Mr. Mizutani:

Please send us information about your
company's electronic air-comfort system. This
system was advertised in the February issue of
Exclusive Electronics.

My company wants to install a new air-
circulation system in all offices. We would like
to evaluate the electronic air-comfort system for
this purpose.

Your company's advertisement states that the
system will operate between 150 and 1,500
revolutions per minute. Also, inlet cones focus
air on the blades, automatically compensating for
temperature changes in winter or summer.

We are eager to learn more about your
company's system. Thank you for your help.

Sincerely,

(Ms.) Mary Coster-Rome
Purchasing Manager

sjt

A Matter of Respect

IF YOU SAY or do something contrary to the customs of your contacts in other countries, you may as well slap the people in the face. That's the way they'll feel. To show proper respect, you have to observe meticulously the usage and practices in each country.

When you study other customs, you may conclude that U.S. customs are very simple by comparison. But that's probably because you've lived in the United States for many years and learned all of the annoying little details a long time ago. American usage and practice are second nature to you. But if you lived in another country and were trying to learn all about U.S. customs, you would likely be frustrated and overwhelmed by the innumerable differences between them and your own.

BUSINESS AND SOCIAL CUSTOMS

No one doubts that it is not only helpful but mandatory to know usage and practice in other countries if you operate in a global marketplace. Most existing guides, however, emphasize what you should *not* do. You should not, for example, criticize your contact or the person's country. People in most countries are very sensitive and consider it downright rude to make critical observations. You also should not impose your pace on others. People in other countries often take a dim view of the stressful, fast-paced nature of American business and social practices.

The other side of the coin is just as significant. It's important to find out what you *should* do to create a favorable impression. Muslims, for example, who tend to be fatalistic, frequently use the phrase "God will-ing" in speech and correspondence and would be pleased if you used it in your letters in appropriate places:

> I am looking forward to visiting your company in August, God willing [or use the Arabic *Inshallah*].

But if you get your countries mixed up some hectic morning or use the phrase out of habit in a letter to one of your Buddhist contacts in Japan, you'll raise some eyebrows—or worse.

One way to show your respect is to include a compliment about something pertaining to your contact's country. In most countries people take great pride in their nation's cultural heritage and artistic achieve-ments. It's always a nice gesture to recognize this:

> I am very happy to be writing to you in the wonderful city of Budapest. I have always admired the magnificent Royal Palace and historic Belvárosi Templom.

Business Negotiations

How easy it would be if all you had to do in international correspondence was to look up the other party's working hours and check the dates of the country's national holidays. But the other, less obvious customs are the ones most likely to snare you and squash your good intentions. Consider the basic matter of discussing business. I can already hear some of you veterans of foreign trade sighing wistfully. Americans, you're thinking, are *so* easy to get along with. They'll get right down to business without wasting your time and will be glad to close a deal with anyone, whatever his or her job title, who has the authority to do so.

The old pros know that you have to learn a whole new set of rules to conduct business with people in other countries. In some Far Eastern nations, most of the Arab world, and various other countries, it's taboo to get down to business in the first letter(s) or the first meeting(s). Try pushing your contacts, and you may push the potential trade opportuni-ties right out the door. No doubt you've also heard stories about busi-nesspeople trying to conclude a deal with top executives in another country, such as Japan, who discovered that the top executives there were actually appalled that such details weren't being handled by subor-dinates.

Language Problems

For good reason, most of this book has focused intently on the language problems in correspondence. Saying the wrong thing or saying the right thing with the wrong emphasis can sound a lot like an insult to someone in another country. Also, some foreign words and phrases have distinctly different meanings from one region to another. You may even run into trouble within English-speaking regions or countries. Did you know that "tabling a proposal" means acting on it immediately to a Briton? To an American, it means delaying the idea indefinitely.

American businesspeople are taught to put their best foot forward in business, which sounds innocent enough. With that type of training, you may be eager to impress your contacts with how wonderful it is to live and work in the United States and how advanced your business is in its field or in the world. But to someone in another country, might this not sound like a put-down?

A businessperson in New York said that two of his contacts in Southeast Asia dropped him and his company before negotiations were barely warm. To this day, he's not completely sure why, but he now suspects that when he tried to convey his credentials and the qualifications of his company to supply the foreign firm with tools, his message came across as "Our companies are better than your companies." The wrong slant or one sentence too many can turn an honest attempt to convey information into unintentionally obnoxious boasting. In countries that place great stock on politeness, as most do, this type of impression would be unforgivable.

Family Ties

In Western cultures, such as the United States, Canada, and northern Europe, business and family ties are kept separate. But in many other countries, for example, the Arab world, Latin America, and the Far East, family ties are clearly the ties that bind. This means that family loyalties take precedence over business loyalties.

In a place with strict traditional customs, the family unit usually includes uncles, aunts, and all sorts of relatives in a male-dominated household. The wife may have control over household matters, such as caring for the house and preparing the meals, but the husband is the final authority in all other matters in the marriage and in the business community. Even in countries where women work outside the home, the major support is usually provided by the husband.

In non-Western regions, such as the Middle East and Asia, women occupy a traditional role in society, which usually means that American businesswomen have a difficult time finding acceptance in business circles there. Often the restrictions on women are based on religious customs that spill over into social and business activities.

Even in countries where women are more readily accepted in business dealings, it behooves them to avoid appearing aggressive and never to flaunt their feelings of equal status. In modern western European cities, women can usually proceed as they would in the United States. In Latin American countries, where male feelings of superiority remain widespread, women should proceed more cautiously. This advice also holds true in eastern European nations, and a woman especially needs to turn up her caution meter as she moves across the globe toward the Middle East and the Far East. For more about the potential problems of women in international communication, refer to Chapter 1.

Business Hours and Holidays

Perhaps you're used to working from 9 a.m. to 5 p.m., Monday through Friday. You may decide to send a fast message to another country programmed to arrive on Friday, only to discover that businesses there are closed on Friday afternoons. Or you may realize later that that particular Friday happens to be a national holiday in that country. This possibility seems like a trivial matter compared with other mishaps, but it will turn into a nagging aggravation if repeated over and over. You'll save wear and tear on everyone by learning the working hours and holidays of your contact in advance. Keep a calendar for each business or country with which you deal next to your own calendar. (The country profiles in Chapter 9 include business hours and principal public holidays.)

Regional Differences

Europe.   Customs vary from the western European countries, such as Great Britain and France, to the eastern European countries, such as Poland and some of the former Soviet republics. Although the Westernized nations have customs similar to those in the United States, it is still necessary to approach everyone with a healthy amount of reserve and formality. Until asked to use first names, for example, use titles of respect appropriate for the country, which may be the scholastic title *Dr.*, a job title such as *Director,* or a personal title such as *Mr., Mrs.,* or *Miss.* Stay away from potentially touchy subjects, such as politics, religion, alcohol, money, and sex. Follow your contact's lead in pacing your business negotiations.

Africa and the Middle East.   The countries in this part of the world vary from other countries in many ways, especially in religious practices. African and Middle Eastern countries that have largely Muslim populations, for example, abide by the very strict social, business, and legal codes of Islam. Some African nations have a mixture of religious and social customs, including numerous tribal customs. South Africa, aside from its racial strife, reveals a European influence. In general, expect this entire region to be much more traditional than Europe, particularly western Europe. This means that in addition to all of the restrictions mentioned for Europe that also apply here, you should be especially sensitive to religious practices and aware of the generally subservient female role.

Asia and the Pacific. The countries in this region also vary greatly from other countries, with practices ranging from the Westernized customs of Australia to the traditional customs of China and Japan. Formal procedures and approaches to business are very important in Eastern cultures, which place strong emphasis on hospitality and proper protocol. Follow the same cautions that you would observe in Europe but increase your attention to matters of business protocol. Pay special attention to titles and the proper use of names (watch for a reverse order of names in many Asian cultures).

Latin America and the Caribbean. Both Central and South America and some islands in the Caribbean Sea demonstrate a strong Spanish or Portuguese influence, not only in language but in names, greetings, and hospitality. European customs prevail in many places, and the same restrictions observed in European countries should be followed here. Although Latin America has clear evidence of Western influence, male feelings of superiority are much stronger there than in most western European countries. Also, punctuality and the strict observance of time may appear much more lax than it is in other parts of the world. Remember, too, that people living in Central and South America consider themselves Americans and resent having U.S. businesspeople imply that only U.S. citizens are Americans.

North America. Mexican customs are more akin to Central and South American customs. Anyone who knows U.S. customs, however, won't have any trouble dealing with Canadian usage and practice. In spite of its numerous ethnic groups, the customs of Canada are similar to those in the United States, though somewhat more conservative. Follow the same cautions recommended for Europe but enjoy a far greater understanding of U.S. usage and practice.

RELIGIOUS CUSTOMS
<hr>

A slightly defensive businessman once said that Americans aren't the only ones who make faux pas. He had just received a letter from someone in Southeast Asia asking him to fax a reply on December 25. But he lamented his own oversight on another occasion, when he wrote to his counterpart in Saudi Arabia about a business trip. He wanted to arrange a luncheon meeting on a date that, he later learned, fell during Ramadan, the sacred Islamic period when fasting is practiced daily from sunrise to sunset. I don't know if any serious consequences resulted on either side, but we can probably assume that the parties in each instance are now more sensitive to each other's religious customs.

The main lesson to learn from tales like this is to do your homework before you commit words to paper. In many countries, religion governs conduct in all facets of life, including business, and you can never be one hundred percent certain that you won't damage a relationship by stepping on someone's religious toes.

The following section contains brief profiles of the world's most prominent and influential religions.

Major World Religions

Christianity. *Where it is found:* With more adherents than any other religion, and practiced in every part of the world, Christianity is the major religion in Europe, the Americas, Australia, New Zealand, and the Pacific Islands.

Major branches or divisions: Catholic, Orthodox, Protestant.

House of worship: Church.

Information to keep in mind: The orthodox belief is in one God revealed in three persons—God the father, God the son, and God the Holy Spirit. The Sabbath is observed on Sundays. Some Christians still abstain from eating meat on Fridays, although most no longer observe this practice. Because the Orthodox church does not use the Gregorian calendar, the dates of its religious holidays and seasons may differ from those in the Catholic and Protestant churches.

Islam. *Where it is found:* The second largest religion, Islam is practiced worldwide but is found primarily in countries stretching from Africa to East Asia, including Egypt, Saudi Arabia, Iran, Pakistan, Bangladesh, and Indonesia.

Major branches or divisions: Sunni, Shiite.

House of worship: Mosque.

Information to keep in mind: The principal weekly worship for Muslims occurs at midday on Fridays. Devout Muslims, who recognize one God, must fast during the month of Ramadan from sunup to sundown. Traditionally, strict rules of conduct are observed, with the sexes segregated in restaurants and other public places and with women expected to appear in modest dress. Devout Muslims also are prohibited from eating pork or drinking alcohol.

Hinduism. *Where it is found:* The third largest religion, Hinduism is practiced mostly in India and other South Asian states, such as Nepal, Sri Lanka, and Indonesia.

Major branches or divisions: Great variety of sects recognizing thousands of gods. Three of the most important sects are those worshipping the gods Vishnu and Shiva and the goddess Shakti.

House of worship: Temple.

Information to keep in mind: Hindus, who believe in reincarnation, are instructed to treat animals with respect, and many Hindus are vegetarians. Cows are held to be especially holy, and devout Hindus are prohibited from eating beef. Since devotion is largely an individual or a family matter, Hindus do not form congregations for worship. The caste system, officially abolished in the 1950s, is still recognized unofficially.

Buddhism. *Where it is found:* Primarily practiced in Asia, Buddhism also exists in Europe and North America. It is the religion with the fourth greatest number of worshippers.

Major branches or divisions: Two important divisions—Theravada and Mahayana.

House of worship: Temple.

Information to keep in mind: The Theravada Buddhists focus on the teachings of one Buddha; the Mahayana Buddhists recognize other enlightened Buddhas. Like Hindus, Buddhists believe in reincarnation and use temples primarily for individual meditation. Practices vary among people and sects. Some Buddhists, for example, practice a form of mental meditation; others emphasize physical discipline. Many Buddhists abstain from eating meat.

Judaism. *Where it is found:* Although practiced worldwide, most Jews today live in North America and Israel. It is the fifth largest world religion.

Major branches or divisions: Orthodox, Conservative, and Reform.

House of worship: Synagogue or (for Reform Jews only) temple.

Information to keep in mind: On the Sabbath (from sundown on Friday to sundown on Saturday), traditional Jews refrain from performing any kind of work, including tasks such as driving and cooking; Jews, who recognize one God, spend Yom Kippur (Day of Atonement) in fasting and in prayer. Traditional dietary laws forbid Jews from mixing milk and meat and from eating ritually unclean foods. Pork, shellfish, many kinds of game, and the blood from any kind of animal are not kosher.

Millions of people do not practice any one of the major religions. If you are doing business in a particular country, consult that country's profile in Chapter 9 ("Around the World from Afghanistan to Zimbabwe") and check what its major and minor religions are. Then turn to "Information Sources" in the Appendix for a list of reference books with information on individual countries and their local religions.

9

Around
the World
from
Afghani-
stan to
Zimbabwe

WHAT DO BUSINESSPEOPLE in all countries have in common? This isn't a riddle or a trick question. The answer is a desire to help their employers prosper. That's not a bad starting point for mutual understanding and cooperation. If everyone has the same objective, the incentive to work successfully with a foreign counterpart should be strong on both sides. But beyond that, don't expect to find that you have the same practices and procedures as your foreign contacts.

Each country, as you know, has its own unique heritage, social and business environment, and political system. Each one observes the practices that are appropriate for and faithful to its own society. Sometimes, though, it seems that even within a particular country the people follow a regimen of complex contradictions. Is that the way others see us? Probably, so it's hardly surprising that writing effective international correspondence is such a challenging task.

Pick almost any country and consider the profound differences between practices and attitudes there and those in the United States. Our foremost trading partner, Japan, remains a puzzle to many American businesspeople. Americans, for example, are often exasperated as they try to cultivate solid business friendships with Japanese businesspeople. Although Americans are proud that they can create almost instant feelings of camaraderie, the Japanese look askance at this; they must first feel what they call *shinyo*—trust and confidence—and it can take a long time for Japanese people to feel that. Until they do, other things will just have to wait.

Etiquette should be one of the easiest subjects to master, but for some reason Americans have trouble with it, possibly because it has never been a top priority in the U.S. business world. In many other societies, however, it not only is essential but is an end in itself.

In Eastern cultures, among others, personal feelings are an important part of business practice. In Japan, for example, human feelings are considered more important than making a profit, whereas in the United States, the objective of making money takes precedence over someone's personal feelings. So we have two diametrically opposed views. Does this mean that the Japanese disregard the pursuit of profit or that the Americans pursue profit without regard for anything or anyone else? Of course not. It's just an example of the innumerable subtle and not-so-subtle differences that have to be taken into account when you prepare your comments for an international audience.

To illustrate the range of differences that could seriously affect your international correspondence, this chapter takes a trip around the world. For each country, it summarizes everything from religions and languages to working hours and holidays to currencies and systems of weights and measures. All of this, however, is only a beginning—a foundation. The hope is that you'll find it easier to build your house if the foundation is already there.

MAJOR COUNTRIES OF THE WORLD

The following profiles can help you improve your international correspondence in two ways: (1) by orienting you globally in your quest for better understanding of the countries you deal with and (2) by enhancing your knowledge of usage and practice in other parts of the world.

None of this material, however, is meant to be so all-inclusive that you never have to read another book—sorry! To expand your knowledge about certain countries or regions, you might start by reading the country descriptions in world almanacs or in world travel or business guides, as well as the profiles in the State Department's *Background Notes* and Brigham Young University's *Culturgrams*. For in-depth information, look for individual books devoted to a particular country or region, such as *Understanding Arabs* or *Japanese Etiquette & Ethics in Business* (refer to the sources listed in the Appendix for further examples). Also, the Departments of State and Commerce have many offices dealing with matters of international trade and communication, and foreign and U.S. consulates, embassies, and various other organizations are likely sources of further useful information. Ask your local reference librarian for additional sources.

The following profiles summarize this information for each country:

Geographical location
Capital city
Official and other languages
Major and other religions
Principal holidays
Business hours
Customs

Each profile begins with the official name of the state, for example, in the case of Greece, "Hellenic Republic"; its global location; and its capital city. The profile next specifies the major administrative units within the country (if any), such as states, provinces, or districts. It then lists the principal languages in the country, including which ones (if any) are the official languages, and the principal religions, including which ones (if any) have a majority of followers. It concludes with the principal holidays, standard business hours, and general customs.

Many holidays fall on a different date each year, so specific dates cannot be given; rather, the holidays are listed according to the Gregorian calendar in order from the first to the last each year. You should fill in the exact dates at the beginning of each new year, keeping in mind that other countries may use a different calendar or may celebrate common holidays on dates that differ from those in the United States. If your local office supplier cannot order country calendars for you, look for current dates in some of the world guides, such as the *World Travel Guide,* updated annually; in the "Travel Notes" sections of some *Background Notes;* or through embassies, consulates, and other organizations involved in international affairs.

The business hours listed in the summaries are fairly standard, but you should routinely ask the companies with which you deal for their specific working hours. Most businesses will be closed on the country's principal holidays, but inquire if you have any doubts. Closings may vary on religious holidays in countries that have more than one major religion, with different businesses observing different religious holidays. Some businesses also may close for other events celebrated only in their locality.

The customs section of the profiles summarizes general attitudes and practices, such as whether the country has strict religious customs or if it has a relatively modern, Western orientation. The phrase "normal business etiquette" means complete courtesy and respect, with polite reserve and formality in attitude and approach; it doesn't mean typical American-style casualness and familiarity.

Some countries are newly formed republics; others are currently engaged in military, political, or religious conflicts that could alter their boundaries at any time. Keeping up to date is a never-ending but necessary task for anyone involved in international communication. Watch for changes and update the following profiles from time to time.

Afghanistan. Republic of Afghanistan, located northwest of Pakistan and India in southwestern Asia, with thirty-one provinces.
Capital: Kabul.
Language: Pushtu (majority), Dari, Persian, Turki, other.
Religion: Sunni Muslim (majority), Shiite Muslim, Hindu, Jewish, Christian.
Principal holidays: Leilat al-Meiraj, Eid al-Fitr, Revolution Day, Workers' Day, Eid al-Adha, Ashoura, Independence Day, Prophet's Birthday.
Business hours: 8–12 and 3–6:30 Sat.–Wed., 8:30–3:30 Thur.; some offices closed Wed. and Thur. afternoon.
Customs: Emphasis on traditional social and religious customs; traditional male-female roles strictly observed.

Albania. Republic of Albania, located in southeastern Europe along the Adriatic and Ionian seas, with twenty-six districts (*rreth*).
Capital: Tirana.
Language: Albanian (official: Tusk dialect), Greek.
Religion: Sunni Muslim (majority), Greek Orthodox, Roman Catholic.
Principal holidays: New Year's Day, Proclamation of the Republic, Labor Day, Independence Day, Liberation Day.
Business hours: April–Sept.: 7–4 Mon.–Sat.; 5–8 Mon.–Tues. Oct.–Mar.: 7:30–2:30 Mon.–Sat.; 4–7 Mon.–Tues.
Customs: Traditional tribal influences and traditional male-female roles.

Algeria. People's Democratic Republic of Algeria, located in northern Africa along the Mediterranean Sea, with forty-eight states (*wilayaat*).
Capital: Algiers.
Language: Arabic (official), French, Berber dialects, English in major business centers.
Religion: Sunni Muslim.
Principal holidays: New Year's Day, Eid al-Fitr, Labor Day, Revolution Day, Eid al-Adha, Ben Bella's Overthrow, Muslim New Year, Indepen-

dence Day, Ashovra, Mouloud (Prophet's Birthday), Revolution Anniversary.

Business hours: 8–12 and 2–6:30 Sat.–Wed.

Customs: Emphasis on traditional religious and social customs and traditional male-female roles; French influence in business circles; emphasis on hospitality.

Andorra. Principality of Andorra, located in the Pyrenees between France and Spain in southwestern Europe, with seven parishes (*parròquia*), under joint supervision of France and Spanish bishops of Urgel; foreign affairs conducted by France.

Capital: Andorra la Vella.

Language: Catalan (official), French, Spanish.

Religion: Roman Catholic.

Principal holidays: New Year's Day, Epiphany, Good Friday, Easter Monday, Easter, National Day, Christmas, New Year's Eve.

Business hours: Substantial variation; inquire in companies.

Customs: Similar to customs in Spain, with traditional male-female roles; emphasis on appearance.

Angola. People's Republic of Angola, located in southwestern Africa along the Atlantic Ocean, with eighteen provinces.

Capital: Luanda.

Language: Portuguese (official), Bantu.

Religion: Animist (majority), Roman Catholic, Protestant.

Principal holidays: New Year's Day, Outbreak of Rebellion Against Portuguese Colonialism, Victory Day, Youth Day, Workers' Day, Armed Forces Day, National Hero's Day, Dr. Agostinho Neto's Birthday, Independence Day, Pioneers' Day, Foundation of Workers' Party (MPLA), Family Day.

Business hours: 8:30–12 and 2–6 Mon.–Fri.; 8:30–12 Sat.

Customs: Traditional social and business etiquette interspersed with local customs and influences.

Antigua and Barbuda. Independent state, located in the Leeward Islands in the eastern Caribbean, including the island of Redonda.

Capital: St. John's.

Language: English.

Religion: Anglican (majority), Roman Catholic, other Christian.

Principal holidays: New Year's Day, Good Friday, Easter Monday, Labor

Day, Whit Monday, Caricom Day, Carnival, Independence Day, Christmas Day, Boxing Day.

Business hours: 8–12 and 1–4 Mon.–Fri.

Customs: Relatively informal atmosphere; normal business etiquette.

Argentina. Argentine Republic, located in southeastern South America along the Atlantic Ocean, with twenty-two provinces and one federal district.

Capital: Buenos Aires.

Language: Spanish (official), English, German, French, Italian.

Religion: Roman Catholic.

Principal holidays: New Year's Day, Maundy Thursday, Good Friday, Easter, Labor Day, National Day, Malvinas Day, Flag Day, Independence Day, San Martin's Death, Student Day, Columbus Day, Feast of the Immaculate Conception, Christmas.

Business hours: 9–7 Mon.–Fri.

Customs: Emphasis on social and economic status; respect for elderly and women; traditional male-female roles.

Armenia. Republic of Armenia, former Soviet republic located in the Caucasus east of Turkey between Europe and Asia.

Capital: Yerevan.

Language: Armenian (official), Russian, Kurdish, Azerbaijani, English, German.

Religion: Armenian Apostolic, Russian Orthodox, Protestant, Muslim.

Principal holidays: Former Soviet holidays: New Year's Day, Army and Navy Day, International Labor Day, International Women's Day, Victory in Europe Day, Constitution Day, October Revolution, Agriculture and Agro-Industrial Workers' Day.

Business hours: 9–6 Mon.–Fri.

Customs: Emphasis on traditional customs and beliefs; evolving national identity.

Australia. Commonwealth of Australia, the smallest continent and largest island in the world, located in the Indian and Pacific oceans, with six federated states.

Capital: Canberra.

Language: English.

Religion: Protestant/Anglican, Roman Catholic, other.

Principal holidays: New Year's Day, Australia Day, Good Friday, Easter,

Easter Monday, Anzac Day (Veterans' Memorial Day), Queen Elizabeth's Birthday, Christmas, Boxing Day.

Business hours: 9–5 Mon.–Fri.

Customs: Casual customs, with North American and European influence in business.

Austria. Republic of Austria, Alpine country located south of Germany in west central Europe, with nine federated states.

Capital: Vienna.

Language: German; English required in schools.

Religion: Roman Catholic.

Principal holidays: New Year's Day, Epiphany, Easter Monday, Labor Day, Ascension Day, Whit Monday, Corpus Christi, Assumption Day, National Day, All Saints' Day, Immaculate Conception, Christmas Day, St. Stephen's Day.

Business hours: 8–4 Mon.–Fri.

Customs: Formal approach, with respect for religion; highest percentage of working mothers in world; emphasis on art and culture.

Azerbaijan. Republic of Azerbaijan, former Soviet republic located in the Caucasus and along the western Caspian Sea between Europe and Asia.

Capital: Baku.

Language: Azerbaijani (official), Russian, Turkish, local dialects.

Religion: Shiite Muslim (majority), Sunni Muslim, Russian Orthodox, Armenian Apostolic.

Principal holidays: Former Soviet holidays: New Year's Day, Army and Navy Day, International Labor Day, International Women's Day, Europe Day, Constitution Day, October Revolution, Agricultural and Agro-Industrial Workers' Day.

Business hours: 9–6 Mon.–Fri.

Customs: Emphasis on traditional customs and beliefs; evolving national identity.

Bahamas. Commonwealth of the Bahamas, located in the Caribbean Sea between Florida and Haiti, with seven hundred islands and one thousand cays.

Capital: Nassau.

Language: English.

Religion: Baptist, Anglican, Roman Catholic, other.

Principal holidays: New Year's Day, Good Friday, Easter Monday, Whit Monday, Labor Day, Independence Day, Emancipation Day, Discovery Day, Christmas Day, Boxing Day.

Business hours: 9–5 Mon.–Fri.

Customs: Informal approach; normal business etiquette.

Bahrain. State of Bahrain, located east of Saudi Arabia in the Middle East and the western Persian Gulf, with about thirty-three islands.

Capital: Manama.

Language: Arabic (official), English, Farsi, Urdu.

Religion: Sunni Muslim (majority), Shiite Muslim, Christian, Bahai, Hindu, Parsee.

Principal holidays: New Year's Day, Leilat al-Meiraj, Eid al-Fitr, Eid al-Adha, Muslim New Year, Ashoura, Mouloud (Prophet's Birthday), National Day.

Business hours: Varies; inquire in companies.

Customs: Formal approach, with emphasis on traditional beliefs and male-female roles, except for slightly more liberal attitudes to women than usual in this region.

Bangladesh. People's Republic of Bangladesh, located in southern Asia northeast of the Indian subcontinent, with four divisions.

Capital: Dhaka.

Language: Bangla (official), English.

Religion: Muslim (majority), Hindu, Buddhist, Christian.

Principal holidays: Shahid Day, Independence Day, Eid al-Fitr, May Day, Eid al-Adha, Jamat Wide, Muslim New Year, National Solidarity Day, Victory Day.

Business hours: 9–4 Sat.–Thur.

Customs: Emphasis on religious and traditional social customs; traditional male-female roles; frequently, instead of offering thanks, a favor is returned.

Barbados. Independent state, easternmost island located in the Windward Islands of the Caribbean Sea.

Capital: Bridgetown.

Language: English (official), local Bajan Creole.

Religion: Anglican (majority), Methodist, Roman Catholic.

Principal holidays: New Year's Day, Errol Barrow Day, Easter, Labor Day, Whit Monday, Kadooment Day, United Nation's Day, Independence Day, Christmas Day, Boxing Day.

Business hours: 8–4 Mon.–Fri., 8–12 Sat.

Customs: Friendly and hospitable attitude, with modern Western influences.

Belarus. Republic of Belarus, former Soviet Republic of Belorussia located west of Russia in northeastern Europe, with six regions.
Capital: Minsk.
Language: Belorussian (official), Russian, Polish, Eastern Slavonic.
Religion: Roman Catholic, Eastern Orthodox, Muslim, Jewish.
Principal holidays: Former Soviet holidays: New Year's Day, Army and Navy Day, International Labor Day, International Women's Day, Victory in Europe Day, Constitution Day, October Revolution, Agricultural and Agro-Industrial Workers' Day.
Business hours: 9–6 Mon.–Fri.
Customs: Emphasis on traditional customs and beliefs; evolving national identity.

Belgium. Kingdom of Belgium, located north of France in northwestern Europe, with nine provinces.
Capital: Brussels.
Language: Flemish (official, over 50 percent) and French (official, about 30 percent), German.
Religion: Roman Catholic (majority), Protestant, Jewish.
Principal holidays: New Year's Day, Easter Monday, May Day, Ascension Day, Whit Monday, National Holiday, Assumption Day, All Saints' Day, Armistice Day, King's Birthday, Christmas, Boxing Day.
Business hours: 8:30–5:30 Mon.–Fri.
Customs: Cosmopolitan Western attitudes; emphasis on art and culture.

Belize. Independent state, formerly British Honduras, located in northeastern Central America along the Caribbean Sea and Gulf of Honduras, with six districts.
Capital: Belmopan.
Language: English (official), Spanish, Maya, Carib.
Religion: Roman Catholic (majority), Protestant.
Principal holidays: New Year's Day, Baron Bliss Day/Commonwealth Day, Easter, Labor Day, Queen's Birthday, St. George's Cay Day, Independence Day, Columbus Day, Garifuna Settlement Day, Christmas.
Business hours: 8–12 and 1–5 Mon.–Thur.; 8:30–12 and 1–6:45 Fri.
Customs: British influence in many customs; normal business etiquette.

Benin. Republic of Benin, located west of Nigeria in western Africa along the Bight of Benin, with six provinces.

Capital: Porto Novo.

Language: French (official), English, Bariba, Fulani, Fon, Yoruba.

Religion: Animist (majority), Roman Catholic, Muslim.

Principal holidays: New Year's Day, Martyrs' Day, Good Friday, Easter Monday, Workers' Day, Ascension Day, Whit Monday, Eid al-Adha, Assumption, Armed Forces Day, All Saints' Day, National Day, Christmas Day, Harvest Day.

Business hours: 8:30–12:30 and 3–6:30 Mon.–Fri.

Customs: Emphasis on religion, including voodoo; normal business etiquette.

Bhutan. Kingdom of Bhutan, located south of China on the Indian subcontinent in southern Asia, with eighteen districts.

Capital: Thimphu.

Language: Dzongkha (official), Sharchop Kha, Nepalese, English.

Religion: Buddhist (majority), Hindu.

Principal holidays: Wesak/Budda Day, Thimphu Tsechu, H. M. Jigme Singye Wangchuk's Birthday, National Day.

Business hours: Varies; inquire in companies.

Customs: Emphasis on religion (Buddhism); traditional social customs but with equal rights for women.

Bolivia. Republic of Bolivia, located north of Argentina in central South America, with nine departments.

Capital: Sucre.

Language: Spanish (official), Quechua, Aymara, English.

Religion: Roman Catholic (majority), Protestant.

Principal holidays: New Year's Day, Carnival, *Dia de Mar*, Good Friday, Labor Day, Corpus Christi, Independence Day, All Saints' Day, Christmas.

Business hours: 9–12 and 2–6 or 3–7 Mon.–Fri.; 9–12 Sat.

Customs: Emphasis on tradition; male superiority; evidence of Western influence; consider themselves Americans; normal business etiquette.

Bosnia-Herzegovina. Former Yugoslav republic, located in southeastern Europe bordering Yugoslavia, Croatia, and the Adriatic Sea.

Capital: Sarajevo.

Language: Serbo-Croatian.

Religion: Eastern Orthodox, Roman Catholic, Muslim.

Principal holidays: New Year, Labor Day, Veterans' Day, Republic Days.

Business hours: 7–3 Mon.–Fri.

Customs: Emphasis on traditional customs and beliefs; disrupted by political instability.

Botswana. Republic of Botswana, located north of South Africa in southern central Africa, with nine districts.

Capital: Gaborone.

Language: English (official), Setswana.

Religion: Christian, indigenous.

Principal holidays: New Year's Day, Easter, Bank Holiday, Ascension Day, President's Day, Botswana Day, Christmas.

Business hours: Apr.–Oct.: 8–5; Oct.–Apr.: 7:30–4:30.

Customs: Emphasis on traditional tribal customs; often unfamiliar with Western ways.

Brazil. Federative Republic of Brazil, located in northeastern central South America along the Atlantic Ocean, with twenty-six states and one federal district.

Capital: Brasília.

Language: Portuguese (official), French, German, Italian, English.

Religion: Roman Catholic.

Principal holidays: New Year's Day, Foundation of Rio de Janeiro, Foundation of São Paulo, Carnival, Easter, Tiradentes Day, Labor Day, Ascension Day, Corpus Christi, Independence Day, Nossa Senhora de Aparecida, All Souls' Day, Proclamation of the Republic, Christmas.

Business hours: 9–6 Mon.–Fri.

Customs: Emphasis on religion, with traditional male-female roles; European influence in business etiquette; casual attitude about time.

Brunei Darussalam. State of Brunei Darussalam, located in southeastern Asia next to the Malaysian states of Sabah and Sarawak on the island of Borneo.

Capital: Bandar Seri Begawan.

Language: Malay (official), Chinese, English.

Religion: Muslim (official: mostly Sunni), Christian, Buddhist, Confucian.

Principal holidays: New Year's Day, Chinese New Year, Anniversary of Revelation of Koran, Hari Raya Puasa, Eid al-Fitr, Anniversary of Royal

Brunei Regiment, Hari Raya Haji, Feast of Sacrifice, Eid al-Adha, Muslim New Year, Sultan's Birthday, Mouloud (Prophet's Birthday), Christmas.

Business hours: 8–12 and 1–5 Mon.–Fri.; 9–12 Sat.

Customs: Emphasis on traditional customs and traditional male-female roles.

Bulgaria.   Republic of Bulgaria, located in southeastern Europe along the Black Sea north of Greece, with nine regions.

Capital: Sofia.

Language: Bulgarian (official), Turkish, Macedonian, Russian, French, German, English.

Religion: Bulgarian (Eastern) Orthodox (majority), Muslim, Roman Catholic, Protestant, Jewish, Gregorian-Armenian.

Principal holidays: New Year's Day, Liberation Day, Orthodox Easter, Labor Day, Education Day, National Day, Christmas.

Business hours: 8–6 Mon.–Sat.

Customs: Emphasis on traditional customs, but with European influence; normal business etiquette.

Burkina Faso.   Formerly Upper Volta, independent state located south of Mali in western Africa, with thirty provinces.

Capital: Ouagadougou.

Language: French (official), tribal languages.

Religion: Animist (majority), Muslim, Roman Catholic.

Principal holidays: New Year's Day, Eid al-Fitr, Easter Monday, Labor Day, Ascension Day, Whit Monday, Eid al-Adha, National Day, Assumption, Mouloud (Prophet's Birthday), All Saints' Day, Christmas.

Business hours: 8–12:30 and 3–5:30 Mon.–Fri.

Customs: Local customs observed; French influence in cities.

Burundi.   Republic of Burundi, located west of Tanzania in central Africa along Lake Tanganyika, with fifteen provinces.

Capital: Bujumbura.

Language: French (official), Kirundi, Swahili.

Religion: Roman Catholic (majority), Protestant, animist.

Principal holidays: New Year's Day, Unity Day, Easter Monday, Labor Day, Ascension Day, Independence Day, Assumption, Anniversary of Third Republic, Victory Day, All Saints' Day, Christmas Day.

Business hours: Inquire in companies.

Customs: Traditional local customs outside cities; normal business etiquette in major urban centers.

Cambodia. State of Cambodia, previously Kampuchea, located north of Vietnam in Southeast Asia along the Gulf of Thailand.

Capital: Phnom Penh.

Language: Khmer (official), French, Chinese, Vietnamese.

Religion: Theravada Buddhist (majority), Muslim, Christian.

Principal holidays: Liberation of Phnom Penh, New Year, Victory over American Imperialism Day, Labor Day, Day of Hatred, Feast of Ancestors, Full Moon Water Festival.

Business hours: Inquire in companies.

Customs: Traditional customs and traditional male-female roles observed; political topics strictly avoided; emphasis on group rather than individual; strong influence of Buddhism in spite of ban during Pol Pot regime of 1970s.

Cameroon. Republic of Cameroon, located in western central Africa along the Gulf of Guinea, with ten provinces.

Capital: Yaoundé.

Language: French and English (official), numerous local African languages.

Religion: Animist, Christian, Muslim.

Principal holidays: New Year's Day, Youth Day, Good Friday, Easter Monday, Eid al-Fitr, Labor Day, National Day, Ascension Day, Eid al-Adha, Festival of the Sheep, Assumption, Christmas Day.

Business hours: East: 8–12 and 2:30–5:30 Mon.–Fri.; West: 7:30–2:30 Mon.–Fri. and 7:30–12 Sat.

Customs: Strong emphasis on traditional and religious beliefs; normal business etiquette in towns.

Canada. Independent state, located in northern North America, with ten provinces and two territories.

Capital: Ottawa.

Language: English, French.

Religion: Roman Catholic (majority), United Church, Anglican, various other.

Principal holidays: New Year's Day, Good Friday, Easter Monday, Victoria Day, Canada Day, Labor Day, Thanksgiving, Remembrance Day.

Business hours: 9–5 Mon.–Fri.

Customs: Modern Western country; normal business etiquette.

Cape Verde. Republic of Cape Verde, located in the Atlantic Ocean off northern and western Africa, with ten islands and five islets.

Capital: Praia.

Language: Portuguese (official), Criuolo, English, French.

Religion: Roman Catholic (majority), Protestant.

Principal holidays: National Heroes' Day, Women's Day, Labor Day, Children's Day, Independence Day, Day of the Nation, Christmas Day.

Business hours: Inquire in companies.

Customs: Evidence of traditional customs, with European influence in business etiquette.

Central African Republic. Central African Republic, located west of Sudan in central Africa, with fourteen prefectures and the autonomous commune of the capital city.

Capital: Bangui.

Language: French (official), Sangho, Arabic, Hansa, Swahili.

Religion: Animist, Muslim, other.

Principal holidays: New Year's Day, Anniversary of Death of Barthélemy Boganda, Easter Monday, Labor Day, Ascension Day, Whit Monday, National Day of Prayer, Independence Day, Assumption, All Saints' Day, National Day, Christmas.

Business hours: 8–1 Mon.–Fri.

Customs: Strong traditional and religious beliefs and traditional male-female roles.

Chad. Republic of Chad, located south of Libya in northern central Africa, with fourteen prefectures.

Capital: N'djaména.

Language: French and Arabic (official), Chadian Arabic, Sara, numerous tribal languages.

Religion: Muslim, animist, Christian.

Principal holidays: New Year's Day, Eid al-Fitr, Easter Monday, Labor Day, Liberation of Africa Day, Anniversary of Organization of African Unity's Foundation, Whit Monday, Eid al-Adha, Independence Day, Assumption, Mouloud (Prophet's Birthday), All Saints' Day, Proclamation of the Republic, Victory of Deby over Habré Day, Christmas Day.

Business hours: 7:30–5 Mon.–Sat.; 7–12 Fri.

Customs: Emphasis on traditional customs and traditional male-female roles.

Chile. Republic of Chile, located in southwestern South America along the Pacific Ocean, with thirteen regions and fifty-one provinces.

Capital: Santiago.

Language: Spanish (official), English.

Religion: Roman Catholic (majority), Protestant.

Principal holidays: New Year's Day, Good Friday, Easter Saturday, Labor Day, Navy Day, Corpus Christi, St. Peter and St. Paul's Day, Assumption, Independence Day, Army Day, Columbus Day, All Saints' Day, Immaculate Conception, Christmas.

Business hours: 9–6 Mon.–Fri. or Sat., with midday breaks.

Customs: Traditional customs combined with progressive, modern attitude; traditional male-female roles modified by increasing influence of women.

China. People's Republic of China, located in eastern Asia along the Caribbean Sea and Pacific Ocean, with twenty-two provinces, five autonomous regions, and three government-controlled municipalities.

Capital: Beijing.

Language: Mandarin Chinese (official), Chinese, local dialects.

Religion: (officially atheist) Buddhist (majority), Taoism, Confucianism, Protestant, Roman Catholic.

Principal holidays: New Year's Day, Lunar New Year, International Working Women's Day, Quing Ming Festival, Founding of Communist Party of China, Army Day, National Day.

Business hours: 8–12 and 2–6 Mon.–Sat.

Customs: Emphasis on reserved manners and hospitality; influence of religious beliefs clearly evident in spite of government-encouraged atheism.

Colombia. Republic of Colombia, located in northwestern South America, with thirty-two departments and the capital district.

Capital: Bogotá.

Language: Spanish (official), English, local Indian dialects.

Religion: Roman Catholic (majority), Jewish, Protestant.

Principal holidays: New Year's Day, Epiphany, St. Joseph's Day, Maundy Thursday, Good Friday, Labor Day, Ascension, Thanksgiving, Corpus Christi, St. Peter and St. Paul's Day, Independence Day, Battle of Boyacá, Assumption Day, Columbus Day, All Saints' Day, Independence of Cartagena, Feast of the Immaculate Conception.

Business hours: 8–12 and 2–5:30 Mon.–Fri.

Customs: Evidence of traditional and religious customs and traditional male-female roles, with North American influence; normal business etiquette.

Comoros. Federal Islamic Republic of the Comoros, archipelago of four main islands located in the Indian Ocean between Africa and Madagascar.

Capital: Moroni.

Language: French and Arabic (official), Comoran (blend of Arabic and Swahili), Shaafi Muslim, Malagasu.

Religion: Sunni Muslim (majority), Roman Catholic.

Principal holidays: Leilat al-Meiraj, Eid al-Fitr, Eid al-Adha, Muslim New Year, Independence Day, Ashoura, Mouloud (Prophet's Birthday), Anniversary of President Abdallah's Assassination.

Business hours: 7–5:30 Mon.–Thur. and 7:30–11 Fri.

Customs: Emphasis on traditional and religious customs, particularly among non-French residents.

Congo. Republic of the Congo, located in western Africa along the Atlantic Ocean, with nine prefectures.

Capital: Brazzaville.

Language: French (official), Lingala, Kikongo, other.

Religion: Animist (majority), Roman Catholic, Protestant, Muslim.

Principal holidays: New Year's Day, General Denis Sassou-Ngeusso Day, National Tree Day, Women's Day, Anniversary of Marien Ngouabi's Death, Good Friday, Easter Monday, Labor Day, Birthday of the Popular Army, Revolution Day, Anniversary of August 1963 Revolution, Independence Day, Christmas Day, Children's Day, Foundation Day.

Business hours: 8–12 and 3–6 Mon.–Fri.; 7–12 Sat.

Customs: Strong emphasis on tradition; European influence in business etiquette.

Costa Rica. Republic of Costa Rica, located in Central America between the Caribbean Sea and the Pacific Ocean, with seven provinces.

Capital: San José.

Language: Spanish (official), English.

Religion: Roman Catholic.

Principal holidays: New Year's Day, Maundy Thursday, Good Friday, Labor Day, Ascension, Corpus Christi, St. Peter and St. Paul's Day, Annexation of Guanacaste, Virgin of Los Angeles, Assumption, Independence Day, Columbus Day, Abolition of the Armed Forces, Feast of the Immaculate Conception, Christmas Day.

Business hours: 8–11:30 and 1:30–5:30 Mon.–Fri.

Customs: Influence of religion evident, with traditional male-female roles; appreciation of individuality.

Croatia. Former Yugoslav republic, located south of Hungary in south-eastern Europe.

Capital: Zagreb.

Language: Serbo-Croatian.

Religion: Roman Catholic.

Principal holidays: New Year's Day, Labor Day, Veterans' Day, Republic Days.

Business hours: 7–3 Mon.–Fri.

Customs: Emphasis on traditional customs and beliefs; disrupted by political instability.

Cuba. Republic of Cuba, largest Caribbean island located in the north-western Caribbean Sea south of Florida, with fourteen provinces and the Isle of Youth municipality.

Capital: Havana.

Language: Spanish (majority), French, English.

Religion: Roman Catholic.

Principal holidays: Liberation Day, Labor Day, Revolution Day, Wars of Independence Day.

Business hours: 8:30–12:30 and 1:30–5:30 Mon.–Fri.; some businesses 8–5 alternate Sat.

Customs: Conservative social views; normal business etiquette modified by government restrictions such as ban on gift giving.

Cyprus. Republic of Cyprus, island located in the eastern Mediterranean Sea south of Turkey.

Capital: Nicosia.

Language: Greek (majority), Turkish, English, German, French.

Religion: Greek Orthodox (majority), Muslim, Maronite Latin.

Principal holidays: New Year's Day, Epiphany, Greek-Cypriot Independence Day, Good Friday, Easter (Greek Orthodox Church), May Day, Kataklysmos, Dormition (Assumption) of the Virgin Mary, Cyprus Independence Day, Christmas.

Business hours: Summer: 8–1 and 4–7 Mon.–Fri.; winter: 8–1 and 2:30–5:30 Mon.–Fri.

Customs: Emphasis on traditional religious beliefs, hospitality, and courtesy.

Czech Republic. Formerly part of Czechoslovakia, independent republic located east of Germany in central Europe, with eight regions.

Capital: Prague.

Language: Czech (official), Slovak, Hungarian, Romany, Russian, German, English.

Religion: Roman Catholic (majority), Protestant, Orthodox, other.

Principal holidays: New Year's Day, Easter Monday, Labor Day, National Day of Liberation, St. Cyril and St. Methodius Day, National Day, Independence Day, Christmas.

Business hours: 8–4 Mon.–Fri.

Customs: Emphasis on traditional customs, with European influence; emerging national identity.

Denmark. Kingdom of Denmark, located in northern Europe along the Baltic and North seas, with fourteen counties and the city of Copenhagen.

Capital: Copenhagen.

Language: Danish (official), Faroese, Greenlandic, German, French, English.

Religion: Evangelical Lutheran (majority), Roman Catholic.

Principal holidays: New Year's Day, Maundy Thursday, Good Friday, Easter Monday, General Prayer Day, Ascension Day, Constitution Day, Whit Monday, Christmas Day, Boxing Day.

Business hours: 8–4 or 5 Mon.–Fri.

Customs: Modern Western customs, with a straightforward approach to business.

Djibouti. Republic of Djibouti, located in northeastern Africa along the Red Sea and Gulf of Aden, with five districts.

Capital: Djibouti.

Language: Arabic and French (official), Afar, Somali, English.

Religion: Muslim (majority), Roman Catholic, Protestant, Greek Orthodox.

Principal holidays: New Year's Day, Eid al-Fitr, Workers' Day, Eid al-Adha, Independence Day, Islamic New Year, Prophet's Birthday, Christmas.

Business hours: 6:30–1 Sat.–Thur.

Customs: Strict emphasis on traditional and religious customs and traditional male-female roles.

Dominica. Commonwealth of Dominica, largest island in the Windward Islands located in the eastern Caribbean Sea north of Martinique.

Capital: Rosean.

Language: English (official), French patois, Creole French, Cocoy.

Religion: Roman Catholic (majority), Anglican, Methodist.

Principal holidays: New Year's Day, Masquerade Carnival, Good Friday, Easter Monday, May Day, Whit Monday, Independence Celebrations, Community Service Day, Christmas, Boxing Day.

Business hours: Inquire in companies.

Customs: Traditional Catholic influence; normal business etiquette.

Dominican Republic. Independent republic located on the island of Hispaniola in the Caribbean Sea east of Cuba, with twenty-six provinces and one national district.

Capital: Santo Domingo.

Language: Spanish (official), English.

Religion: Roman Catholic (majority), Protestant, Jewish.

Principal holidays: New Year's Day, Epiphany, La Altagracia, Duarte's Birthday, Independence Day, Pan-American Day, Good Friday, Labor Day, Corpus Christi, Foundation of Sociedad la Trinitaria, Restoration Day, Las Mercedes, Columbus Day, United Nations Day, All Saints' Day, Christmas.

Business hours: 8:30–12 and 2–6 Mon.–Fri.

Customs: Noticeable American influence; informal atmosphere, but initial contacts formal.

Ecuador. Republic of Ecuador, located in northwestern South America along the Pacific Ocean, with twenty-one provinces.

Capital: Quito.

Language: Spanish (official), Quechua, other Indian dialects.

Religion: Roman Catholic.

Principal holidays: New Year's Day, Good Friday, Easter Saturday, Labor Day, Anniversary of the Battle of Pichincha, Anniversary of the Birth of Simón Bolívar, Independence Day, Anniversary of the Independence of Guayaquil, Discovery of America, Anniversary of the Independence of the Cuenca, Foundation of Quito, Christmas Day.

Business hours: 9–1 and 3–7 Mon.–Fri.; 8:30–12:30 Sat.

Customs: Considerable ethnic diversity; formal, traditional social and business values, but with Western influence in urban areas.

Egypt. Arab Republic of Egypt, located in northeastern Africa and the Middle East along the Mediterranean and Red seas, with twenty-six governorates.

Capital: Cairo (El Qahira).

Language: Arabic (official), English, French.

Religion: Muslim (majority: mostly Sunni), Coptic church, other Christian.

Principal holidays: New Year's Day, Leilat al-Meiraj (Ascension of Mohammed), Eid al-Fitr, lst Bairam, Sinai Liberation Day, Sham el-Nassim (Coptic Easter Monday), Eid al-Fitr, Workers' Day, Eid al-Adha, 2nd Bairam, Evacuation Day, Islamic New Year, Revolution Day, Prophet Mohammed's Birthday, Armed Forces Day, Victory Day.

Business hours: 9–2 Mon.–Thur. and Sat.–Sun.

Customs: Strong emphasis on traditional and religious customs and traditional male-female roles.

El Salvador. Republic of El Salvador, located in western Central America along the Pacific Ocean, with fourteen departments.

Capital: San Salvador.

Language: Spanish (official), Nahua, English.

Religion: Roman Catholic (majority), various other Christian.

Principal holidays: New Year's Day, Easter, Labor Day, Corpus Christi, School Teachers' Day, Bank Holiday (banks only), August Festivities (banks and commerce), Independence Day, Columbus Day (business only), All Souls' Day, First Call for Independence (business only), Christmas.

Business hours: 8–12:30 and 2:30–5:30 Mon.–Fri.

Customs: Primarily traditional values, with Western influence among educated; consider themselves Americans.

Equatorial Guinea. Republic of Equatorial Guinea, located in western Africa along the Gulf of Guinea and two islands located in the Gulf, with two regions and seven provinces.

Capital: Malabo.

Language: Spanish (official), pidgin English, Fang, Bubi, other African dialects.

Religion: Roman Catholic (majority), animist.

Principal holidays: New Year's Day, Good Friday, Easter Monday, May Day, Christmas.

Business hours: Inquire in companies.

Customs: Traditional and religious customs; normal business etiquette.

Estonia. Republic of Estonia, former Soviet republic located west of Russia in northeastern Europe along the Gulfs of Finland and Riga, with fifteen districts.

Capital: Tallinn.

Language: Estonian (official), Russian, English, German, Finnish.

Religion: Protestant (majority: mostly Lutheran), Orthodox.

Principal holidays: New Year's Day, Good Friday, Easter Monday, May Day, Christmas.

Business hours: Inquire in companies.

Customs: Emphasis on cultural heritage; normal business etiquette.

Ethiopia. People's Democratic Republic of Ethiopia, located north of Kenya in northeastern Africa along the Red Sea, with fourteen regions.

Capital: Addis Ababa.

Language: Amharic (official), English, Arabic, Tigrinya, Orominga.

Religion: Muslim, Ethiopian Orthodox, Coptic, animist.

Principal holidays: Christmas, Epiphany, Battle of Adowa Day, Eid al-Fitr, Victory Day, Easter Monday (Christian), Palm Monday (Coptic), May Day, Eid al-Adha, Mouloud (Prophet's Birthday), New Year's Day (Julian 1984), Revolution Day, Feast of Masgel (Coptic).

Business hours: 8–12 and 1–4 Mon.–Fri.; 8–12 Sat.

Customs: Emphasis on traditional and religious customs and traditional male-female roles; normal business etiquette in major trade centers, with formal approach.

Fiji. Republic of Fiji, more than three islands located in the western South Pacific Ocean southeast of the Solomon Islands, with fourteen provinces.

Capital: Suva.

Language: English (official), Fijian, Hindustani.

Religion: Methodist, Hindu, Roman Catholic, Muslim.

Principal holidays: New Year's Day, Good Friday, Easter Monday, Queen's Birthday, Bank Holiday, Prophet's Birthday, Independence Day, Diwali, Prince of Wales' Birthday, Christmas.

Business hours: 9–4:30 Mon.–Fri.

Customs: Emphasis on hospitality; normal business etiquette.

Finland. Republic of Finland, located in Scandinavia in northern Europe along the Baltic Sea and Gulfs of Finland and Bothnia, with twelve provinces.

Capital: Helsinki.

Language: Finnish (majority) and Swedish (both official), Lapp, English.

Religion: Evangelical Lutheran (majority), Eastern Orthodox, other Christian, Jewish, Muslim.

Principal holidays: New Year's Day, Epiphany, Good Friday, Easter, May Day Eve and Day, Ascension Day, Whitsun, Midsummer's Eve and Day, All Saints' Day, Independence Day, Christmas Eve and Day, Boxing Day.

Business hours: 8–4:30 Mon.–Fri.

Customs: Western customs, including women's rights, but more reserved approach.

France. French Republic, located in western Europe between the English Channel and the Mediterranean Sea, with twenty-two regions.

Capital: Paris.

Language: French (official), English, regional dialects.

Religion: Roman Catholic (majority), Protestant, Jewish, Muslim.

Principal holidays: New Year's Day, Easter Monday, Labor Day, VE Day, Ascension Day, Whit Monday, Bastille Day, Feast of Assumption, All Saints' Day, Remembrance Day, Christmas Day.

Business hours: 9–12 and 2–6 Mon.–Fri.

Customs: Modern Western nation, with emphasis on culture and heritage; reserved approach to business.

Gabon. Gabonese Republic, located in western Africa along the Atlantic Ocean, with nine provinces.

Capital: Libreville.

Language: French (official), Fang, Myene, Bateke, Bapounou, Eschira, Bandjabi.

Religion: Christian (majority), Muslim, animist.

Principal holidays: New Year's Day, Renovation Day, Eid al-Fitr, Good Friday, Easter Monday, Labor Day, Whit Monday, Eid al-Adha, Independence Day, Mouloud (Prophet's Birthday), Christmas.

Business hours: 7:30–12 and 2:30–6 Mon.–Fri.

Customs: Traditional and religious customs, but with some Western influence, particularly from France.

The Gambia. Republic of The Gambia, located in western Africa along the Atlantic Ocean, with thirty-five districts.

Capital: Banjul.

Language: English (official), Mandinka, Fulu, Wollof, Jola, Serahule.

Religion: Muslim (majority), Christian, animist.

Principal holidays: New Year's Day, Independence Day, Eid al-Fitr, Easter, Labor Day, Eid al-Adha, Assumption, Mouloud (Prophet's Birthday), Christmas.

Business hours: 9–4 Mon.–Thur.; 9–12 Fri.–Sat.

Customs: Emphasis on traditional and religious customs, particularly Muslim, but some knowledge of Western ways in trade circles.

Georgia. Republic of Georgia, former Soviet republic, located north of Turkey in the Caucasus between Europe and Asia.

Capital: Tbilisi.

Language: Georgian (official), Russian, Ossetian, Abkhazian, Adzharian.

Religion: Georgian Orthodox, Muslim, Jewish.

Principal holidays: New Year's Day, Army and Navy Day, International Labor Day, International Women's Day, Victory in Europe Day, Constitution Day, October Revolution, Agricultural and Agro-Industrial Workers' Day.

Business hours: 9–6 Mon.–Fri.

Customs: Emphasis on traditional customs and beliefs; evolving national identity.

Germany. Federal Republic of Germany, located in western central Europe along the Baltic and North seas, with sixteen states (*Länder*).

Capital: Berlin (seat of government: Bonn).

Language: German (official), Sorbian, English, French.

Religion: Protestant, Roman Catholic.

Principal holidays: New Year's Day, Epiphany, Easter, Labor Day, Ascension Day, Whit Monday, Corpus Christi, Ascension of Virgin Mary, Day of Unity, All Saints' Day, Day of Prayer and Repentance, Christmas.

Business hours: 8–5 Mon.–Fri.

Customs: Western customs (especially in western Germany), with traditional values and emphasis on privacy and skill; normal business etiquette; ongoing adjustment to reunification.

Ghana. Republic of Ghana, located in western Africa along the Atlantic Ocean, with ten regions.

Capital: Accra.

Language: English (official), Akan, Moshi-Dagomba, Ewe, Ga, Fante, Twi.

Religion: Christian, Muslim, indigenous beliefs.

Principal holidays: New Year's Day, Independence Day, Good Friday, Easter Monday, May Day, Anniversary of the 1979 Uprising, Republic Day, Christmas, Revolution Day.

Business hours: 8–12 and 2–5 Mon.–Fri.; 8:30–12 Sat.

Customs: Strong emphasis on traditional and religious customs; various ethnic practices, but generally traditional male-female roles; formality in business dealings.

Greece. Hellenic Republic, located in southeastern Europe along the Mediterranean Sea, with thirteen regions.

Capital: Athens.

Language: Greek (official), English, French, German, Italian, Turkish.

Religion: Greek Orthodox (majority), Muslim, Roman Catholic.

Principal holidays: New Year's Day, Epiphany, Independence Day, Orthodox Easter, Labor Day, Day of the Holy Spirit, Assumption, Ohi Day, Christmas Eve and Day, St. Stephen's Day.

Business hours: 8:30–1:30 and 5–8 Mon.–Fri.

Customs: Relatively modern nation, but emphasis on traditional and religious customs; traditional male-female roles; normal business etiquette.

Grenada. Independent state in British Commonwealth, the most southerly of the Windward Islands located in the southeastern Caribbean Sea.

Capital: St. George's.

Language: English (official), French patois.

Religion: Roman Catholic (majority), Anglican, Protestant.

Principal holidays: New Year's Day, Independence Day, Easter, Labor Day, Whit Monday, Corpus Christi, Emancipation Holiday, Carnival, Thanksgiving Day, Christmas.

Business hours: 8–11:45 and 1–4 Mon.–Fri.

Customs: Emphasis on traditional and religious customs, with noticeable diversity of local culture and colonial and African history.

Guatemala. Republic of Guatemala, located in Central America between the Gulf of Honduras and the Pacific Ocean, with twenty-two departments.

Capital: Guatemala City.

Language: Spanish (official), English, Indian dialects.

Religion: Roman Catholic (majority), Protestant, Mayan.

Principal holidays: New Year's Day, Epiphany, Easter, Labor Day, Anniversary of the Revolution, Assumption, Independence Day, Columbus Day, Revolution Day, All Saints' Day, Christmas Eve and Day, New Year's Eve.

Business hours: 8–6 Mon.–Fri.; 8–12 Sat.

Customs: Traditional and religious customs observed, with formal, conservative approach in business; some Western influence in cities.

Guinea. Republic of Guinea, located in western Africa along the Atlantic Ocean, with thirty-three provinces and the capital city.

Capital: Conakry.

Language: French (official), Susu, Malinke, Fula.

Religion: Muslim (majority), Christian, animist.

Principal holidays: New Year's Day, Eid al-Fitr, Easter Monday, Labor Day, Anniversary of Women's Revolt, Mouloud (Prophet's Birthday), Referendum Day, Republic Day, All Saints' Day, Day of 1970 Invasion, Christmas Day.

Business hours: Inquire in companies.

Customs: Traditional and religious customs and traditional male-female roles observed.

Guinea-Bissau. Republic of Guinea-Bissau, located in northwestern Africa along the Atlantic Ocean, with eight regions and the capital city.

Capital: Bissau.

Language: Portuguese (official), Creole, French, African languages.

Religion: Animist (majority), Muslim, Christian.

Principal holidays: New Year's Day, Death of Amilcar Cabral, Eid al-Fitr, Korité, Labor Day, Eid al-Adha, Tabaski, Anniversary of the Killing of Pidjiguiti, National Day, Anniversary of the Movement of Readjustment, Christmas Day.

Business hours: May–Oct.: 8–3 Mon.–Fri.; Oct.–May: 8–12 and 3–6 Mon.–Fri.

Customs: Traditional and religious customs observed, particularly in Muslim areas; formal and reserved, but hospitable, approach to outsiders.

Guyana.   Co-operative Republic of Guyana, located in northeastern South America along the Atlantic Ocean, with ten regions.

Capital: Georgetown.

Language: English (official), Hindi, Urdu, Amerindian.

Religion: Christian (majority), Hindu, Muslim.

Principal holidays: New Year's Day, Republic Day, Eid al-Fitr, Good Friday, Easter Monday, Labor Day, Indian Heritage Day, Eid al-Adha, Caribbean Day, Freedom Day, Yum an-Nabi (Prophet's Birthday), Deepavali (Divali), Christmas.

Business hours: 8–11:30 and 1–4:30 Mon.–Fri.

Customs: Traditional and religious customs observed, with Caribbean influence.

Haiti.   Republic of Haiti, located in the Caribbean Sea on the western side of the island of Hispaniola, with nine departments.

Capital: Port-au-Prince.

Language: French (official), Creole, French patois.

Religion: Roman Catholic (majority: with voodoo influence), Protestant.

Principal holidays: New Year's Day, Heroes of Independence Day, Shrove Monday and Tuesday, Pan-American Day, Good Friday, National Sovereignty Day, Assumption, United Nations Day, All Souls' Day, Army Day, Discovery Day, Christmas.

Business hours: Summer: 7–4 Mon.–Fri.; winter: 7–5 Mon.–Fri.

Customs: Traditional and religious customs observed; normal business etiquette.

Honduras.   Republic of Honduras, located in Central America between the Caribbean Sea and the Pacific Ocean, with eighteen departments and the central district with the capital city.

Capital: Tegucigalpa.

Language: Spanish (official), English, Indian dialects.

Religion: Roman Catholic (majority), Mormon, Evangelist.

Principal holidays: New Year's Day, Day of Americas, Maundy Thursday, Good Friday, Labor Day, Day of the Student, Independence Day, Birth of General Morazán, Discovery of America Day, Armed Forces Day, Christmas Day, New Year's Eve.

Business hours: 8–12 and 2–5 Mon.–Fri.; 8–11 Sat.

Customs: Traditional and religious customs and traditional male-female roles observed, with Spanish influence in urban areas; normal business etiquette.

Hungary. Hungarian Republic, located south of the Czech and Slovak republics in eastern central Europe, with nineteen countries and the capital city.

Capital: Budapest.

Language: Hungarian (Magyar: official), German, French, English.

Religion: Roman Catholic (majority), Protestant, Eastern Orthodox, Jewish.

Principal holidays: New Year's Day, Anniversary of 1848 Uprising Against Austrian Rule, Easter, Labor Day, Constitution Day, Proclamation Day of the Republic, Christmas.

Business hours: 8–5 Mon.–Fri.

Customs: Emphasis on cultural heritage; traditional values, with Western influence from Europe.

Iceland. Republic of Iceland, located in Atlantic Ocean near the Arctic Circle, with eight regions.

Capital: Reykjavík.

Language: Icelandic (official), Danish, English.

Religion: Evangelical Lutheran (majority), other Protestant, Roman Catholic.

Principal holidays: New Year's Day, Maundy Thursday, Good Friday, Easter Monday, First Day of Summer, Labor Day, Ascension Day, Whit Monday, National Day, Bank Holiday, Christmas, New Year's Eve.

Business hours: 9–5 Mon.–Fri.

Customs: Relatively modern Western attitudes; emphasis on equal opportunities and literate populace.

India. Republic of India, located on the Indian and Asian subcontinent along the Arabian Sea, the Bay of Bengal, and the Indian Ocean, with twenty-five states and seven territories.

Capital: New Delhi.

Language: Hindi and fourteen other official languages, English, other.

Religion: Hindu (majority), Muslim, Sikh, Christian, Buddhist.

Principal holidays: New Year's Day, Eid al-Fitr, Mahabiar Jayanti, Good Friday, Buddha Purnima, Eid uz-Zuha, Muharram (Islamic New Year), Independence Day, Mahatma Gandhi's Birthday, Dussehra, Diwali, Guru Nannak's Birthday, Christmas.

Business hours: 9:30–5:30 Mon.–Fri.

Customs: Strong emphasis on traditional and religious customs, with local cultural diversity but national democratic values.

Indonesia. Republic of Indonesia, located between Southeast Asia and Australia, with six main islands and more than thirteen thousand smaller islands.

Capital: Jakarta (Java).

Language: Bahasa Indonesian (official), Dutch, English, numerous local dialects.

Religion: Muslim (majority), Protestant, Roman Catholic, Hindu.

Principal holidays: New Year's Day, Eid al-Fitr, Good Friday, Ascension Day, Waisak Day, Eid al-Adha, Islamic New Year, Independence Day, Mouloud (Prophet's Birthday), Christmas Day.

Business hours: 7–3 Mon.–Fri.

Customs: Traditional and religious customs observed, with high respect for individual and family; formal approach preferred; patient, unassuming nature essential.

Iran. Islamic Republic of Iran, located in western Asia and the Middle East between the Caspian Sea and the Persian Gulf, with twenty-four provinces.

Capital: Tehran.

Language: Persian (official: Farsi), Arabic, Turkish, English, French, German.

Religion: Muslim (official: mostly Shiite), Christian, Jewish, Zoroastrian, Baha'i.

Principal holidays: Leilat al-Meiraj, National Day (Fall of Shah), Oil Nationalization Day, Ruz (Iranian New Year), Islamic Republic Day, Revolution Day, Eid al-Fitr, Birthday of Twelfth Imam, Eid al-Adha, Ashoura, Martyrdom of Imam Ali, Mouloud (Prophet's Birthday).

Business hours: 8–2 Sat.–Wed.; 8–12 Thur.

Customs: Strong emphasis on traditional and religious customs and traditional male-female roles, with restrictions on women's dress; emphasis on courtesy; Western influence discouraged by government.

Iraq. Republic of Iraq, located north of Saudi Arabia in Western Asia and the Middle East, with eighteen governorates (*liwa*).

Capital: Baghdad.

Language: Arabic (official), Kurdish (official in Kurdish areas), Assyrian, Armenian.

Religion: Muslim (majority: mostly Shiite), Christian, Druze.

Principal holidays: New Year's Day, Army Day, Leilat al-Meiraj, Eid al-Fitr, Eid al-Adha, Muslim New Year, Ashoura, Republic Day, Mouloud (Prophet's Birthday).

Business hours: 8–2 Sat.–Wed.; 8–1 Thur.

Customs: Traditional and religious customs and traditional male-female roles observed, with conservative dress required; formal courtesy necessary.

Ireland.   Republic of Ireland, located in North Atlantic Ocean west of Britain and southwest of Northern Ireland, with four provinces. (*Note*: Northern Ireland is part of the United Kingdom.)

Capital: Dublin.

Language: Irish (Gaelic) and English (both official).

Religion: Roman Catholic (majority), Protestant, Anglican.

Principal holidays: New Year's Day, St. Patrick's Day, Good Friday, Easter Monday, Bank Holiday, Christmas Day, Boxing Day.

Business hours: 9–5 Mon.–Fri.

Customs: Traditional customs, with some liberal influence slowly becoming evident; informal business approach.

Israel.   State of Israel, located in western Asia along the Mediterranean Sea, with six districts.

Capital: Jerusalem.

Language: Hebrew and Arabic (official), English, French, Spanish, German, Yiddish, Polish, Hungarian, Russian.

Religion: Jewish (majority), Muslim (mostly Sunni), Christian, Druze.

Principal holidays: Arbor Day (Tu B'Shvat), Purim, Shushan Purim, Passover (Pesach), Holocaust Day, Memorial Day, Independence Day (Yom Ha'Atzmaut), Jerusalem Day, Pentecost (Shavuot), Fast of the 9th Av (Tisha B'av), New Year (Rosh Hashanah), Day of Atonement (Yom Kippur), Tabernacles (Succot), Rejoicing of the Law (Simchat Torah), Feast of Lights (Hanukkah).

Business hours: Nov.–May: 8–1 and 3–6 Sun.–Thur.; Jun.–Oct.: 7:30–2:30 Sun.–Thur.; some businesses open a half day on Fri.

Customs: Traditional and religious customs observed; European-style hospitality, but with less formality in business.

Italy.   Italian Republic, peninsula located in western and southern Europe along the Mediterranean, Adriatic, and Ionian seas, with twenty regions.

Capital: Rome.

Language: Italian (official), German, French, Slovenian, English.

Religion: Roman Catholic (majority), Protestant.

Principal holidays: New Year's Day, Epiphany, Easter Monday, Liberation Day, Labor Day, Festival of the Tricolor, Assumption of the Virgin (Ferragosto), All Saints' Day, National Unity Day, Immaculate Conception, Christmas.

Business hours: 9–1 and 2–6 Mon.–Fri.

Customs: Western nation, with strong Roman Catholic influence and very strong family ties; leisurely approach in southern Italy but more pressure in industrial North; normal business etiquette.

Ivory Coast (Côte d'Ivoire).   Republic of the Ivory Coast, located in western Africa along the Atlantic Ocean, with thirty-four departments.

Capital: Abidjan.

Language: French (official), Dioula, Baoule, other African languages.

Religion: Indigenous (majority), Muslim, Christian.

Principal holidays: New Year's Day, Eid al-Fitr, Easter Monday, Labor Day, Ascension Day, Whit Monday, Eid al-Adha, Assumption, All Saints' Day, Peace Day, National Day, Christmas Day.

Business hours: 7:30–12 and 2:30–5:30 Mon.–Fri.; 8–12 Sat.

Customs: Numerous ethnic customs; normal business etiquette in major business circles.

Jamaica.   Independent state in British Commonwealth, located in the West Indies in the northern Caribbean Sea south of Cuba.

Capital: Kingston.

Language: English (official), French patois, Creole.

Religion: Protestant (majority), Roman Catholic, Jewish, Muslim, Hindu, Baha'i.

Principal holidays: New Year's Day, Ash Wednesday, Good Friday, Easter Monday, Labor Day, Independence Day, National Heroes' Day, Christmas.

Business hours: 8:30–4:30 or 5:30 Mon.–Fri.

Customs: Former British influence evident, but wide acceptance of many cultures as a result of tourism; very friendly and hospitable, but not tolerant of personal curiosity or too much familiarity; casual attitudes in some areas.

Japan.   Constitutional monarchy, located off the Asian continent between the Sea of Japan and the western Pacific Ocean, with four major islands and more than three thousand minor islands.

Capital: Tokyo.

Language: Japanese (official), some English in large urban areas.

Religion: Shintoist and Buddhist (majority), Christian.

Principal holidays: New Year's Day, Coming of Age Day, National Foundation Day, Greenery Day, Constitution Memorial Day, Children's Day, Respect for the Aged Day, Autumn Equinox, Health and Sports Day, Culture Day, Labor Thanksgiving Day, Birthday of the Emperor.

Business hours: 9–5 Mon.–Fri.

Customs: Asian customs and etiquette observed, with strict code of conduct and strong emphasis on formality and politeness; group more important than individual; word *no* absent from Japanese language.

Jordan. Hashemite Kingdom of Jordan, located east of Israel in western Asia and the Middle East, with eight governorates.

Capital: Amman.

Language: Arabic (official), English, French.

Religion: Sunni Muslim (majority), Shiite Muslim, Christian.

Principal holidays: New Year's Day, Arbor Day, Leilat al-Meiraj, Arab League Day, Eid al-Fitr, Independence Day, Eid al-Adha, Islamic New Year, Accession of King Hussein, Mouloud (Prophet's Birthday), King Hussein's Birthday, Christmas Day.

Business hours: Muslim: 8–2 and 4–7 Sat.–Thur.; Christian: 8–2 and 4–7 Mon.–Thur. and Sat.

Customs: Traditional and religious customs and traditional male-female roles observed, but some Western influence evident; Palestinian residents object to being considered Jordanians.

Kazakhstan. Republic of Kazakhstan, former Soviet republic located north of Iran in central Asia.

Capital: Alma-Ata.

Language: Kazakh (official), Russian, Uighur, regional dialects.

Religion: Sunni Muslim, Eastern Orthodox.

Principal holidays: Former Soviet holidays: New Year's Day, Army and Navy Day, International Women's Day, International Labor Day, October Revolution, Agricultural and Agro-Industrial Workers' Day.

Business hours: 9–6 Mon.–Fri.

Customs: Emphasis on traditional customs and beliefs; evolving national identity.

Kenya. Republic of Kenya, located in eastern Africa along the Indian Ocean, with eight provinces.

Capital: Nairobi.

Language: Swahili and English (official), Kikuyu, Luo, other indigenous languages.

Religion: Protestant, Roman Catholic, Muslim, indigenous beliefs.

Principal holidays: New Year's Day, Eid al-Fitr, Good Friday, Easter Monday, Labor Day, Madaraka Day, Eid al-Adha, Kenyatta Day, Independence Day, Christmas.

Business hours: 8–1 and 2–5 Mon.–Fri.; 8:30–12 Sat.

Customs: Friendly, patriotic people; European influences; group and family orientation.

Kirghizia (Kyrgyzstan). Republic of Kirghizia, former Soviet republic located north of Afghanistan in central Asia.

Capital: Frunze.

Language: Kirghizian (official), Russian, Uzbek, Kazakh, local dialects.

Religion: Sunni Muslim.

Principal holidays: Former Soviet holidays: New Year's Day, Army and Navy Day, International Women's Day, International Labor Day, Victory in Europe Day, Constitution Day, October Revolution, Agricultural and Agro-Industrial Workers' Day.

Business hours: 9–6 Mon.–Fri.

Customs: Emphasis on traditional customs and beliefs; evolving national identity.

Kiribati. Republic of Kiribati, located over a large area of the central Pacific Ocean, with three groups of coral atolls and one volcanic island.

Capital: Tarawa.

Language: English and Swahili (both official), Kiribati, Gilbertese.

Religion: Roman Catholic, Protestant, Baha'i, Seventh-Day Adventist.

Principal holidays: New Year's Day, Easter, Independence Day, In Honor of Independence Day, Youth Day, Christmas.

Business hours: 8–12:30 and 1:30–4:15 Mon.–Fri.

Customs: Traditional and local customs, with European influence, in a casual atmosphere.

Korea (North). Democratic People's Republic of Korea, northern part of Korean peninsula located southeast of China in eastern Asia, with thirteen administrative units (nine provinces and four cities).

Capital: Pyongyang.

Language: Korean.

Religion: (no official religion) Buddhist, Confucian, Christian, Chundo Kyo.

Principal holidays: New Year, Kim Jong Il's Birthday, International Women's Day, Kim Il Sung's Birthday, May Day, Anniversary of Liberation, Independence Day, Anniversary of the Foundation of Korean Workers' Party, Anniversary of the Constitution.

Business hours: Inquire: Businesses in form of government-mobilized cooperatives.

Customs: Intensely nationalistic people loyal to the state above all else, but with belief in self-reliance; contacts require caution and discretion.

Korea (South). Republic of Korea, southern part of Korean peninsula located southeast of China in eastern Asia, with fifteen provinces, six of them cities with provincial status.

Capital: Seoul.

Language: Korean (official), English.

Religion: Mahayana Buddhist, Confucian, Daoist, Chundo Kyo, Christian, folk religions.

Principal holidays: New Year, Folklore Day, Independence Movement Day, Arbor Day, Children's Day, Buddha's Birthday, Memorial Day, Constitution Day, Liberation Day, Thanksgiving Day, National Foundation Day, Christmas Day.

Business hours: 9–12 and 1–6 Mon.–Fri.; 9–1 Sat.

Customs: Traditional and religious customs observed, with emphasis on courtesy, modesty, and respect for others' feelings; quiet, formal approach in business.

Kuwait. State of Kuwait, located in the Middle East in the northeastern Arabian peninsula along the Persian Gulf, with four governorates.

Capital: Kuwait City.

Language: Arabic (official), English.

Religion: Muslim (majority), Christian, Hindu, Parsee.

Principal holidays: New Year's Day, Leilat al-Meiraj, National Day, Eid al-Fitr, Eid al-Adha, Islamic New Year, Prophet's Birthday.

Business hours: Winter: 8–1 and 4–8 Sat.–Thur.; summer: 8–1 and 3–7 Sat.–Thur.

Customs: Strong emphasis on traditional and religious customs and traditional male-female roles; familiarity with Western customs in business circles.

Laos. Lao People's Democratic Republic, located south of China in Southeast Asia.

Capital: Vientiane.

Language: Lao (official), French, English, Vietnamese.

Religion: Buddhist (majority), Confucian, Christian, animist.

Principal holidays: New Year's Day, New Year (Water Festival), Labor Day, Buddhist Memorial Day, National Day.

Business hours: 8–12 and 2–5 Mon.–Fri., 8–12 Sat.

Customs: Traditional and religious customs observed; emphasis on courtesy and respect for feelings of others.

Latvia. Republic of Latvia, former Soviet republic located in northeastern Europe along the Baltic Sea.

Capital: Riga.

Language: Latvian (official), Russian, ethnic languages.

Religion: Protestant (majority: Lutheran), Roman Catholic.

Principal holidays: New Year's Day, Good Friday, Easter Monday, May Day, St. John's Day, National Day, Christmas.

Business hours: Inquire in companies.

Customs: Traditional customs; hospitable, but reserved, approach; evolving national identity.

Lebanon. Republic of Lebanon, located in western Asia and the Middle East along the Mediterranean Sea, with six governorates.

Capital: Beirut.

Language: Arabic and French (both official), Armenian, English, Kurdish.

Religion: Muslim (majority: Shiite), Roman Catholic, other Christian, Jewish.

Principal holidays: New Year's Day, Leilat al-Meiraj, Feast of St. Marron, Arab League Anniversary, Eid al-Fitr, Easter, Ascension Day, Eid al-Adha, Islamic New Year, Ashoura, Assumption, Mouloud (Prophet's Birthday), All Saints' Day, Independence Day, Christmas, Evacuation Day.

Business hours: Jun.–Oct.: 8–1 Mon.–Sat.; Nov.–May: 8:30–12:30 and 3–6 Mon.–Fri. and 8:30–12:30 Sat.

Customs: Traditional and religious customs and traditional male-female roles observed, but with widespread awareness of Western customs.

Lesotho. Kingdom of Lesotho, located in southern Africa surrounded on all sides by South Africa, with ten districts.

Capital: Masera.

Language: Sesotho and English (both official), Zulu, Xhosa.

Religion: Roman Catholic (majority), Lesotho, Evangelical, Anglican.

Principal holidays: New Year's Day, Army Day, Moshoeshoe's Day, Good Friday, Easter Monday, Ascension Day, Family Day, King's Birthday, Independence Day, National Sports Day, Christmas Day, Boxing Day.

Business hours: 8–1 and 2–5 Mon.–Fri.; 8–1 Sat.

Customs: Emphasis on traditional customs, with courteous, although formal, approach.

Liberia. Republic of Liberia, located in western Africa along the Atlantic Ocean, with thirteen counties.

Capital: Monrovia.

Language: English (official), Bassa, Kpelle, Kru, other African languages.

Religion: Indigenous (majority), Muslim, Christian.

Principal holidays: New Year's Day, Armed Forces Day, Decoration Day, J. J. Roberts' Birthday, Good Friday, Fast and Prayer Day, National Redemption Day, Anniversary of the 1980 Coup, Good Friday, National Unification Day, Independence Day, Flag Day, Thanksgiving Day, National Memorial Day, President Tubman's Birthday, Christmas Day.

Business hours: 8–12 and 2–4 Mon.–Fri.

Customs: Traditional and religious customs and traditional male-female roles observed, particularly in Muslim areas.

Libya. Great Socialist People's Libyan Arab Republic, located in northern Africa along the Mediterranean Sea.

Capital: Tripoli.

Language: Arabic (official), English, Italian.

Religion: Sunni Muslim.

Principal holidays: Leilat al-Meiraj, British Evacuation Day, Eid al-Fitr, Evacuation Day, Eid al-Adha, Islamic New Year, Ashoura, Revolution Day, Mouloud (Prophet's Birthday).

Business hours: 7–2 Sat.–Thur.

Customs: Traditional and religious customs and traditional male-female roles observed, with strong socialist principles applied; caution and discretion required.

Liechtenstein. Principality of Liechtenstein, located between Austria and Switzerland in western central Europe, with eleven communes.

Capital: Vaduz.

Language: German (official), Alemannic dialect, English.

Religion: Roman Catholic (majority), Protestant, other.

Principal holidays: New Year's Day, Epiphany, Shrove Tuesday, St. Joseph Day, Good Friday, Easter Monday, Labor Day, Ascension Day, Whit Monday, Corpus Christi, Feast of the Assumption, Nativity of Our Lady, Immaculate Conception, Christmas Day, Boxing Day.

Business hours: 8–12 and 2–6 Mon.–Fri.

Customs: Western customs similar to those in northern Europe; formal approach to business.

Lithuania. Republic of Lithuania, former Soviet republic located in northeastern Europe along the Baltic Sea, with twenty-two urban and forty-four rural districts.

Capital: Vilnius.

Language: Lithuanian (official), Polish, English, Russian, ethnic dialects.

Religion: Roman Catholic (majority), Evangelical Lutheran, Evangelical Reformist, Jewish.

Principal holidays: New Year's Day, Day of Independence, Good Friday, Easter Monday, May Day, National Day (Mindaugas Coronation), Christmas.

Business hours: Inquire in companies.

Customs: Traditional customs; people with strong sense of cultural and national heritage; evolving national identity.

Luxembourg. Grand Duchy of Luxembourg, located west of Germany in western Europe.

Capital: Luxembourg.

Language: Luxembourgish (official: a German-Moselle-Frankish dialect), French, German.

Religion: Roman Catholic (majority), Protestant, Jewish.

Principal holidays: New Year's Day, Carnival Monday, Easter Monday, May Day, Ascension Day, Whit Monday, National Day, Assumption, All Saints' Day, All Souls' Day, Christmas Day, St. Stephen's Day.

Business hours: 8:30–12 and 2–6 Mon.–Fri.

Customs: Western nation with customs similar to those in western Europe, but with slower pace; friendly, formal approach.

Macedonia. Former Yugoslav republic seeking recognition as independent nation, located at the far southern end of Yugoslavia in southern central Europe.

Capital: Skopje.

Language: Macedonian, Latin, Cyrillic.

Religion: Orthodox, Roman Catholic, Muslim.

Principal holidays: Yugoslav holidays: New Year, Labor Day, Veterans' Day, Republic Days.

Business hours: 7–3 Mon.–Fri.

Customs: Traditional customs; hospitable, but reserved, people; evolving national identity.

Madagascar. Democratic Republic of Madagascar, island located off southeastern Africa in the western Indian Ocean, with six provinces.

Capital: Antananarivo.

Language: French and Malagasy (both official).

Religion: Animist (majority), Christian, Muslim.

Principal holidays: New Year's Day, Martyrs of 1947 Day, Good Friday, Easter Monday, Labor Day, Ascension Day, Whit Monday, Independence Day, Assumption, All Saints' Day, Christmas, Anniversary of the Democratic Republic of Madagascar.

Business hours: Inquire in companies.

Customs: Emphasis on hospitality and casual atmosphere, without strict regard for punctuality.

Malawi. Republic of Malawi, located west of Mozambique in southeastern Africa along Lake Malawi.

Capital: Lilongwe.

Language: English and Chichewa (both official), Tombuka, local languages.

Religion: Protestant (majority), Roman Catholic, Muslim, Hindu.

Principal holidays: New Year's Day, Martyrs' Day, Good Friday, Easter Monday, Kamuzu Day (President Banda's Birthday), Republic Day, Mothers' Day, National Tree Planting Day, Christmas Day, Boxing Day.

Business hours: 7:30–5 Mon.–Fri.

Customs: Emphasis on traditional customs and traditional male-female roles; European influence in business circles.

Malaysia. Federation of Malaysia, located in central Southeast Asia, including peninsular Malaysia along the South China Sea and the north coast of the island of Borneo, shared with Indonesia, with eleven states and one federal territory on peninsular Malaysia.

Capital: Kuala Lumpur.

Language: Bahasa Malaysia (official), English, Chinese, Tamil, Iban, Mandarin and Hakka dialects, tribal languages.

Religion: Muslim (majority), Buddhist, Taoist, Confucian, Hindu, Christian.

Principal holidays: Chinese New Year, Hari Raya Puasa (Eid al-Fitr), Labor Day, Wesak Day, Yang di-Pertuan Agong's Birthday, Hari Raya Haji (Eid al-Adha), Maal Hijrah, National Day, Mouloud (Prophet's Birthday), Deepavali, Christmas Day.

Business hours: 8:30–4 or 5:30 Mon.–Fri., closed 12–2; 8:30–12 Sat.

Customs: Traditional and religious customs and traditional male-female roles observed, particularly in Muslim areas; emphasis on respect and courtesy; often fatalistic attitude; minor European influence.

Maldives. Republic of the Maldives, chain of more than 1,200 small coral islands located in the Indian Ocean southwest of India, with twenty districts including the capital city.

Capital: Malé.

Language: Dhivehi (official), English.

Religion: Sunni Muslim.

Principal holidays: New Year's Day, Martyrs' Day, Ramadan, Eid al-Fitr, Hajj Day, Eid al-Adha, Islamic New Year, Independence Day, National Day, Mohammed's Birthday, Victory Day, Fisheries' Day, Republic Day, Huravee Day.

Business hours: 7:30–1 Sat.–Thur.

Customs: Traditional and religious customs and traditional male-female roles observed; informal business practices.

Mali. Republic of Mali, located south of Algeria in northwestern Africa, with nine regions including the capital district.

Capital: Bamako.

Language: French (official), Bambara, Arabic, other local languages.

Religion: Muslim (majority), Christian, animist.

Principal holidays: New Year's Day, Armed Forces Day, Eid al-Fitr/Korité, Easter Monday, Labor Day, Africa Day, Anniversary of the Organization of African Unity's Foundation, Eid al-Adha/Tabaski (Feast of the Sacrifice, Mouloud (Prophet's Birthday), Independence Day, Baptism of the Prophet, Anniversary of the 1968 Coup, Christmas.

Business hours: 7:30–2:30 Mon.–Thur. and Sat., 7:30–12:30 Fri.

Customs: Traditional and religious customs and traditional male-female roles observed; courteous, reserved people.

Malta. Republic of Malta, archipelago located in the Mediterranean Sea south of Sicily.

Capital: Valletta.

Language: Maltese and English (official), Italian.

Religion: Roman Catholic.

Principal holidays: New Year's Day, St. Paul's Shipwreck, St. Joseph's Day, Good Friday, May Day, Memorial Day, Feast of St. Peter and St. Paul, Assumption, Our Lady of Victories Day, Independence Day, Feast of the Immaculate Conception, Republic Day, Christmas Day.

Business hours: 8:30–12:45 and 2:30–5:30 Mon.–Fri.; 8:30–12 Sat.

Customs: Traditional and religious customs observed, with European influence; conservative approach in business.

Marshall Islands. Republic of the Marshall Islands, two groups of islands spread over a half million square miles of the western Pacific Ocean.

Capital: Majuro.

Language: English (official), Marshallese (Malay-Polynesian dialects), Japanese.

Religion: Protestant.

Principal holidays: New Year's Day, Memorial and Nuclear Victim's Day, Constitution Day, Fishermen's Day, Workers' Day, Independence Day, President's Day, Kamolo (Thanksgiving) Day, Christmas.

Business hours: 8–5 Mon.–Fri.

Customs: Local island customs observed; courteous, somewhat informal business atmosphere.

Mauritania. Islamic Republic of Mauritania, located in northwestern Africa along the Atlantic Ocean, with twelve regions and a capital district.

Capital: Nouakchott.

Language: Arabic and French (official), local dialects.

Religion: Muslim.

Principal holidays: New Year's Day, Leilat al-Meiraj, Korité (Eid al-Fitr), Labor Day, African Liberation Day, Anniversary of the Organization of African Unity's Foundation, Tabaski (Eid al-Adha), Islamic New Year, Mouloud (Prophet's Birthday), National Day.

Business hours: 8 or 9–12 and 3–6 Sat.–Wed.

Customs: Emphasis on traditional and religious customs and traditional male-female roles; French influence in business practices.

Mauritius. Republic of Mauritius, eight islands located in the southwestern Indian Ocean off the southeast coast of Africa, with nine districts on the main island of Mauritius.

Capital: Port Louis.

Language: English (official), Creole, French, Hindi, Urdu, Hakka, Bojpoori, Arabic, Chinese.

Religion: Hindu (majority), Christian, Muslim.

Principal holidays: New Year, Cavadee, Maha Shivaratree, Chinese Spring Festival, Independence Day, Ougadi, Eid al-Fitr, Good Friday.

Business hours: 9–4 Mon.–Fri. and 9–12 Sat.

Customs: Traditional and religious customs observed; friendly, relaxed approach in business; familiarity with Western ways.

Mexico. United Mexican States, located south of the United States in southernmost North America, with thirty-one states and the federal district.

Capital: Mexico City.

Language: Spanish (official), English.

Religion: Roman Catholic (majority), Protestant.

Principal holidays: New Year's Day, Constitution Day, Birth of Benito Juárez, Good Friday, Easter Monday, Labor Day, Anniversary of Battle of Puebla, Independence Day, Discovery of America, President's Annual Message, All Souls' Day, Anniversary of the Mexican Revolution of 1910, Day of Our Lady of Guadalupe, Christmas Day.

Business hours: 8–3 Mon.–Fri.

Customs: Local customs and traditional male-female roles observed, with emphasis on religion and family; punctuality less important than hospitality and respect for individual.

Micronesia. Federated States of Micronesia, archipelago of 607 widely scattered islands located in the western Pacific Ocean, with four states (Kosrae, Pohnpei, Chuuk, Yap).

Capital: Kolonia.

Language: English (official), Japanese, local languages.

Religion: Roman Catholic and Protestant (majority).

Principal holidays: New Year's Day, Yap Day, Federated States of Micronesia Day, Liberation Day (Kosrae), Liberation Day (Pohnpei), Charter Day (Chuuk), Independence Day, Constitution Day (Pohnpei), Constitution Day (Yap), Christmas Day.

Business hours: Inquire in companies.

Customs: Variety of local customs observed, with emphasis on religion.

Moldova. Republic of Moldova, former Soviet republic located east of Romania in southeastern Europe.
Capital: Kishinev.
Language: Romanian (official), Moldovian, Russian, ethnic languages.
Religion: Eastern Orthodox, Russian Orthodox.
Principal holidays: Former Soviet holidays: New Year's Day, Army and Navy Day, International Labor Day, International Women's Day, Victory in Europe Day, Constitution Day, October Revolution, Agriculture and Agro-Industrial Workers' Day.
Business hours: Inquire in companies.
Customs: Emphasis on traditional customs and beliefs; evolving national identity.

Monaco. Principality of Monaco, located in western Europe along the Mediterranean Sea, with four districts.
Capital: Monaco.
Language: French (official), English, Italian, Monégasque.
Religion: Roman Catholic (majority), Anglican.
Principal holidays: New Year's Day, Feast of St. Dévote, Easter Monday, Labor Day, Ascension Day, Whit Monday, Corpus Christi, Assumption, All Saints' Day, Monaco National Day, Immaculate Conception, Christmas.
Business hours: Inquire in companies.
Customs: Western nation, with European customs; formality in business matters.

Mongolia. State of Mongolia, located north of China in central Asia, with eighteen provinces and three city administrative units.
Capital: Ulan Bator.
Language: Mongolian Khalkha (official), Russian, Turkic, Chinese, local dialects.
Religion: Tibetan Buddhist (majority), Muslim.
Principal holidays: New Year's Day, Tsagaan Sar Mongolian New Year, Women's Day, Naadam (anniversary of revolution), Constitution Day.
Business hours: 9–6 Mon.–Fri.; 9–3 Sat.
Customs: Emphasis on traditional and religious customs; changing national identity since collapse of communism in 1989.

Morocco. Kingdom of Morocco, located in northwestern Africa along the Atlantic Ocean, with forty-nine provinces and prefectures.

Capital: Rabat.

Language: Arabic (official), Berber, French, Spanish.

Religion: Muslim (majority), Christian, Jewish.

Principal holidays: New Year's Day, Feast of the Throne, Eid el-Seghir (Eid al-Fitr), Labor Day, Eid el-Kebir (Eid al-Adha), Muslim New Year, Ashoura, Oued Eddahab Day, Mouloud (Prophet's Birthday), Anniversary of the Green March, Independence Day.

Business hours: Sat–Thur.—Winter (Sept.–Jul. except Ramadan): 8:30–12 and 2:30–6; Ramadan: 9–3 or 4; summer (Jul.–early Sept.): 8–3 or 4.

Customs: Traditional and religious customs and traditional male-female roles observed; French customs common in some business circles.

Mozambique. Republic of Mozambique, located in southeastern Africa along the Indian Ocean, with ten provinces and the capital city.

Capital: Maputo.

Language: Portuguese (official), local African languages.

Religion: Indigenous beliefs (majority), Christian, Muslim, Hindu.

Principal holidays: New Year's Day, Heroes' Day, Women's Day, Labor Day, Independence and Foundation of Frelimo Day, Victory Day, Armed Forces Day, Family Day.

Business hours: 8–12 and 2–5 Mon.–Fri.; 8–12 Sat.

Customs: Traditional local customs observed, with Portuguese and other Latin influences in business circles.

Myanmar. Union of Myanmar (formerly Burma), located southeast of India in Southeast Asia, with seven states and seven divisions.

Capital: Yangon (formerly Rangoon).

Language: Burmese (official), English, more than a hundred other languages and dialects.

Religion: Theravada Buddhist (majority), Hindu, Muslim, Christian, animist.

Principal holidays: Independence Day, Union Day, Peasants' Day, Full Moon of Tabaung, Armed Forces Day, Maha Thingyan (water festival), Burmese New Year, Workers' Day, Full Moon of Kason, Eid al-Adha, Full Moon of Waso, Martyrs' Day, Full Moon of Thadingyut, Devali, Tazaungdaing Festival, National Day, Christmas Day.

Business hours: 9:30–4:30 Mon.–Fri.

Customs: Traditional and religious customs observed; emphasis on courtesy and respect for others.

Namibia. Republic of Namibia, located in southwestern Africa along the Atlantic Ocean, with twenty-six districts including the capital city.
Capital: Windhoek.
Language: English (official), Afrikaans, German, indigenous languages.
Religion: Christian (majority), indigenous beliefs.
Principal holidays: New Year's Day, Independence Day, Good Friday, Easter Monday, Workers' Day, Ascension Day, Namibia Day, Human Rights Day, Christmas Day.
Business hours: 7:30–5 Mon.–Fri.
Customs: Western customs widely observed; normal business etiquette.

Nauru. Republic of Nauru, coral island located in the southern central Pacific Ocean west of Kiribati.
Capital: No city; government in Yaren District.
Language: Nauruan (official), English, French.
Religion: Protestant (majority), Roman Catholic.
Principal holidays: New Year's Day, Independence Day, Easter, Angam Day, Christmas Day, Boxing Day.
Business hours: Inquire in companies.
Customs: Traditional local customs observed, with widespread European influence; casual atmosphere combined with courtesy and tact.

Nepal. Kingdom of Nepal, located south of China in the Himalayan mountains of central Asia, with fourteen zones.
Capital: Kathmandu.
Language: Nepali (official), twenty other languages and numerous dialects.
Religion: Hindu (majority), Buddhist, Muslim, Christian.
Principal holidays: Unity Day, Martyrs' Day, Tribhuvan Jiyanti (King Tribhuvan's Birthday), Navabarsha (New Year's Day), Teachers' Day, Baishakh Purnima (Birthday of lord Buddha), Indra Jatra (Festival of the Rain God), Durga Paja Festival, United Nations Day, Tihr (Festival of Lights), Queen Aishworya's Birthday, Constitution Day, Mahendra Jayanti, King Birendra's Birthday.
Business hours: Summer: 10–5 Sun.–Fri.; winter: 10–4 Sun.–Fri.
Customs: Strong emphasis on traditional and religious customs, with numerous superstitions, many concerning visitors; humility and modesty important values.

The Netherlands. Kingdom of the Netherlands, located in northwestern Europe along the North Sea, with thirteen provinces, one consisting of a register of people who have no fixed residence.

Capital: Amsterdam.

Language: Dutch (official), English, French, German.

Religion: Roman Catholic, Protestant, unaffiliated.

Principal holidays: New Year's Day, Good Friday, Easter Monday, Queen's Birthday, National Liberation Day, Ascension Day, Whit Monday, Christmas.

Business hours: 8:30–5 Mon.–Fri.

Customs: Western nation, with European-style hospitality; respect for hard work and clean, attractive environment.

New Zealand.   Independent state in British Commonwealth, located in the southern Pacific Ocean southeast of Australia, with fifty-nine district authorities, twenty city authorities, and fourteen regional authorities.

Capital: Wellington.

Language: English (official), Maori.

Religion: Christian (majority), Hindu, Confucian, other.

Principal holidays: New Year, Waitangi Day, Good Friday, Easter Monday, Anzac Day, Queen's Birthday, Labor Day, Christmas.

Business hours: 9–5 Mon.–Fri.

Customs: Western nation, with relaxed informal lifestyle; conservative British influence in business.

Nicaragua.   Republic of Nicaragua, isthmus located in Central America between the Caribbean Sea and the Pacific Ocean, with three zones containing sixteen administrative departments.

Capital: Managua.

Language: Spanish (official), English, indigenous Indian languages.

Religion: Roman Catholic.

Principal holidays: New Year's Day, Maundy Thursday, Good Friday, Labor Day, Liberation Day, Managua local holiday, Battle of San Jacinto, Independence Day, All Souls' Day, Christmas Day.

Business hours: 8–12 and 2:30–5:30 Mon.–Fri.; 8–1 Sat.

Customs: Traditional and religious customs and traditional male-female roles observed in family-oriented Latin society; modern influences in urban areas.

Niger.   Republic of Niger, located south of Algeria and Libya in western central Africa, with seven departments and the capital district.

Capital: Niamey.

Language: French (official), Hausa, Djerma, Manga, Zarma, Tuareg.

Religion: Muslim (majority), Christian, animist.

Principal holidays: New Year's Day, Eid al-Fitr, Easter Monday, Anniversary of 1974 Coup, Labor Day, Eid al-Adha, Islamic New Year, Independence Day, Mouloud (Prophet's Birthday), Republic Day, Christmas.

Business hours: 7:30–12:30 and 3–6 or 6:30 Mon.–Fri.; 7:30–12:30 Sat.

Customs: Traditional and religious customs and traditional male-female roles observed.

Nigeria. Federal Republic of Nigeria, located on the western coast of Africa along the Bight of Benin and Bight of Biafra, with thirty states and a federal capital territory.

Capital: Abuja.

Language: English (official), Hausa, Yoruba, Ibo, more than 250 other local languages.

Religion: Muslim (majority), Christian, numerous local religions.

Principal holidays: New Year's Day, Eid al-Fitr, Easter, Eid al-Kebir, Mouloud (Prophet's Birthday), National Day, Christmas.

Business hours: 7:30–3:30 Mon.–Fri.

Customs: Emphasis on traditional and religious customs and traditional male-female roles, but with multicultural variations in local customs; relaxed atmosphere and relatively slow pace in business.

Norway. Kingdom of Norway, located in northern Europe in the western Scandinavian peninsula along the Arctic Ocean and the North Sea, with nineteen counties (*fylker*).

Capital: Oslo.

Language: Norwegian (official), Lapp, English.

Religion: Evanagelical Lutheran (majority), Roman Catholic, other Christian.

Principal holidays: New Year's Day, Palm Sunday, Maundy Thursday, Good Friday, Easter, Easter Monday, May Day, National Independence Day, Ascension Day, Whit Sunday, Whit Monday, Christmas Day, St. Stephen's Day.

Business hours: 8–4 Mon.–Fri.

Customs: Western customs observed, with reserved approach; punctuality important in business.

Oman. Sultanate of Oman, located in the Middle East on the southeastern tip of the Arabian peninsula along the Gulf of Oman and the Arabian Sea, with seven planning regions.

Capital: Muscat.

Language: Arabic (official), English, Baluchi, Urdu, Indian dialects.

Religion: Ibadhi Muslim (majority), Sunni Muslim, Shiite Muslim, Hindu.

Principal holidays: Leilat al-Meiraj (Ascension of the Prophet), Ramadan, Eid al-Fitr, Eid al-Adha, Muharram, Islamic New Year, Ashoura, Mouloud (Prophet's Birthday), National Day, Sultan's Birthday.

Business hours: 7:30–2 Sat.–Wed.; 8–1 Thur.; some 4–7 Sat.–Wed.

Customs: Emphasis on traditional and religious customs and traditional male-female roles.

Pakistan. Islamic Republic of Pakistan, located northwest of India in southern Asia, with four provinces, federally administered tribal areas, and the capital territory.

Capital: Islamabad.

Language: Urdu and English (official), Punjabi, Sindhi, Pashtu, Saraiki, Baluchi, other.

Religion: Sunni Muslim (majority), Shiite Muslim, Hindi, Christian.

Principal holidays: Ramadan, Pakistan Day, Good Friday, Easter Monday, Labor Day, Eid al-Fitr, Eid al-Adha, Islamic New Year, Ashoura, Independence Day, Defense of Pakistan Day, Eid-e-Milad-un-Nabi (Prophet's Birthday), Anniversary of Death of Quaid-i-Azam, Iqbal Day, Quaid-i-Azam's Birthday, Christmas, Boxing Day.

Business hours: 9–4 Sat.–Thur.

Customs: Emphasis on traditional and religious customs and traditional male-female roles; different social classes recognized; acceptance of Islamic law tempered with the desire for more Western-style business practices.

Panama. Republic of Panama, located in southern Central America between the Caribbean Sea and the Pacific Ocean, with nine provinces and the San Blas Special Territory.

Capital: Panama City.

Language: Spanish (official), English.

Religion: Roman Catholic (majority), Protestant.

Principal holidays: New Year's Day, National Martyrs' Day, Shrove Tuesday, Good Friday, Labor Day, Foundation of Panama City, Columbus Day, National Anthem Day, All Souls' Day, Independence from Colombia, National Flag Day, Independence Day (Colón), First Call of Independence, Independence from Spain, Mother's Day, Immaculate Conception, Christmas Day.

Business hours: 8–12 and 2–5 Mon.–Fri.

Customs: Traditional customs and traditional male-female roles observed, with emphasis on individuality; blend of Spanish and American lifestyles.

Papua New Guinea. Independent state, more than six hundred islands located in the southern Pacific Ocean north of Australia, with twenty provinces including the national capital district.

Capital: Port Moresby.

Language: English (official), pidgin English, Motu, more than seven hundred other languages and dialects.

Religion: Christian (majority), indigenous beliefs.

Principal holidays: New Year's Day, Good Friday, Easter Monday, Queen's Birthday, Remembrance Day, Independence Day, Constitution Day, Christmas Day, Boxing Day.

Business hours: 8–5 Mon.–Fri.

Customs: Traditional local customs observed, with some very primitive cultures; informality in business.

Paraguay. Republic of Paraguay, located north of Argentina in central South America, with nineteen departments and the capital city.

Capital: Asunción.

Language: Spanish (official), Guarani.

Religion: Roman Catholic (majority), Mennonite, other Protestant.

Principal holidays: New Year's Day, San Blás (national saint), Heroes' Day, Maundy Thursday, Good Friday, Labor Day, National Independence Day, Ascension Day, Peace of Chaco, Corpus Christi, Founding of Asunción, Constitution Day, Battle of Boquerón, Columbus Day, All Saints' Day, Immaculate Conception, Christmas Day.

Business hours: 8–12 and 3–5:30 or 3–7 Mon.–Fri.; 8–12 Sat.

Customs: Latin culture, with traditional male superiority; hospitable people who consider themselves Americans.

Peru. Republic of Peru, located in western South America along the Pacific Ocean, with twenty-four departments and the constitutional province of Callao.

Capital: Lima.

Language: Spanish and Quechua (official), Aymara, English.

Religion: Roman Catholic.

Principal holidays: New Year's Day, Shrove Tuesday (half day), Maundy Thursday, Good Friday, Labor Day, Day of the Peasant, St. Peter and St. Paul's Day, National Independence Day, Santa Rosa of Lima Day, Battle of Angamos, All Saints' Day, Immaculate Conception, Christmas Day.

Business hours: 9–5 Mon.–Fri.

Customs: Latin culture with traditional male superiority; nationalistic attitude, but with local customs observed.

Philippines. Republic of the Philippines, archipelago of more than seven hundred islands located in the Pacific Ocean and South China Sea off the southeastern coast of Asia, with fourteen regions.

Capital: Manila.

Language: Filipino and English (both official), more than a hundred other languages and dialects.

Religion: Roman Catholic (majority), Protestant, Muslim, Buddhist.

Principal holidays: New Year's Day, Freedom Day, Anniversary of the People's Revolution, Maundy Thursday, Good Friday, Easter Monday, Labor Day, Araw ng Kagitingan, Independence Day, National Heroes' Day, Barangay Day, National Thanksgiving Day, All Saints' Day, Andres Bonifacio Day, Christmas Day, Rizal Day, Last Day of the Year.

Business hours: 8 or 9–12 and 3–5 or 6 Mon.–Fri.

Customs: Local customs observed, with emphasis on family over individual; American-style business practices in most places, but with more relaxed attitude about time.

Poland. Polish Republic, located in eastern central Europe east of Germany, with forty-nine voivodships (*wojewodztwo*).

Capital: Warsaw.

Language: Polish (official), German, French, English.

Religion: Roman Catholic (majority), Orthodox, Protestant.

Principal holidays: New Year's Day, Easter Monday, Labor Day, Polish National Day, Victory Day, Corpus Christi, Assumption, All Saints' Day, Christmas.

Business hours: 7–3 Mon.–Fri.

Customs: Traditional and religious customs observed; reserved, formal approach in business.

Portugal. Republic of Portugal, located in southwestern Europe on the

Iberian Peninsula along the Atlantic Ocean, with eighteen districts and the autonomous regions of the Azores and Madeira.

Capital: Lisbon.

Language: Portuguese.

Religion: Roman Catholic (majority), Protestant.

Principal holidays: New Year's Day, Shrove Tuesday, Good Friday, Easter Monday, National Day, Labor Day, Camões, Portugal Day, Corpus Christi, Assumption Day, Republic Day, All Saints' Day, Portuguese Independence Day, Immaculate Conception, Christmas Day, Bank Holiday.

Business hours: 9–1 and 3–7 Mon.–Fri.

Customs: Traditional and religious customs observed; leisurely Latin-southern Europe lifestyle; emphasis on courtesy and strong friendships.

Qatar. State of Qatar, peninsula located in the Middle East along the Persian Gulf, with nine municipalities.

Capital: Doha.

Language: Arabic (official), English.

Religion: Muslim.

Principal holidays: Leilat al-Meiraj, Accession of the Emir, Ramadan, Eid al-Fitr, Eid al-Adha, Islamic New Year, National Day.

Business hours: 7:30–12 and 3–6 Sat.–Thur.

Customs: Emphasis on traditional and religious customs and traditional male-female roles.

Romania. Independent republic, located in southeastern Europe along the Black Sea.

Capital: Bucharest.

Language: Romanian (official), German, Hungarian, French, English.

Religion: Romanian Orthodox (majority), Roman Catholic, Lutheran, Muslim, Jewish.

Principal holidays: New Year, Orthodox Easter, Good Friday, Easter Monday, International Labor Day, Christmas.

Business hours: 7–3:30 Mon.–Fri.; 7–12:30 Sat.

Customs: Traditional society striving toward standard of other European nations; traditional male-female roles; conservative business approach.

Russia. Russian Federation, located in northeastern Europe and northern Asia, stretching across the continent to the Sea of Japan, with forty-nine regions, six territories, and sixteen autonomous republics.

Capital: Moscow.

Language: Russian (official), ethnic languages.

Religion: Russian Orthodox (majority), Muslim, Buddhist, Jewish.

Principal holidays: Former Soviet holidays: New Year's Day, Army and Navy Day, International Women's Day, International Labor Day, Victory in Europe Day, Constitution Day, October Revolution, Agricultural and Agro-Industrial Workers' Day.

Business hours: 9–6 Mon.–Fri.

Customs: Traditional customs observed, with considerable economic pressures resulting from conversion to nontotalitarian society; pessimistic and fatalistic attitudes.

Rwanda. Republic of Rwanda, located in central Africa west of Tanzania, with ten prefectures.

Capital: Kigali.

Language: Kinyarwanda and French (both official), Kiswahili.

Religion: Roman Catholic (majority), Protestant, Muslim, animist.

Principal holidays: New Year's Day, Democracy Day, Easter Monday, Labor Day, Ascension Day, Whit Monday, Independence Day, National Peace and Unity Day, Anniversary of 1973 Coup, Assumption, Kamarampaka (anniversary of 1961 referendum), Armed Forces Day, All Saints' Day, Christmas.

Business hours: 7–12 and 2–5 Mon.–Fri.; 7–12 Sat.

Customs: Traditional and religious customs observed, including tribal customs; normal business etiquette.

Saint Kitts and Nevis. Federation of Saint Kitts and Nevis, two islands, part of the Lesser Antilles, located in the eastern Caribbean Sea. (Saint Kitts, formerly Saint Christopher, in the northern part of the Leeward Islands, lies about two miles north of Nevis.)

Capital: Basseterre.

Language: English.

Religion: Anglican, Roman Catholic, Protestant.

Principal holidays: New Year's Day, Carnival Day, Good Friday, Easter Monday, Labor Day, Whit Monday, Queen's Birthday, Emancipation Day, Culturama (Nevis), Independence Anniversary, Christmas Day, Boxing Day.

Business hours: 8–12 and 1–4 Mon.–Sat.; fewer hours Thur.

Customs: Traditional island customs influenced by developing tourism; relaxed lifestyle.

Saint Lucia. Independent state, island of the Lesser Antilles located in the southeastern Caribbean Sea and bounded on the east by the Atlantic Ocean, with eight regions.

Capital: Castries.

Language: English (official), French patois.

Religion: Roman Catholic (majority), Protestant.

Principal holidays: New Year, Independence Day, Carnival, Good Friday, Easter Monday, Labor Day, Whit Monday, Corpus Christi, Emancipation Day, Thanksgiving Day, National Day, Christmas.

Business hours: 8–4 Mon.–Fri.

Customs: Traditional West Indian customs, with French influence; relaxed island lifestyle.

Saint Vincent and the Grenadines. Independent state, island of Saint Vincent and about fifty smaller islands, part of the Windward Islands, located in the eastern Caribbean Sea southwest of Saint Lucia.

Capital: Kingstown.

Language: English, French patois.

Religion: Roman Catholic, Anglican, Methodist, other Christian.

Principal holidays: New Year's Day, Saint Vincent and the Grenadines, Good Friday, Easter Monday, Labor Day, Whit Monday, Caricom Day, Carnival Tuesday, Emancipation Day, Independence Day, Christmas.

Business hours: 8–4 Mon.–Fri.

Customs: Traditional West Indian customs, with English influence; relaxed island lifestyle.

San Marino. Republic of San Marino, located in western Europe in the northern Appennine part of the Italian peninsula, with eleven districts.

Capital: San Marino.

Language: Italian.

Religion: Roman Catholic.

Principal holidays: New Year's Day, Liberation Day, St. Joseph's Day, Anniversary of the Arengo, Captains-Regent Investiture, Easter Monday, Labor Day, Corpus Christi, Anniversary of the Fall of Fascism, Assumption, San Marino Day, Republic Day, All Saints' Day, Commemoration of the Dead, Immaculate Conception, Christmas, St. Stephen's Day.

Business hours: Inquire in companies.

Customs: Traditional southern European customs, with Italian influence; normal business etiquette.

São Tomé and Príncipe. Democratic Republic of São Tomé and Príncipe, two main islands and several islets located in the Gulf of Guinea off the western coast of Africa, with two provinces.

Capital: São Tomé.

Language: Portuguese (official), French, English, local dialects.

Religion: Roman Catholic (majority), Protestant.

Principal holidays: New Year's Day, Commemoration of the 1953 Massacre, Shrove Tuesday, Good Friday, Easter Monday, Workers' Day, Ascension, Corpus Christi, Independence Day, Assumption, Agricultural Nationalization Day, All Saints' Day, People's Popular Power Day, Christmas.

Business hours: Inquire in companies.

Customs: Traditional, relaxed island culture, with Portuguese influence; normal business etiquette.

Saudi Arabia. Kingdom of Saudi Arabia, located in the Middle East on the Arabian peninsula of southwestern Asia along the Red Sea.

Capital: Riyadh.

Language: Arabic (official), English.

Religion: Sunni Muslim (majority), Shiite Muslim.

Principal holidays: Leilat al-Meiraj, Eid al-Fitr, Eid al-Adha, Islamic New Year, Ashoura, Mouloud (Prophet's Birthday).

Business hours: 8–12 and 3–6 Sat.–Thur. (nighttime hours during Ramadan).

Customs: Emphasis on traditional and religious customs; traditional male-female roles; conservative business practices, with a slower pace than in Western nations.

Senegal. Republic of Senegal, located in northwestern Africa along the Atlantic Ocean, with ten regions.

Capital: Dakar.

Language: French (official), Wolof, other local languages.

Religion: Muslim (majority), Roman Catholic, Protestant, indigenous beliefs.

Principal holidays: New Year's Day, Good Friday, Easter Monday, National Day, Eid al-Fitr, Ascension Day, Whit Monday, Eid al-Adha, Day of Association, Assumption Day, Mouloud (Prophet's Birthday), All Saints' Day, Christmas.

Business hours: 9–12 and 2:30–6 Mon.–Fri.; 8–12 Sat. (nighttime during Ramadan).

Customs: Emphasis on traditional and religious customs and traditional male-female roles, with various ethnic customs as well; respect for family and attention to courtesy.

Seychelles. Republic of Seychelles, nearly a hundred islands located in the western Indian Ocean off the east coast of Africa.

Capital: Victoria.

Language: Creole (official), French, English.

Religion: Roman Catholic (majority), Anglican, Muslim.

Principal holidays: New Year, Good Friday, Easter Monday, Labor Day, Liberation Day, Corpus Christi, Independence Day, Assumption Day, All Saints' Day, Immaculate Conception, Christmas Day.

Business hours: 8–12 and 1–4 Mon.–Fri.

Customs: Traditional local customs observed in a relaxed island atmosphere.

Sierra Leone. Republic of Sierra Leone, located in western central Africa along the Atlantic Ocean, with three provinces and the Western Area.

Capital: Freetown.

Language: English (official), Krio, other local languages.

Religion: Animist (majority), Muslim, Christian.

Principal holidays: New Year's Day, Eid al-Fitr, Good Friday, Easter Monday, Independence Day, Eid al-Adha, Mouloud (Prophet's Birthday), Christmas.

Business hours: 8–12 or 12:30 and 2–4:30 or 5 Mon.–Fri.

Customs: Traditional and religious customs and traditional male-female roles observed; normal business etiquette.

Singapore. Republic of Singapore, one relatively large island and nearly sixty islets located in southwestern Asia off the tip of the Malay peninsula (connected by a long causeway).

Capital: Singapore.

Language: English (official), Mandarin Chinese, Malay, Tamil, Indian.

Religion: Chinese: Buddhist and atheist (majority); Malays: Muslim (majority), Christian, Hindu, Sikh, Taoist, Confucian.

Principal holidays: New Year, Chinese New Year, Hari Raya Haji, National Day, Deepavali, Christmas Day.

Business hours: 8:30–4:30 Mon.–Fri.; 8:30–12:30 Sat.

Customs: Traditional and religious customs observed in multicultural society; emphasis on industriousness.

Slovak Republic. Formerly part of Czechoslovakia, located north of Austria and Hungary in central Europe.

Capital: Bratislava.

Language: Slovak (official), Czech, Hungarian, Romany, Russian, German, English.

Religion: Catholic (majority), Protestant, Orthodox, various other religions.

Principal holidays: New Year's Day, Easter Monday, Labor Day, National Day of Liberation, St. Cyril and St. Methodius Day, National Day, Independence Day, Christmas.

Business hours: 8–4 Mon.–Fri.

Customs: Emphasis on traditional customs, with European influence; emerging national identity.

Slovenia. Republic of Slovenia, former Yugoslav republic, located north of Croatia in southern central Europe.

Capital: Ljubljana.

Language: Slovene (official), Macedonian, Serbian, Croatian.

Religion: Roman Catholic (majority), Orthodox, Muslim.

Principal holidays: New Year, Labor Day, Veterans' Day, Republic Days, Christmas.

Business hours: 7–3 Mon.–Fri.

Customs: Emphasis on traditional customs and beliefs; disrupted by political instability in region.

Solomon Islands. Independent nation, archipelago scattered across the southwestern Pacific Ocean east of Papua New Guinea, with seven provinces and the capital territory.

Capital: Honiara.

Language: English (official), Pidgin English, more than a hundred indigenous languages.

Religion: Anglican, Roman Catholic, South Sea Evangelical, other Protestant.

Principal holidays: New Year's Day, Good Friday, Easter, Queen's Official Birthday, Whit Monday, Independence Day, Christmas.

Business hours: 8–12 and 1–4:30 Mon.–Fri.; 7:30–12 Sat.

Customs: Blend of European and local traditional customs; relaxed island atmosphere.

Somalia. Somali Democratic Republic, located on the eastern coast of Africa along the Indian Ocean, with eighteen regions.

Capital: Mogadishu.

Language: Somali (official), Arabic, Swahili, Italian, English.

Religion: Sunni Muslim (majority), Roman Catholic.

Principal holidays: New Year's Day, Eid al-Fitr, Labor Day, Eid al-Adha, Independence Day, Foundation of the Republic, Ashoura, Mouloud (Prophet's Birthday), Anniversary of 1969 Revolution.

Customs: Emphasis on traditional and religious customs and traditional male-female roles; business disrupted by civil turmoil throughout country, with no effective central government.

South Africa. Republic of South Africa, located in the southern tip of Africa along both the Atlantic Ocean and the Indian Ocean, with four provinces.

Capital: Cape Town (legislative); Pretoria (administrative).

Language: Afrikaans and English (both official); Zulu, Xhosa, Sesotho, other African languages.

Religion: Christian (majority), Hindu, Muslim, Jewish.

Principal holidays: New Year's Day, Founders' Day, Good Friday, Family Day, Workers' Day, Ascension Day, Republic Day, Kruger Day, Day of the Vow, Christmas Day, Day of Goodwill.

Business hours: 8–5 Mon.–Fri.

Customs: Numerous ethnic groups, with diverse customs; changing social climate and attitudes as country moves toward reform and the end of apartheid.

Spain. Kingdom of Spain, mainland located in southwestern Europe on the Iberian peninsula next to Portugal and two island groups, the Balearic Islands in the Mediterranean Sea and the Canary Islands off the West Coast of Africa, with seventeen autonomous communities.

Capital: Madrid.

Language: Castilian Spanish (official), Catalan, Galician, Basque.

Religion: Roman Catholic.

Principal holidays: New Year's Day, Three Kings' Day, Maundy Thursday, Good Friday, Easter Monday, Labor Day, Corpus Christi, King Juan Carlos's Saint's Day, St. James of Compostela, Assumption Day, National Day, All Saints' Day, Constitution Day, Immaculate Conception, Christmas Day, Boxing Day.

Business hours: Varies; inquire in companies.

Customs: Traditional and religious customs and traditional male-female roles observed, with more modern customs in urban areas; strong emphasis on appearances and social position.

Sri Lanka. Socialist Republic of Sri Lanka, island located southeast of India in the Indian Ocean, with nine provinces and twenty-five districts.

Capital: Colombo.

Language: Sinhala and Tamil (both official), English.

Religion: Buddhist (majority), Hindu, Christian, Muslim.

Principal holidays: New Year's Day, Tamil Thai Pongal Day, Independence Commemoration Day, Maha Sivarathri Day, Eid al-Fitr, Good Friday, Easter Monday, May Day, National Heroes' Day, Eid al-Adha, Hadji Festival Day, Special Bank Holiday, Prophet's Birthday, Deepavali Festival Day, Christmas Day, Boxing Day, Special Bank Holiday.

Business hours: 8:30 or 9–4:30 or 5 Mon.–Fri.

Customs: Traditional ethnic customs and traditional male-female roles; caste system declining in importance among modern elements of society.

Sudan. Republic of Sudan, located south of Egypt in northeastern Africa along the Red Sea, with nine regions.

Capital: Khartoum.

Language: Arabic (official), English, numerous local dialects.

Religion: Sunni Muslim (majority), Christian, animist.

Principal holidays: Independence Day, Eid al-Fitr, Uprising Day (anniversary of the 1985 Coup), Sham an-Nassim (Coptic Easter Monday), Mouloud (Prophet's Birthday), Christmas.

Business hours: 8:30–2 Sat.–Thur.

Customs: Emphasis on traditional and religious customs and traditional male-female roles; evidence of social class distinctions and economic inequalities; formal but hospitable approach to outsiders.

Suriname. Republic of Suriname, located on the northern coast of South America along the Atlantic Ocean.

Capital: Paramaribo.

Language: Dutch (official), English, Sranan, Tongo (Taki-Taki), Hindi, Javanese, Chinese French, Spanish.

Religion: Christian (majority), Hindu, Muslim, indigenous beliefs.

Principal holidays: New Year's Day, Revolution Day, Phagwa, Eid al-Fitr, Easter, Labor Day, National Union Day, Independence Day, Christmas.

Business hours: 7–3 Mon.–Fri., 7–2:30 Sat.

Customs: Traditional and local customs observed; normal business etiquette.

Swaziland. Kingdom of Swaziland, located north of South Africa in southern Africa, with four regions.

Capital: Mbabane.

Language: English and Siswati (both official).

Religion: Christian (majority), animist.

Principal holidays: New Year's Day, Good Friday, Easter Monday, King's Birthday, National Flag Day, Ascension Day, Birthday of (the late) King Sobhuza, Umhlanga Day, Somhlolo (Independence) Day, Christmas Day, Boxing Day, Incwala Day.

Business hours: 8–1 and 2–5 Mon.–Fri.; 8:30–12:30 Sat.

Customs: Emphasis on traditional and religious customs; strong ties to South Africa.

Sweden. Kingdom of Sweden, located in northwestern Europe in the Scandinavian peninsula along the Baltic Sea, with twenty-four counties.

Capital: Stockholm.

Language: Swedish (majority), Lapp, Finnish, English, German.

Religion: Evangelical Lutheran (majority), Roman Catholic, other Protestant, Muslim, Jewish.

Principal holidays: New Year's Day, Epiphany, Good Friday, Easter Monday, Labor Day, Ascension Day, Whit Monday, Midsummer's Day, All Saints' Day, Christmas.

Business hours: 9–5 Mon.–Fri.

Customs: Modern society, with strong social welfare system; reserved approach in business.

Switzerland. Swiss Confederation, located east of France and South of Germany in western Europe, with twenty-three cantons.

Capital: Bern.

Language: German (official), French, Italian, Romansh.

Religion: Roman Catholic, Protestant.

Principal holidays: New Year, Good Friday, Easter Monday, Ascension Day, Whit Monday, Christmas.

Business hours: 8–12 and 2–5 Mon.–Fri.

Customs: Modern, politically neutral nation, with movement toward greater economic participation in Europe; European business etiquette and practices.

Syria. Syrian Arab Republic, located in the Middle East along the Mediterranean Sea, with fourteen districts.

Capital: Damascus.

Language: Arabic (official), French, English, Kurdish, Armenian.

Religion: Sunni Muslim (majority), Christian, other Muslim.

Principal holidays: New Year's Day; Leilat al-Meiraj; Revolution Day; Eid al-Fitr; Easter (Greek Orthodox); Eid al-Adha; Islamic New Year; Egypt's Revolution Day; Union of Syria, Egypt, and Libya; Mouloud (Prophet's Birthday); October War; National Day; Christmas Day.

Business hours: 8–2:30 Sat.–Thur.

Customs: Emphasis on traditional and religious customs and traditional male-female roles; hospitable and courteous people, with conservative, reserved attitudes.

Taiwan. Republic of China, one main island and more than seventy-five small islands located off the coast of the People's Republic of China in Southeast Asia between the Formosa Strait and the Pacific Ocean.

Capital: Taipei.

Language: Mandarin Chinese (official), Taiwanese dialects, English, Japanese.

Religion: Buddhist (majority), Taoist, Confucian, Christian.

Principal holidays: National Holiday and Founding Day, Chinese New Year, Youth Day, Ching Ming, Tomb-Sweeping Day, Dragon Boat Festival, Mid-Autumn Moon Festival, Confucius' Birthday, Teachers' Day, Double Tenth National Day, Retrocession Day, Birthday of Chiang Kai-Shek, Dr. Sun Yat-sen's Birthday, Constitution Day.

Business hours: 8:30–5:30 Mon.–Fri.; 8:30–12:30 Sat.

Customs: Traditional customs observed; emphasis on proper behavior and courtesy; reserved, polite approach in business.

Tajikistan. Republic of Tajikistan, former Soviet republic located west of China in southeastern central Asia.

Capital: Dushanbe.

Language: Tajik (official), Russian, Uzbek, ethnic languages.

Religion: Sunni Muslim, Russian Orthodox, Jewish.

Principal holidays: Former Soviet holidays: New Year's Day, Army and Navy Day, International Labor Day, International Women's Day, Victory in Europe Day, Constitution Day, October Revolution, Agriculture and Agro-Industrial Workers' Day.

Business hours: Inquire in companies.

Customs: Emphasis on traditional customs and beliefs; evolving national identity.

Tanzania. United Republic of Tanzania, located in eastern Africa along the Indian Ocean, with twenty-five regions.

Capital: Dodoma.

Language: Swahili and English (both official), Bantu, other African languages.

Religion: Christian, Muslim, Hindu, indigenous beliefs.

Principal holidays: New Year's Day, Zanzibar Revolution Day, Chama Cha Mapinduzi Day, Eid al-Fitr, Easter, Union Day, Labor Day, Eid al-Haji, Saba Saba Peasants' Day, Maulidi (Prophet's Birthday), Independence Day, Christmas Day.

Business hours: 8:30–11:30 and 2–6 Mon.–Fri.

Customs: Traditional and religious customs observed, with group considered more important than individual; normal business etiquette.

Thailand. Kingdom of Thailand, located south of China in southeastern Asia along the Gulf of Thailand and the Indian Ocean, with seventy-five provinces (*changwads*).

Capital: Bangkok.

Language: Thai (official), English, Malay, Tachew Chinese.

Religion: Theravada Buddhist (majority), Muslim, Christian.

Principal holidays: New Year's Day, Makhabuja Day, Chinese New Year, Chakri Day, Songkran (Water Festival), Coronation Day, Royal Ploughing Ceremony, Visakha Puja, Asalha Puja, Khao Phansa, Queen's Birthday, Chulalongkorn Day, King's Birthday, Constitution Day, New Year's Eve.

Business hours: 8:30–4:30 Mon.–Fri.

Customs: Emphasis on traditional and religious customs, with open acceptance of numerous mistresses for males; signs of Western influence, such as respect for wealth and education.

Togo. Repulic of Togo, located east of Ghana in western Africa along the Atlantic Ocean, with five regions.

Capital: Lomé.

Language: French (official), Ewe, Mina, Dagomba, Kabyè.

Religion: Traditional and animist (majority), Christian, Muslim.

Principal holidays: New Year's Day, Liberation Day, Day of Victory (at Sarakawa), Eid al-Fitr, Easter Monday, Victory Day, Independence Day, Labor Day, Ascension Day, Whit Monday, Eid al-Adha (Tabaski), Assumption, Anniversary of Failed Attack on Lomé, All Saints' Day, Christmas Day.

Business hours: 7–12 and 2:30–5:30 Mon.–Fri.

Customs: Emphasis on traditional and religious customs, with strong voodoo influence; normal business etiquette.

Tonga.   Kingdom of Tonga, archipelago located in the South Pacific Ocean, with about 170 islands consisting of five administrative divisions.
Capital: Nuku'alofa.
Language: Tongan and English (both official).
Religion: Wesleyan Church, Roman Catholic, Anglican.
Principal holidays: New Year's Day, Easter, Anzac Day, Crown Prince's Birthday, Independence Day, His Majesty the King's Birthday, Constitution Day, King George Tupou I Day, Christmas, Boxing Day.
Business hours: 9–5 Mon.–Fri.
Customs: Traditional island customs and traditional male-female roles observed; relaxed lifestyle.

Trinidad and Tobago.   Republic of Trinidad and Tobago, two islands located in the southeastern Caribbean Sea off the coast of northeastern South America, with three municipalities, eight counties, and Tobago.
Capital: Port of Spain.
Language: English (official), Hindi, French, Spanish, Chinese.
Religion: Roman Catholic, Hindu, Protestant, Muslim.
Principal holidays: New Year's Day, Carnival, Eid al-Fitr, Good Friday, Easter Monday, Whit Monday, Corpus Christi, Labor Day, Emancipation Day, Independence Day, Republic Day, Divali, Christmas.
Business hours: 8–4 Mon.–Fri.
Customs: Traditional island customs, with relaxed lifestyle; hospitable approach to visitors.

Tunisia.   Republic of Tunisia, located in northern Africa along the Mediterranean Sea, with twenty-three *gouvernorats*.
Capital: Tunis.
Language: Arabic (official), French, English.
Religion: Muslim (majority), Roman Catholic, Protestant, Jewish.
Principal holidays: New Year's Day, Independence Day, Youth Day, Eid el-Kebir, Ras El Am Hejri (Muslim New Year's Day), Republic Day, Women's Day, El Mouled (Prophet's Birthday), New Era Day.
Business hours: Sept.–Jun.: 8–12:30 and 2–6 Mon.–Thur.; 8–1 Fri.–Sat. Jul.–Aug.: 7–1 Mon.–Sat.
Customs: Traditional and religious customs and traditional male-female

roles observed; reserved approach in business; loose concept of time.

Turkey. Republic of Turkey, located in southeastern Europe and western Asia between the Black Sea and the Mediterranean Sea, with seventy-three provinces.

Capital: Ankara.

Language: Turkish (official), Kurdish, Arabic, French, German, English.

Religion: Sunni Muslim (majority), Christian, Jewish.

Principal holidays: New Year's Day, Feast of Ramazan, National Independence and Children's Day, Seker Bayram, Spring Day, Atatürk's Commemoration Day, Youth and Sports Day, Kurban Bayrami (Feast of Sacrifice), Victory Day, Republic Day.

Business hours: 8:30–12 and 1–5:30 Mon.–Fri.

Customs: Emphasis on traditional and religious customs and traditional male-female roles; influence of both Europe and Asia because of location.

Turkmenistan. Republic of Turkmenistan, former Soviet republic located north of Iran in southwestern central Asia along the Caspian Sea.

Capital: Ashkhabad.

Language: Turkmenian (official), Russian, ethnic languages.

Religion: Sunni Muslim (majority), shamanism, Sufi mysticism.

Principal holidays: Former Soviet holidays: New Year's Day, Army and Navy Day, International Labor Day, International Women's Day, Victory in Europe Day, Constitution Day, October Revolution, Agriculture and Agro-Industrial Workers' Day.

Business hours: Inquire in companies.

Customs: Emphasis on traditional customs and beliefs; evolving national identity.

Tuvalu. Independent nation, formerly Ellice Islands, nine small atolls located in the southern and western Pacific Ocean east of the Solomon Islands.

Capital: Fongafale.

Language: Tuvaluan, English.

Religion: Protestant (majority), other Christian.

Principal holidays: New Year, Commonwealth Day, Easter, Queen's Birthday, National Children's Day, Tuvalu Day, Prince of Wales' Birthday, Christmas, Boxing Day.

Business hours: 7:30–4:30 Mon.–Thur.; 7:30–12:30 Fri.

Customs: Traditional and religious customs observed; relaxed island atmosphere, but with emphasis on etiquette and proper business practices.

Uganda. Republic of Uganda, located south of Sudan in central and eastern Africa along Lake Victoria, with thirty-four districts.

Capital: Kampala.

Language: English (official), Luganda, Swahili, other African languages.

Religion: Christian (majority), animist, Muslim.

Principal holidays: New Year's Day, Leilat al-Meiraj, Eid al-Fitr, Easter, Labor Day, Martyrs' Day, Eid al-Adha, Independence Day, Christmas Day.

Business hours: 8–12:30 and 2–5 Mon.–Fri.

Customs: Traditional customs observed, with familiarity with Western ways; normal business etiquette.

Ukraine. Republic of Ukraine, located west of Russia in southeastern central Europe, with twenty-five regions.

Capital: Kiev.

Language: Ukrainian (official), Russian, ethnic languages.

Religion: Ukrainian Orthodox, Roman Catholic, Protestant, Jewish, Muslim.

Principal holidays: Former Soviet holidays: New Year's Day, Army and Navy Day, International Labor Day, International Women's Day, Victory in Europe Day, Constitution Day, October Revolution, Agriculture and Agro-Industrial Workers' Day.

Business hours: Inquire in companies.

Customs: Emphasis on traditional customs and beliefs; evolving national identity.

United Arab Emirates. Independent nation, located north of Saudi Arabia in the Middle East along the Persian Gulf, with seven emirates.

Capital: Abu Dhabi.

Language: Arabic (official), Hindi, Urdu, Farsi, English.

Religion: Sunni Muslim (majority), Shiite Muslim, Christian, Hindu.

Principal holidays: Leilat al-Meiraj, Ramadan, Eid al-Fitr, Eid al-Adha, Islamic New Year, Accession of His Highness Shaikh Zayed, Mouloud (Prophet's Birthday), National Day.

Business hours: 8–1 and 4–7 Sat.–Wed.; 7–12 Thur. (closed during Ramadan).

Customs: Emphasis on traditional and religious customs and traditional male-female roles; normal business etiquette, with respect for Islamic restrictions.

United Kingdom. United Kingdom of Great Britain and Northern Ireland, located in northwestern Europe on Great Britain (England, Scotland, and Wales) and east of the Republic of Ireland along the Atlantic Ocean and the North Sea.

Capital: London.

Language: English (official), Welsh, Gaelic, ethnic languages.

Religion: Protestant (majority), other Christian, Jewish, Muslim, Hindu.

Principal holidays: New Year's Day, Good Friday, Easter Monday, May Day, Bank Holiday, Spring Bank Holiday, Summer Bank Holiday, Late Summer Bank Holiday, Christmas Day, Boxing Day.

Business hours: 9–5 Mon.–Fri.

Customs: Leading industrialized Western nation, with many practices similar to those in the United States; ongoing unrest in Northern Ireland; reserved approach in business.

Uruguay. Oriental Republic of Uruguay, located east of Argentina along the Atlantic Ocean, with nineteen departments.

Capital: Montevideo.

Language: Spanish (official), English.

Religion: Roman Catholic (majority), Protestant, Jewish.

Principal holidays: New Year's Day, Epiphany, Landing of the 33 Patriots, Labor Day, Anniversary of Battle of Las Piedras, Birth of General Artigas, Constitution Day, Independence Day, Columbus Day, All Souls' Day, Blessing of the Waters, Christmas Day.

Business hours: 9–12 and 2:30–7 Mon.–Fri.

Customs: Traditional Latin customs and traditional male-female roles observed, but with increasing influence of women; punctuality not strictly observed.

Uzbekistan. Republic of Uzbekistan, former Soviet republic located north of Afghanistan in central Asia, with thirteen regions.

Capital: Tashkent.

Language: Uzbek (official), Russian, ethnic languages.

Religion: Sunni Muslim, Orthodox Christian, Jewish.

Principal holidays: Former Soviet holidays: New Year's Day, Army and Navy Day, International Labor Day, International Women's Day, Victory in Europe Day, Constitution Day, October Revolution, Agriculture and Agro-Industrial Workers' Day.

Business hours: Inquire in companies.

Customs: Emphasis on traditional customs and beliefs; evolving national identity.

Vanuatu.   Republic of Vanuatu, formerly the New Hebrides, about eighty islands located in the southwestern Pacific Ocean east of Australia.

Capital: Vila.

Language: English and French (official), Pidgin English (Bislama), local dialects.

Religion: Christian.

Principal holidays: New Year's Day, Easter, Labor Day, Ascension Day, Independence Day, Assumption, Constitution Day, Unity Day, Christmas Day.

Business hours: Inquire in companies.

Customs: Traditional island customs; relaxed lifestyle and casual business practices.

Venezuela.   Republic of Venezuela, located in northern South America along the Caribbean Sea and the Atlantic Ocean, with twenty states and four federal areas.

Capital: Caracas.

Language: Spanish (official), English, French, Portuguese, German, Indian dialects.

Religion: Roman Catholic (majority), Protestant.

Principal holidays: New Year's Day, Carnival, Good Friday, Easter Monday, Declaration of Independence, Labor Day, Carabobo Day, Independence Day, Bolívar's Birthday, Columbus Day, Christmas.

Business hours: 8–6 (up to 2-hr. midday break) Mon.–Fri.

Customs: Cosmopolitan Latin country, but with traditional male dominance; some Portuguese influence; punctuality not strictly observed.

Vietnam.   Socialist Republic of Vietnam, located east of Laos and Cambodia in southeastern Asia along the South China Sea, with forty provinces.

Capital: Hanoi.

Language: Vietnamese (official), Khmer, Chinese, Russian, French, English.

Religion: Buddhist (majority), Confucian, Taoist, Roman Catholic.

Principal holidays: New Year, Têt, Lunar New Year, Emperor-Founder Hung Vuong, Liberation of Saigon.

Business hours: 7:30–12 and 1–4:30 Mon.–Fri.

Customs: Traditional customs observed, with emphasis on the extended family unit and respect for ancestors; progressive attitude toward global relations.

Western Samoa. Independent State of Western Samoa, nine islands located in the South Pacific Ocean northeast of New Zealand.

Capital: Apia.

Language: Samoan (official), English.

Religion: Congregational Church, Roman Catholic, Methodist, Latter Day Saints.

Principal holidays: New Year's Day, Good Friday, Easter Monday, Anzac, Independence Day, Whit Monday, National Women's Day, Christmas Day, Boxing Day.

Business hours: 8–12 and 1:30–4:30 Mon.–Fri.

Customs: Traditional and religious customs observed, with emphasis on character and proper behavior.

Yemen. Republic of Yemen, located in the Middle East on the Arabian peninsula along the Gulf of Aden and the Red Sea, with eleven provinces (*Liwa'*).

Capital: Sana'a.

Language: Arabic (official), English.

Religion: Muslim (majority), Christian, Hindu.

Principal holidays: New Year's Day, Leilat al-Meiraj, Eid al-Fitr, Labor Day, Eid al-Adha, Corrective Movement Anniversary, Muharram, Islamic New Year, Mouloud (Prophet's Birthday), National Day.

Business hours: 8–12:30 and 4–7 Mon.–Wed.; 8–11 Thur.

Customs: Emphasis on traditional and religious customs and traditional male-female roles; normal business etiquette, with respect for Islamic practices.

Yugoslavia. Federal Republic of Yugoslavia (Serbia and Montenegro), newly created republic located in the southern half of former Yugoslavia in southern central Europe along the Adriatic Sea.

Capital: Belgrade.

Language: Serbian (official), Macedonian, Slovenian, Albanian, Hungarian.

Religion: Eastern Orthodox (majority), Roman Catholic, Muslim.

Principal holidays: New Year's Day, Labor Days, Veterans' Day, Republic Days.

Business hours: 7–3 Mon.–Fri.

Customs: Traditional and religious customs observed, with social and business activities severely disrupted by war against the former Yugoslav republics of Bosnia-Herzegovina and Croatia.

Zaïre. Republic of Zaïre, located south of the Central African Republic in central Africa, with ten regions and the capital city.

Capital: Kinshasa.

Language: French (official), Swahili, Lingala, other African dialects.

Religion: Roman Catholic (majority), Protestant, Muslim, local traditional beliefs.

Principal holidays: New Year's Day, Day of the Martyrs of Independence, Labor Day, Anniversary of the Popular Movement of the Revolution, Fishermen's Day, Independence Day, Parents' Day, Youth Day, Three-Z Day (anniversary of name change to Zaïre), Army Day, Anniversary of the Second Republic, Christmas Day.

Business hours: 7–5 Mon.–Fri.; 7:30–12 Sat.

Customs: Numerous traditional ethnic customs observed; emphasis on courtesy and respect for others.

Zambia. Republic of Zambia, located south of Zaïre in southern central Africa, with nine provinces.

Capital: Lusaka.

Language: English (official), about seventy native languages.

Religion: Christian (majority), Muslim, Hindu, indigenous beliefs.

Principal holidays: New Year's Day, Youth Day, Easter, Labor Day, Africa Freedom Day, Heroes' Day, Unity Day, Farmers' Day, Independence Day, Christmas Day.

Business hours: 8–1 and 2–5 Mon.–Fri.

Customs: Traditional customs observed, with both matriarchal and patriarchal extended families; emphasis on respect for others, particularly elderly and tribal heads.

Zimbabwe. Republic of Zimbabwe, located north of South Africa in southern Africa, with eight provinces.

Capital: Harare.

Language: English (official), numerous indigenous languages.

Religion: Christian (majority), Hindu, Muslim, indigenous beliefs.

Principal holidays: New Year's Day, Easter, Independence Day, Workers' Day, Africa Day, Heroes' Day, Christmas.

Business hours: 8 or 8:30–5 or 5:30 Mon.–Fri.

Customs: Blend of traditional and modern, Western-style customs (in urban areas); emphasis on courteous, conservative behavior, with European influences but less formality in business.

NATIONALITY AND ETHNIC DESIGNATIONS

When you are writing to people in other countries, it is very important to use the proper nationality designations and to know the correct ethnic group to which your contacts belong. Most people are sensitive about their nationality and ethnicity; even those who aren't will expect you to describe them accurately, just as citizens of the United States expect to be called Americans, not United Stateans.

The following list provides the proper noun and adjective forms for the different nationalities throughout the world:

He is a *Filipino* [noun] and observes *Philippine* [adjective] customs.

Principal ethnic groups in each country are also listed, and the majority group is indicated when it comprises more than 50 percent of the population.

NATIONALITY

Country	Noun	Adjective	Ethnic Group
Afghanistan	Afghan(s)	Afghan	Pashtun, Tajik, Uzbek, Hazara
Albania	Albanian(s)	Albanian	Albanian (majority), Greek, Vlach, Gypsy, Serb, Bulgarian
Algeria	Algerian(s)	Algerian	Arab (majority), Berber, European
Andorra	Andorran(s)	Andorran	Catalan (majority), Spanish, Andorran, French

NATIONALITY

Country	Noun	Adjective	Ethnic Group
Angola	Angolan(s)	Angolan	Ovimbundu, Kimbundu, Bakongo, Mestico, European
Antigua and Barbuda	Antiguan(s)	Antiguan	African (majority), Lebanese, Syrian, European
Argentina	Argentine(s)	Argentine	European (majority: Spanish, Italian), Indian, Mestizo, Arab
Armenia	Armenian(s)	Armenian	Armenian (majority), Kurd, Russian
Australia	Australian(s)	Australian	European (majority), Asian, aborigine
Austria	Austrian(s)	Austrian	German (majority), Croatian, Slovene
Azerbaijan	Azerbaijani(s) *or* Azeri(s)	Azerbaijani	Azerbaijani (majority), Armenian, Russian, Lezhi, Avar, Ukrainian, Tatar, Jewish
Bahamas	Bahamian(s)	Bahamian	Black (majority), white (British, North American)
Bahrain	Bahraini(s)	Bahraini	Bahraini (majority), Asian, Iranian, other Arab
Bangladesh	Bangladeshi(s)	Bangladesh	Bengali (majority), Bihari, tribals
Barbados	Barbadian(s)	Barbadian	African (majority), white, mixed
Belarus	Belorussian(s)	Belorussian	Belorussian (majority), Russian, Ukrainian, Polish, Jewish
Belgium	Belgian(s)	Belgian	Fleming (majority), Walloon, mixed
Belize	Belizean(s)	Belizean	Creole, Mestizo, Maya, Garifuna
Benin	Beninese	Beninese	African (Fon, Adja, Bariba, Yoruba)
Bhutan	Bhutanese	Bhutanese	Bhote (majority), Nepalese, tribals

NATIONALITY

Country	Noun	Adjective	Ethnic Group
Bolivia	Bolivian(s)	Bolivian	Quechua, Aymara, European, mixed
Bosnia-Herzegovina	Bosnian(s)	Bosnian	Muslim Slav, Serbian, Croatian
Botswana	Motswana (*sing.*) or Batswana (*pl.*)	Batswana *or* Botswanan	Batswana, Kalanga, Basarwa, Kgalagadi
Brazil	Brazilian(s)	Brazilian	Portuguese, Italian, German, Japanese, Amerindian, African, Jewish, Arab
Brunei Darussalam	Bruneian(s)	Bruneian	Malay (majority), Chinese
Bulgaria	Bulgarian(s)	Bulgarian	Bulgarian (majority), Turk, Gypsy, Macedonian, Armenian, Russian
Burkina Faso	Burkinabe	Burkinabe	Mossi, Gurunsi, Senufo, Lobi, Bobo, Mande, Fulan
Burundi	Burundian(s)	Burundi	Hutu (majority: Bantu), Tutsi (Hamitic), Twa (pygmy), Rwandan, Zairian, European, South Asian
Cambodia (formerly Kampuchea)	Cambodian(s) (Kampuchean[s])	Cambodian (Kampuchean)	Khmer (majority: Cambodian), Chinese
Cameroon	Cameroonian(s)	Cameroonian	Cameroon Highlander, Bantu, Kirdi, Fulani, Nigritic, other African
Canada	Canadian(s)	Canadian	British, French, other European, mixed
Cape Verde	Cape Verdean(s)	Cape Verdean	Creole (majority: Mulatto), African, European
Central African Republic	Central African(s)	Central African	Baya, Banda, Mandija, Sara, Mboum, M'Baka, European

NATIONALITY

Country	Noun	Adjective	Ethnic Group
Chad	Chadian(s)	Chadian	200 groups, including Arab, Toubou, Fulbe, Sara, Ngambaye, and nonindigenous
Chile	Chilean(s)	Chilean	European (majority), Indian
China	Chinese	Chinese	Han Chinese (majority), Zhuang, Uygur, Korean, other
Colombia	Colombian(s)	Colombian	Mestizo (majority), Caucasian, Mulatto
Comoros	Comoran(s)	Comoran	Arab, African, East Indian
Congo	Congolese	Congolese *or* Congo	75 groups (majority: Bantu), European
Costa Rica	Costa Rican(s)	Costa Rican	Spanish, Indian
Croatia	Croatian(s)	Croatian	Croatian
Cuba	Cuban(s)	Cuban	Spanish, African
Cyprus	Cypriot(s)	Cypriot	Greek (majority), Turk
Czech Republic	Czech(s)	Czech	Czech (majority), Slovak, Hungarian, German, Polish, Ukrainian, Russian
Denmark	Dane(s)	Danish	Scandinavian, Eskimo, Faeroese, German
Djibouti	Djiboutian	Djiboutian	Somali (majority: Issa), Afar, French, Italian, Arab, Ethiopian
Dominica	Dominican(s)	Dominican	Black, Carib-Indian
Dominican Republic	Dominican(s)	Dominican	White, black, mixed
Ecuador	Ecuadorian(s)	Ecuadorian	Mestizo (majority), Indian, Spanish, African
Egypt	Egyptian(s)	Egyptian	Eastern Hamitic (majority), Bedouin, Nubian
El Salvador	Salvadoran(s)	Salvadoran	Mestizo (majority), Indian

NATIONALITY

Country	Noun	Adjective	Ethnic Group
Equatorial Guinea	Equatorial Guinean(s)	Equatorial Guinean	Fang (majority), Bubi
Estonia	Estonian(s)	Estonian	Estonian (majority), Russian, Ukrainian, Belorussian, Finn, Jewish
Ethiopia	Ethiopian(s)	Ethiopian	Oromo, Amhara, Tigrean, Sidama, Shankella
Fiji	Fijian(s)	Fijian	Indian, Fijian, European
Finland	Finn(s)	Finnish	Finn (majority), Swede, Lapp, Gypsy
France	Frenchman, Frenchwoman (*sing.*), French (*pl.*)	French	European, Mediterranean, North African, Indochinese, Basque
Gabon	Gabonese	Gabonese	Fang, Eshira, Bapounou, Bateke, other African, European
The Gambia	Gambian(s)	Gambian	Mandinka, Fula, Wolof, Jola, other
Georgia	Georgian(s)	Georgian	Georgian (majority), Armenian, Russian, Azerbaijani, Ossetian, Greek, Abkhazian
Germany	German(s)	German	German (majority), Slavic, Danish
Ghana	Ghanaian	Ghanaian	Akan, Moshi-Dagomba, Ewe, Ga, other
Greece	Greek(s)	Greek	Greek (majority), Turk
Grenada	Grenadian(s)	Grenadian	African descent
Guatemala	Guatemalan(s)	Guatemalan	Maya (majority), Mestizo
Guinea	Guinean(s)	Guinean	Foulah, Malinke, Soussous, other tribal
Guinea-Bissau	Guinea-Bissauan(s)	Guinea-Bissauan	African (majority), European, Mulatto
Guyana	Guyanese	Guyanese	East Indian, (majority), African, mixed

NATIONALITY

Country	Noun	Adjective	Ethnic Group
Haiti	Haitian(s)	Haitian	African descent, Mulatto, European
Honduras	Honduran(s)	Honduran	Mestizo (majority), Indian
Hungary	Hungarian(s)	Hungarian	Hungarian (majority), German, Slovak, Romanian, Gypsy
Iceland	Icelander(s)	Icelandic	Descendants of Norwegian and Celtic
India	Indian(s)	Indian	Indo-Aryan (majority), Dravidian, Mongoloid
Indonesia	Indonesian(s)	Indonesian	Malay, Chinese, Irianese
Iran	Iranian(s)	Iranian	Persian (majority), Azerbaijani, Kurd
Iraq	Iraqi(s)	Iraqi	Arab (majority), Kurd, Turk
Ireland	Irishman, Irish-woman (*sing.*), Irish (*pl.*)	Irish	Celtic, English
Israel	Israeli(s)	Israeli	Jewish (majority), Arab
Italy	Italian(s)	Italian	Italian (majority), German, French, Slovene, Albanian
Ivory Coast (Côte d'Ivoire)	Ivorian(s)	Ivorian	Baule, Bete, Senufo, Malinke, other African, Lebanese, French
Jamaica	Jamaican(s)	Jamaican	African (majority), Chinese, white, East Indian, mixed
Japan	Japanese	Japanese	Japanese (majority), Korean
Jordan	Jordanian(s)	Jordanian	Arab (majority), Circassian, Armenian
Kazakhstan	Kazakh(s)	Kazakh	Kazakh (majority), Russian, German, Ukrainian
Kenya	Kenyans(s)	Kenyan	Kikuyu, Luo, Luhya, other tribal, Asian, European, Arab

NATIONALITY

Country	Noun	Adjective	Ethnic Group
Kirghizia (Kyrgyzstan)	Kirghiz (Kyrgyz)	Kirghiz (Kyrgyz)	Kirghiz (Kyrgyz), Russian, Uzbek, Ukrainian, German, Tatar
Kiribati	Kiribatian(s)	Kiribati	Micronesian (majority), Polynesian
Korea (North)	Korean(s)	Korean	Korean
Korea (South)	Korean(s)	Korean	Korean (majority), Chinese
Kuwait	Kuwaiti(s)	Kuwaiti	Kuwaiti, other Arab, Iranian, Indian, Pakistani
Laos	Lao	Laotian *or* Lao	Lao, Mon-Khmer, Thai, Meo, Yao, other
Latvia	Latvian(s)	Latvian	Latvian (majority), Russian, Belorussian, Ukrainian, Polish
Lebanon	Lebanese	Lebanese	Arab (majority), Armenian, Palestinian
Lesotho	Mosotho (*sing.*), Basotho (*pl.*)	Basotho	Sotho (majority), European, Asian
Liberia	Liberian(s)	Liberian	Indigenous tribal (majority), Americo-Liberian
Libya	Libyan(s)	Libyan	Berber and Arab (majority), Egyptian, Pakistani, Greek, Turk, Indian, other
Liechtenstein	Liechtensteiner(s)	Liechtenstein	Alemannic (majority), Italian
Lithuania	Lithuanian(s)	Lithuanian	Lithuanian (majority), Russian, Belorussian, Ukrainian, Polish, Jewish
Luxembourg	Luxembourger(s)	Luxembourg	Celtic base with French and German mixture, other European
Macedonia	Macedonian(s)	Macedonian	Macedonian

NATIONALITY

Country	Noun	Adjective	Ethnic Group
Madagascar	Malagasy	Malagasy	Malayan-Indonesian tribes (majority), Arab, African
Malawi	Malawian(s)	Malawian	Chewa (majority), Nyanja, Lomwe, other Bantu
Malaysia	Malaysian(s)	Malaysian	Malay (majority), Chinese, Indian
Maldives	Maldivian(s)	Maldivian	Sinhalese, Dravidian, Arab mixture
Mali	Malian(s)	Malian	Mande, Peul, Voltaic, Songhai, Tuareg, Moor
Malta	Maltese	Maltese	Italian, Arab, French, Spanish, English
Marshall Islands	Marshallese	Marshallese	Micronesian
Mauritania	Mauritanian(s)	Mauritanian	Arab-Berber (majority), Moor, black, mixed
Mauritius	Mauritian(s)	Mauritian	Indo-Mauritian (majority), Creole, Sino-Mauritian, Franco-Mauritian
Mexico	Mexican(s)	Mexican	Mestizo (majority), Amerindian, white
Micronesia	Micronesian(s)	Micronesian	Micronesian, Polynesian
Moldova	Moldovian(s)	Moldovian	Moldovian (majority), Ukrainian, Russian, Gagauz, Jewish, Bulgarian
Monaco	Monacan(s) or Monégasque(s)	Monacan or Monégasque	French (majority), Italian, Monégasque
Mongolia	Mongolian(s)	Mongolian	Mongol (majority), Kazakh, Chinese, Russian
Morocco	Moroccan(s)	Moroccan	Arab-Berber (majority), Jewish, other
Mozambique	Mozambican(s)	Mozambican	Bantu tribes (majority), Euro-African, Indian, European

NATIONALITY

Country	Noun	Adjective	Ethnic Group
Myanmar (formerly Burma)	Burmese	Burmese	Burman (majority), Karen, Shan, Rakhine, Chinese, other
Namibia	Namibian(s)	Namibian	Ovambo (majority), Kavango, Herero, Damara, other
Nauru	Nauruan(s)	Nauruan	Nauruan (majority), other Pacific Islanders, Chinese, European
Nepal	Nepalese	Nepalese	Tribal descendants of Indian, Tibetan, and Central Asian migrants
The Netherlands	Dutchman, Dutchwoman (*sing.*), Dutch (*pl.*)	Dutch	Dutch (majority), Indonesian
New Zealand	New Zealander(s)	New Zealand	European (majority), Maori, Pacific Islander
Nicaragua	Nicaraguan(s)	Nicaraguan	Mestizo (majority), white, black, Indian
Niger	Nigerian(s)	Nigerian	Hausa (majority), Djerma, Fulani, Tuareg, Arab, French, other
Nigeria	Nigerian(s)	Nigerian	250 tribal groups (including Hausa, Fulani, Yoruba, Ibos), other
Norway	Norwegian(s)	Norwegian	Germanic, Lapp
Oman	Omani(s)	Omani	Arab (majority), Baluchi, Zanzibari, Indian, Pakistani
Pakistan	Pakistani(s)	Pakistani	Punjabi (majority), Sindhi, Pushtun (Iranian), Urdu, Baluchi, Muhajir
Panama	Panamanian(s)	Panamanian	Mestizo (majority), West Indian, white, Indian
Papua New Guinea	Papua New Guinean(s)	Papua New Guinean	Papuan, Melanesian, Pygmy, Chinese, Australian, Polynesian

NATIONALITY

Country	Noun	Adjective	Ethnic Group
Paraguay	Paraguayan(s)	Paraguayan	Mestizo (majority), white, Indian, black
Peru	Peruvian(s)	Peruvian	Indian, Mestizo, white, black, Asian
Philippines	Filipino(s)	Philippine	Christian Malay (majority), Muslim Malay, Chinese, American, Spanish
Poland	Pole(s)	Polish	Polish (majority), Ukrainian, Belorussian
Portugal	Portuguese	Portuguese	Homogeneous Mediterranean stock, African descendants
Qatar	Qatari(s)	Qatari	Arab, Pakistani, Indian, Iranian, other
Romania	Romanian(s)	Romanian	Romanian (majority), Hungarian, German, Ukrainian, other
Russia	Russian(s)	Russian	Russian (majority), Tatar, Ukrainian, Chuvash, Belorussian, Baskir, Jewish
Rwanda	Rwandan(s)	Rwandan	Hutu (majority), Tutsi, Twa (Pygmy)
Saint Kitts and Nevis	Kittsian(s), Nevisian(s)	Kittsian, Nevisian	Black African
Saint Lucia	Saint Lucian(s)	Saint Lucian	African, East Indian, Caucasian, mixed
Saint Vincent and the Grenadines	St. Vincentian(s) *or* Vincentian(s)	St. Vincentian *or* Vincentian	Black African descendants, mixed
San Marino	Sanmarinese	Sanmarinese	Sanmarinese (majority), Italian
São Tomé and Príncipe	São Toméan(s)	São Toméan	Portuguese-African (majority), African
Saudi Arabia	Saudi(s)	Saudi *or* Saudi Arabian	Arab (majority), Afro-Asian

NATIONALITY

Country	Noun	Adjective	Ethnic Group
Senegal	Senegalese	Senegalese	Wolof, Serer, Fulani, Diola, Toucouleur, Mandingo, European, Lebanese
Seychelles	Seychellois	Seychelles	Seychellois (Creole)
Sierra Leone	Sierra Leonean(s)	Sierra Leonean	African (majority), European, Asian
Singapore	Singaporean(s)	Singapore	Chinese (majority), Malay, Indian, other
Slovak Republic	Slovak(s)	Slovak	Slovak (majority), Czech, Hungarian, German, Polish, Ukrainian, Russian
Slovenia	Slovene(s)	Slovene	Slovene
Solomon Islands	Solomon Island-er(s)	Solomon Islander	Melanesian (majority), Polynesian, Micronesian, European
Somalia	Somali(s)	Somali	Somali (majority), Bantu, Arab, European, Asian
South Africa	South African(s)	South African	Black (majority), white, Asian, Indian
Spain	Spaniard(s)	Spanish	Spanish (majority), Catalan, Galician, Basque
Sri Lanka	Sri Lankan(s)	Sri Lankan	Sinhalese (majority), Tamil, Moor, Burgher, Malay, Veddha
Sudan	Sudanese	Sudanese	Black (majority), Arab, Beja, other
Suriname	Surinamer(s)	Surinamese	Hindustani, Creole, Javanese, Bush black
Swaziland	Swazi(s)	Swazi	African (majority), European, other
Sweden	Swede(s)	Swedish	Swedish (majority), Finnish, Lapp, European
Switzerland	Swiss	Swiss	German (majority), French, Italian, other European

NATIONALITY

Country	Noun	Adjective	Ethnic Group
Syria	Syrian(s)	Syrian	Arab (majority), Kurd, Armenian, other
Taiwan	Chinese	Chinese	Taiwanese (majority), mainland Chinese, aborigine
Tajikistan	Tajik(s)	Tajik	Tajik (majority), Uzbek, Russian, Tatar
Tanzania	Tanzanian(s)	Tanzanian	African (majority: over 100 groups), Asian, European, Arab
Thailand	Thai	Thai	Thai (majority), Chinese, other
Togo	Togolese	Togolese	Ewe, Mina, Kabye, other African, European, Syrian, Lebanese
Tonga	Tongan(s)	Tongan	Tongan (majority), other Polynesian, European
Trinidad and Tobago	Trinidadian(s), Tobagonian(s)	Trinidadian, Tobagonian	African, East Indian, mixed
Tunisia	Tunisian(s)	Tunisian	Arab (majority), European
Turkey	Turk(s)	Turkish	Turk (majority), Kurd
Turkmeni-stan	Turkmen	Turkmen	Turkmen (majority), Russian, Uzbek, Kazakh, Tatar, Ukrainian, Azerbaijani
Tuvalu	Tuvaluan(s)	Tuvaluan	Polynesian
Uganda	Ugandan(s)	Ugandan	African tribes (majority), European, Asian, Arab
Ukraine	Ukrainian(s)	Ukrainian	Ukrainian (majority), Russian, Belorussian, Moldavian, Polish
United Arab Emirates	Emirian(s)	Emirian	Emirian and other Arab, Iranian, Pakistani, Indian
United King-dom	Briton(s), British (*collective pl.*)	British	English (majority), Scottish, Irish, Welsh, Ulster, West Indian, Indian, Pakistani, other

NATIONALITY

Country	Noun	Adjective	Ethnic Group
United States of America	American(s)	American	White (majority), black, Asian, Pacific Islander, American Indian, Eskimo, Hispanic
Uruguay	Uruguayan(s)	Uruguayan	White (majority), Mestizo, black, Mulatto
Uzbekistan	Uzbek(s)	Uzbek	Uzbek (majority), Russian, Tadzhik, Kazakh, Tatar
Vanuatu	Vanuatuan(s)	Vanuatuan	Melanesian (majority), European, Polynesian, Micronesian
Venezuela	Venezuelan(s)	Venezuelan	Mestizo (majority), white, black, Indian
Vietnam	Vietnamese	Vietnamese	Vietnamese (majority), Chinese, Thai, Muong, Khmer, other
Western Samoa	Western Samoan(s)	Western Samoan	Samoan, Euronesian, other Pacific Islander, European
Yemen	Yemini(s)	Yemini	Arab (majority), Indian, Somali, European
Yugoslavia (Serbia and Montenegro)	Yugoslav(s)	Yugoslav	Serb (majority), Albania, Montenegrin, Hungarian
Zaïre	Zairian(s)	Zairian	Bantu tribes (majority), over 200 other tribes
Zambia	Zambian(s)	Zambian	Bantu tribes (majority), European
Zimbabwe	Zimbabwean(s)	Zimbabwean	Shona (majority), Ndebele, white, Asian, mixed

FOREIGN CURRENCIES

When your letters mention monetary amounts, it will be helpful to your foreign contacts if you enclose in parentheses after the U.S. dollars the equivalent amount in the other country's currency. Call your bank for up-to-the minute exchange rates.

The following list includes major denominations and fractional units (if any). Watch for changes in newly independent countries as they introduce their own currencies. Established countries also issue new currencies from time to time. (The *MRI Bankers' Guide to Foreign Currencies*, which describes the currencies of the world in detail, is updated regularly. It is available from Monetary Research International in Houston, Texas, by single copy or subscription.)

Country	Currency
Afghanistan	afghani (Af) = 100 puls
Albania	lek (ALL) = 100 quindars
Algeria	Algerian dinar (DZD) = 100 centimes
Andorra	franc (FFr) = 100 centimes; peseta (Pta) = 100 centimes
Angola	kwanza (AKZ) = 100 lwei
Antigua and Barbuda	East Caribbean dollar (EC$) = 100 cents
Argentina	peso (ARP), formerly austral (ARA) = 100 centavos
Armenia	ruble (Rub) = 100 kopeks (new currency to be introduced)
Australia	Australian dollar (A$) = 100 cents
Austria	Austrian schilling (Sch) = 100 groschen
Azerbaijan	ruble (Rub) = 100 kopeks (new currency to be introduced)
Bahamas	Bahamian dollar (Ba$) = 100 cents
Bahrain	Bahraini dinar (BHD) = 1,000 fils
Bangladesh	taka (BDT) = 100 poishas
Barbados	Barbados dollar (BBD) = 100 cents
Belarus	ruble (Rub) = 100 kopeks (new currency to be introduced)
Belgium	Belgian franc (BFr) = 100 centimes
Belize	Belizean dollar (B$) = 100 cents
Benin	CFA franc (CFA Fr) = 100 centimes
Bhutan	Ngultrum (Re) = 100 chetrums
Bolivia	boliviano (B$) = 100 centavos
Bosnia-Herzegovina	dinar (D) = 100 para
Botswana	pula (Pu) = 100 thebes

Brazil	cruzeiro (Cr) = 100 centavos
Brunei Darussalam	Brunei dollar (Br$) = 100 cents
Bulgaria	lev (Lv) = 100 stotinki
Burkina Faso	CFA franc (CFA Fr) = 100 centimes
Burundi	Burundi franc (BurFr) = 100 centimes
Cambodia	riel (CRI) = 100 sen
Cameroon	CFA franc (CFA Fr) = 100 centimes
Canada	Canadian dollar (Can$) = 100 cents
Cape Verde	Cape Verde escudo (CVE) = 100 centavos
Central African Republic	CFA franc (CFA Fr) = 100 centimes
Chad	CFA franc (CFA Fr) = 100 centimes
Chile	Chilean peso (Ch$) = 100 centavos
China	yuan (¥) = 10 jiao/mao or 100 fen
Colombia	Colombian peso (Col$) = 100 centavos
Comoros	Comoran franc (CFA Fr) = 100 centimes
Congo	CFA franc (CFA Fr) = 100 centimes
Costa Rica	Costa Rican colón (CRC) = 100 centimos
Croatia	Croatian dinar (D) = 100 para
Cuba	Cuban peso (Cub$) = 100 centavos
Cyprus	Cyprus pound (C£) = 100 cents
Czech Republic	koruna (Kcs) = 100 haler(u)
Denmark	Danish krone (DKr) = 100 øre
Djibouti	Djibouti franc (DjFr) = 100 centimes
Dominica	East Caribbean dollar (EC$) = 100 cents
Dominican Republic	Dominica peso (RD$) = 100 centavos
Ecuador	sucre (Su) = 100 centavos
Egypt	Egyptian pound (E£) = 100 piastres
El Salvador	colón (ES¢) = 100 centavos
Equatorial Guinea	CFA franc (CFA Fr) = 100 centimes
Estonia	ruble (Rub) = 100 kopeks, to be replaced with kroon
Ethiopia	Ethiopian birr (ETB) = 100 cents

Fiji	Fiji dollar (F$) = 100 cents
Finland	markka (F Mk) = 100 penni(a)
France	franc (FFr) = 100 centimes
Gabon	CFA franc (CFA Fr) = 100 centimes
The Gambia	Gambian dalasi (Di) = 100 bututs
Georgia	ruble (Rub) = 100 kopeks (new currency to be introduced)
Germany	deutsche mark (DM) = 100 pfennigs
Ghana	cedi (C) = 100 pesewas
Greece	drachma (Dr) = 100 leptae
Grenada	East Caribbean dollar (EC$) = 100 cents
Guatemala	quetzal (Q) = 100 centavos
Guinea	Guinea franc (FG)
Guinea-Bissau	peso (GBP) = 100 centavos
Guyana	Guyana dollar (Guy$) = 100 cents
Haiti	gourde (Gde) = 100 centimes
Honduras	lempira (L)= 100 centavos
Hungary	forint (Ft) = 100 fillér
Iceland	Icelandic krona (IKr) = 100 aurar
India	rupee (RS) = 100 paise
Indonesia	rupiah (Rp) = 100 sen
Iran	Iranian rial (RL) = 1/10 toman (1 toman = 10 rial)
Iraq	Iraqi dinar (ID) = 20 dirhams = 1,000 fils
Ireland	Irish pound (IR£) = 100 pence (penny)
Israel	New Israel shekel (NIS) = 100 agorot (*sing.* agora)
Italy	Italian lira (Lit) = 100 centisimi
Ivory Coast (Côte d'Ivoire)	CFA franc (CFA Fr) = 100 centimes
Jamaica	Jamaican dollar (J$) = 100 cents
Japan	Japanese yen (¥) = 100 sen
Jordan	Jordan dinar (JD) = 1,000 fils
Kazakhstan	ruble (Rub) = 100 kopeks (new currency to be introduced)

Kenya	Kenyan shilling (KSh) = 100 cents
Kirghizia (Kyrgyzstan)	ruble (Rub) = 100 kopeks (new currency to be introduced)
Kiribati	Australian dollar (A$) = 100 cents
Korea (North)	won (NKW) = 100 chon
Korea (South)	won (SKW) = 10 hwan = 100 chun
Kuwait	Kuwaiti dinar (KD) = 1,000 fils
Laos	Laotian kip (LAK) = 100 att
Latvia	ruble (Rub) = 100 kopeks (new currency to be introduced)
Lebanon	Lebanese pound (L£) = 100 piastres
Lesotho	loti (LSM) = 100 lisente
Liberia	Liberian dollar (L$) = 100 cents
Libya	Libyan dinar (LD) = 1,000 dirhams
Liechtenstein	Swiss franc (SFr) = 100 centimes
Lithuania	ruble (Rub) = 100 kopeks, to be replaced with litas
Luxembourg	Luxembourg franc (LFe) = 100 centimes
Macedonia	dinar (D) = 100 para (Yugoslav currency)
Madagascar	Malagasy franc (MGF) (1 ariary = 5 francs)
Malawi	kwacha (MK) = 100 tambala
Malaysia	ringgit (M$) = 100 sen
Maldives	Maldivian rufiyaa (MRF) = 100 laari
Mali	CFA franc (CFA Fr) = 100 centimes
Malta	Maltese lira (liri, Lm) = 100 cents
Marshall Islands	U.S. dollar (US$) = 100 cents
Mauritania	Mauritanian ouguiya (U) = 5 khoums
Mauritius	Mauritian rupee (MRe) = 100 cents
Mexico	Mexican peso (Mex$) = 100 centavos
Micronesia	U.S. dollar (US$) = 100 cents
Moldova	ruble (Rub) = 100 kopeks (leu to be introduced)
Monaco	French franc (FFr) = 100 centimes

Mongolia	tugrik (Tug) = 100 mongos
Morocco	Moroccan dirham (DH) = 100 centimes
Mozambique	Mozambique metical (M) = 100 centavos
Myanmar (formerly Burma)	kyak (Kt) = 100 pyas
Namibia	rand (R) = 100 cents (Namibian to be introduced)
Nauru	Australian dollar (A$) = 100 cents
Nepal	Nepalese rupee (Rs) = 100 paisa
The Netherlands	gulden (Gld) = 100 cents
New Zealand	New Zealand dollar (NZ$) = 100 cents
Nicaragua	Nicaraguan córdoba (C$) = 100 centavos
Niger	CFA franc (CFA Fr) = 100 centimes
Nigeria	naira (N) = 100 kobo
Norway	Norwegian krone (NKr) = 100 øre
Oman	Omani rial (RO) = 1,000 baiza
Pakistan	Pakistan rupee (Re) = 100 paisa
Panama	balboa (Ba) = 100 centesimos
Papua New Guinea	kina (K) = 100 toea
Paraguay	guaraní (G), replacing peso (1 guaraní = 100 pesos)
Peru	nuevo sol (PES) = 100 centavos, replacing inti (1,000 soles = 1 inti)
Philippines	Philippine peso (PP) = 100 centavos
Poland	zloty (Zl) = 100 groszy
Portugal	escudo (Esc) = 100 centavos
Qatar	Qatari riyal (QR) = 100 dirhams
Romania	leu (lei) = 100 ban(i)
Russia	ruble (Rub) = 100 kopeks
Rwanda	Rwanda franc (RwFr) = 100 centimes
Saint Kitts and Nevis	East Caribbean dollar (EC$) = 100 cents
Saint Lucia	East Caribbean dollar (EC$) = 100 cents

Saint Vincent and the Grenadines	East Caribbean dollar (EC$) = 100 cents
San Marino	Italian lira (L) and national coins
São Tomé and Príncipe	dobra (Db) = 100 centimos
Saudi Arabia	Saudi Arabian rial (SAR) = 100 halalas
Senegal	CFA franc (CFA Fr) = 100 centimes
Seychelles	Seychelles rupee (SR) = 100 cents
Sierra Leone	leone (Le) = 100 cents
Singapore	Singapore dollar (S$) = 100 cents
Slovak Republic	koruna (Kcs) = 100 haler(u)
Slovenia	tola(r), replacing Yugoslav dinar (D)
Solomon Islands	Solomon Islands dollar (SI$) = 100 cents
Somalia	Somali shilling (SoSh) = 100 cents
South Africa	rand (R) = 100 cents
Spain	peseta (Pta) = 100 centimos
Sri Lanka	Sri Lankan rupee (SL Re) = 100 cents
Sudan	Sudanese pound (Sud£) = 100 piastres
Suriname	Suriname guilder (S Gld) = 100 cents
Swaziland	lilangeni (E) = 100 cents
Sweden	krona (SKr) = 100 öre
Switzerland	Swiss franc (SFr) = 100 rappen or centimes
Syria	Syrian pound (S£) = 100 piastres
Taiwan	New Taiwan dollar (NT$) = 100 cents
Tajikistan	ruble (Rub) = 100 kopeks (new currency to be introduced)
Tanzania	Tanzanian shilling (TSh) = 100 cents
Thailand	baht (Bt) = 100 satangs
Togo	CFA franc (CFA Fr) = 100 centimes
Tonga	pa'anga (T$) = 100 senti
Trinidad and Tobago	Trinidad and Tobago dollar (TT$) = 100 cents
Tunisia	Tunisian dinar (TD) = 1,000 millimes
Turkey	Turkish lira (TL)

Turkmenistan	ruble (Rub) = 100 kopeks (new currency to be introduced)
Tuvalu	Australian dollar (A$) = 100 cents (*also* Tuvaluan dollar = 100 cents)
Uganda	Uganda shilling (USh) = 100 cents
Ukraine	ruble (Rub) = 100 kopeks (new currency to be introduced)
United Arab Emirates	dirham (Dh) = 100 fils
United Kingdom	pound sterling (£) = 100 pence (penny)
Uruguay	Uruguayan nuevo peso (UN$) = 100 centesimos
Uzbekistan	ruble (Rub) = 100 kopeks (new currency to be introduced)
Vanuatu	vatu (VT) = 100 centimes
Venezuela	bolívar (VBO) = 100 centimos
Vietnam	new dong (ND)
Western Samoa	Western Samoa dollar (S$) or tala (WST) = 100 sene
Yemen	Yemen riyal (YR) = 100 fils and Yemeni dinar (YD) = 1,000 fils
Yugoslavia	dinar (D) = 100 para
Zaïre	zaïre (Z) = 100 makuta
Zambia	Zambian kwacha (ZK) = 100 ngwee
Zimbabwe	Zimbabwe dollar (Z$) = 100 cents

SYSTEMS OF WEIGHTS AND MEASURES

Most countries have adopted the metric system, although traditional systems are still used in some countries or in certain localities within a country. The metric system, also called the International System, or SI (*Système internationale*), is used in the United States along with U.S. customary measures, a traditional system derived from the British imperial system. When you write to someone in another country, use metric rather than U.S. customary weights and measures. If the country or locality uses a traditional system, place the equivalent traditional amount in parentheses after your metric figure. If your guidebooks covering the country of interest to you do not include a complete table of its traditional weights and measures, contact the appropriate embassy or consulate for a list or inquire at the company with which you deal. Since some countries are still debating whether to adopt the SI system, you should periodically update the following list of selected countries.

Country	System of Weights and Measures
Afghanistan	Traditional
Albania	Metric
Algeria	Metric
Angola	Metric
Argentina	Metric
Armenia	Metric
Australia	Conversion to metric in progress
Austria	Metric
Azerbaijan	Metric
Bahamas	U.K. imperial
Bahrain	Metric
Bangladesh	Metric and U.K. imperial
Belarus	Metric
Belgium	Metric
Bolivia	Metric and old Spanish
Bosnia- Herzegovina	Metric
Botswana	Metric
Brazil	Metric
Bulgaria	Metric
Burundi	Metric and traditional
Canada	Metric and U.K. imperial
Chile	Metric and old Spanish
China	Metric and traditional
Colombia	Metric and old Spanish
Comoros	Metric
Costa Rica	Metric and old Spanish
Cuba	Metric, U.S., and old Spanish
Cyprus	Metric
Czech Republic	Metric
Denmark	Metric
Dominican Republic	Metric, U.K. imperial, and old Spanish

Ecuador	Metric and old Spanish
Egypt	Metric and traditional
El Salvador	Metric and traditional
Estonia	Metric
Ethiopia	Metric and traditional
Finland	Metric
France	Metric
Georgia	Metric
Germany	Metric
Greece	Metric
Guatemala	Metric and traditional
Haiti	Metric, U.K. imperial, and U.S.
Honduras	Metric, U.K. imperial, and old Spanish
Hungary	Metric
Iceland	Metric
India	Metric and traditional
Indonesia	Metric and traditional
Iran	Metric
Iraq	Metric
Ireland	Conversion to metric in progress
Israel	Metric
Italy	Metric
Japan	Metric
Jordan	Metric and traditional
Kazakhstan	Metric
Kirghizia (Kyrgyzstan)	Metric
Korea (North)	Metric and traditional
Korea (South)	Metric and traditional
Kuwait	Metric
Latvia	Metric
Lebanon	Metric and traditional
Liberia	Metric, U.K. imperial, and U.S.
Libya	Metric and traditional
Liechtenstein	Metric
Lithuania	Metric

Luxembourg	Metric
Macedonia	Metric and traditional
Madagascar	Metric
Malawi	Metric
Malaysia	Metric and U.K. imperial
Mexico	Metric
Moldova	Metric
Monaco	Metric
Mongolia	Metric
Morocco	Metric
Mozambique	Metric
Myanmar (Burma)	Metric and traditional
The Netherlands	Metric
New Zealand	Metric
Nicaragua	Metric
Nigeria	Metric
Norway	Metric
Oman	Metric
Pakistan	Metric
Panama	Metric and U.K. imperial
Papua New Guinea	Metric
Paraguay	Metric
Peru	Metric
Philippines	Metric and traditional
Poland	Metric
Portugual	Metric and traditional
Qatar	Metric
Romania	Metric and traditional
Russia	Metric
Singapore	Metric
Slovak Republic	Metric
Solomon Islands	Metric
Somalia	Metric
South Africa	Metric

Spain	Metric
Sri Lanka	Metric
Sudan	Metric
Suriname	Metric
Sweden	Metric
Switzerland	Metric
Syria	Metric and traditional
Tajikistan	Metric
Tanzania	Metric
Thailand	Metric and traditional
Tunisia	Metric and traditional
Turkey	Metric
Turkmenistan	Metric
Ukraine	Metric
United Kingdom	Metric and U.K. imperial
Uruguay	Metric
Uzbekistan	Metric
Vanuatu	Metric
Vietnam	Metric
Yugoslavia	Metric
Zaïre	Metric
Zimbabwe	Metric and U.S.

Appendix
    International Mail
    Information Sources

Index of Terms to Avoid or Consider Carefully

Subject Index

INTERNATIONAL MAIL

Regular mail is sent to other countries through the U.S. Postal Service and private carriers. Fast messages are frequently sent by fax, E-mail, telex, or cable. Information on U.S. Postal Service regulations pertaining to correspondence is given here, followed by information on private delivery services and a list of international dialing codes and time-zone differences for use in transmitting fax and other fast messages.

Postal Mail

The U.S. Postal Service has three categories of international mail:

1. Postal Union Mail is governed by the regulations of the Convention of the Universal Postal Union. It includes these classes of mail:

> LC mail (*Lettres et Cartes,* or letters and cards) includes letters, letter packages, postcards, and aerogrammes.
> AO mail (*Autres Objets,* or other articles) includes regular printed matter, books and sheet music, publishers' periodicals, matter for the blind, and small packets.

2. Parcel post, also called CP mail (*Colis Postaux,* or postal parcels), has one class of mail similar to domestic fourth-class, zone-rated parcel post.

3. Express Mail International Service, arranged by agreements with the postal authorities

in other countries, is a reliable, high-speed service to certain countries. It includes two classes, and items are insured against loss, damage, and rifling at no extra cost.

> Custom Designed Service may be picked up from any address or mailed at designated Express Mail postal facilities in accordance with the service agreement (Form 5631) between the mailer and the Postal Service.

> On Demand Service is available at designated Express Mail facilities for nonscheduled, expedited service to countries offering Express Mail International Service.

Most standard business letters transmitted through the U.S. Postal Service are sent as Postal Union LC mail (by air or ship). LC mail *Letters and letter packages* refers to mail containing personal handwritten or typewritten communications having the character of *current* correspondence. This mail may not contain current correspondence between persons other than the sender and addressee or persons residing with the addressee.

Size and Weight Limits. Letter envelopes and packages must be at least $5^1/2$ by $3^1/2$ inches and .007 inch thick and no more than 24 inches long or a total of 36 inches when the length is added to the sum of the girth, or height and depth combined.

Aerogrammes must be $3^9/16$ by $7^1/4$ inches in length and height folded. Private stock, which must be submitted to the Postal Service for approval, must consist of 18-pound, nonslippery, light blue paper with three sealing flaps. Inquire at your local post office for requirements concerning the printing on the enclosures.

Postcards must be at least $5^1/2$ by $3^1/2$ inches and .007 inch thick and no more than 6 by $4^1/4$ inches and .0095 inch thick.

The weight limit for letters and letter packages is 4 pounds. Weight and size limits for Express Mail International Service depend on regulations in the destination country.

Envelope Addresses. On airmail letters, either (1) write the words *PAR AVION* both on the address side to the left of the destination address and on the reverse side, or (2) affix Label 19 (available from your post office) on the front and back. Consult your local post office for appropriate labels to use with Express Mail International Service.

The right half of the address side of an envelope or card should be reserved for the destination address, postage, labels, and postal notations. Addresses in Russian, Greek, Arabic, Hebrew, Cyrillic, Japanese, or Chinese characters must have an interline English translation of the names of the post office and country of the addressee. The country name usually must be on the last line in all capitals:

Mrs. C. P. Lopez
The Lopez Company
46807 Puerto Vallarta, Jalisco
MEXICO

But addresses may follow either of the following styles if a postal delivery zone number is included:

Mr. David Hall
The Hall Company
1010 Clear Street
Ottawa On Canada
K1A 0B1

Mr. David Hall
The Hall Company
1010 Clear Street
Ottawa On K1A 0B1
CANADA

The return address, which should appear in the upper left corner of the envelope, must be complete and include the zip code and country of origin.

Special International Services for Letters.   For a fee, various services are available through Postal Union mail.

Certificates of mailing furnish evidence of mailing but no delivery receipt.

Registered mail gives added protection and security from dispatch to delivery. A delivery record is held at the destination post office unless the sender requests that it be sent back to the originating post office (Form 2865). A modest indemnity is provided on registered mail to most countries. (A relatively higher limit applies to Canada.)

Restricted delivery, depending on the rules of the destination country, limits who may receive an item.

Recall of an item to change an address is possible if the destination country provides this service.

Special delivery is available depending on the regulations of the destination country.

International reply coupons, which the addressee can exchange for postage in the destination country, enable the sender to prepay a reply.

International business reply service is similar to domestic business reply mail. Envelopes and cards can be distributed in other countries for return to the United States, with postage paid for by the business-reply mailer (follow the printing requirements of the Postal Service).

The *International Mail Manual,* published by the U.S. Postal Service, contains all current regulations and fees pertaining to every country of the world and is available by subscription from the Superintendent of Documents, U.S. Government Printing Office, Washington, DC 20402.

Private Mail

Private companies, such as Federal Express, United Parcel Service, Airborne Express, and DHL Worldwide Express, provide rapid courier service for letters and documents to most places in the world. Depending on the destination, delivery is often made in one to three days. Frequently, a document is delivered overnight to a distribution center, such as Amsterdam, and routed from there to its final destination.

Each company has its own regular and special services and its own set of rates and regulations. Since prices, services, and areas covered may vary from one company to another and since all of these items may change from time to time, periodically request new booklets or brochures so that you can compare schedules and prices. For telephone numbers, look under "Delivery Services" in your local *Yellow Pages.*

Although the major private courier services will set up an account for you and provide pickup services, you can also deliver your letters and documents to a local mail service, such as Mail Boxes Etc. or Nationwide Postal Centers. Such services frequently offer a variety of mail alternatives, including postal mail, private mail, and fax service.

If you need to monitor delivery at the destination, private courier companies have sophisticated computer-tracking systems and can usually tell you exactly when a letter or document arrived and who signed for it. The service company can clear your material through customs when needed or work with your receiver's broker. Check with each company for specific regulations concerning insurance coverage and declarations procedure.

Dialing Codes and Time Differences

To send fax or other dial-in fast messages, you need to know the country code, city code, and local number. The following list provides dialing codes and time differences for most countries and their major cities throughout the world. (*Note*: The two countries of former Czechoslovakia are listed together as Czech and Slovak republics. The listing for former Yugoslavia includes the emerging republics. Countries of the former USSR are listed individually.) To call a number in another country, dial as follows: 011 + country code + city code + local number. If your system or subscriber service requires additional access codes, follow the instructions of the system or service.

To determine the time in another country, check the time differences, calculated from eastern standard time, given in the following list. (Check with your contacts to determine whether standard time or a form of daylight savings time applies in their country.) For example, if you want to know if a fax being sent to Bonn will arrive the same day and it is 9 a.m. eastern standard time, add six hours (+6) to determine the time in Bonn: 3 p.m.

International dialing codes change from time to time, particularly as new ones are added each year. Contact your long-distance telephone company periodically and request a current list to update the following information.

Country Code	City Code	Time Difference (EST)
Albania 355	Durres 52, Elbassan 545, Gjirocastra 726, Korce 824, Tirane 42	+7
Algeria 213	None required	+6
Andorra 33	All points 628	+6
Angola 244	All points area code 2 plus 6 digits	+6
Argentina 54	Buenos Aires 1, Cordoba 51, La Plata 21, Rosario 41	+2
Armenia 7	All points 885	+8
Australia 61	Adelaide 8, Brisbane 7, Melbourne 3, Sydney 2	+15
Austria 43	Graz 316, Linz Donau 732, Vienna 1 or 222	+6

Azerbaijan 7	Bakic 8922, Sumgait 89264	+8
Bahrain 973	None required	+8
Bangladesh 880	Barisal 431, Chittagong 31, Dhaka 2, Khulna 41	+11
Belarus 7	Minsk 0172, Mogilev 0222	+8
Belgium 32	Antwerp 3, Brussels 2, Ghent 91, Liège 41	+6
Belize 501	Belize City 2, Corozal Town 4, Punta Gorda 7	−1
Benin 229	None required	+6
Bhutan 975	None required	+10$^{1/2}$
Bolivia 591	Cochabamba 42, La Paz 2, Santa Cruz 3 plus 6 digits	+1
Botswana 267	Francistown 21, Jwaneng 380, Kanye 340, Lobatse 330, Gaborone—none required	+7
Brazil 55	Belo Horizonte 31, Rio de Janeiro 21, São Paulo 11	+2
Brunei Darussalam 673	Bandar Seri Begawan 2, Kuala Belait 3, Tutong 4	+13
Bulgaria 359	Plovdiv 32, Rousse (Ruse) 82, Sofia 2, Varna 52	+7
Burkina Faso 226	None required	+5
Burundi 257	Bubanza 42, Bujumbura 22, Bururi 50, Cibitoke 41, Gitega 40, Muramuya 43, Muvaro 44, Ngarara 23, Ngozi 30	+7
Cambodia 855	Phnom Penh 23	+12
Cameroon 237	None required	+6
Canada	Dial 1 + area code + local number	0 (Ottawa)
Cape Verde 238	None required	+4
Central African Republic	All points area code 61 plus 4 digits	+6
Chad 235	Abeche and Mondou 69 plus 4 digits, Faya 50 plus 4 digits, N'djamena 51 plus 4 digits, Sarh 68 plus 4 digits	+6

Chile 56	Concepción 41, Santiago 2, Valparaiso 32	+1
China 86	Beijing (Peking) 1, Fuzhou 591, Ghuangzhou (Canton) 20, Shanghai 21	+13
Colombia 57	Barranquilla 58, Bogotá 1, Cali 23, Medellin 4	0
Comoros 269	Anjouan 71, Moheli 72, Moroni 73	+9
Congo 242	None required	+6
Costa Rica 506	None required	−1
Cyprus	Limassol 51, Nicosia 2, Paphos 61	+7
Czech and Slovak Republics 42	Bratislava 7, Brno 5, Havirov 6994, Ostrava 69, Prague (Praha) 2	+6
Denmark 45	Aalborg 8, Aarhus 6, Copenhagen 3 plus 7 digits (suburbs 4 plus 7 digits), Oddense 7	+6
Djibouti 253	None required	+8
Ecuador 593	Ambato 2, Cuenca 7, Guayaquil 4, Quito 2	0
Egypt 20	Alexandria 3, Aswan 97, Asyut 88, Benha 13, Cairo 2	+7
El Salvador 503	None required	−1
Equatorial Guinea 240	Bata 8 plus 4 digits, Malabo 9 plus 4 digits	+6
Estonia 7	Tallinn 0142	+8
Ethiopia 251	Addis Ababa 1, Akaki 1, Asmara 4, Assab 3, Awassa 6	+8
Fiji 679	None required	+17
Finland 358	Espoo (Esbo) 0, Helsinki 0, Tampere (Tammerfors) 31, Turku (Abo) 21	+7
France 33	Lyon 7, Marseilles 91, Nice 93, Paris 1 plus 8 digits beginning with 3, 4, or 6	+6
Gabon 241	None required	+6

The Gambia 220	None required	+5
Georgia 7	Sukhumi 88122, Tblisi 8832	+8
Germany: East 37, Vest 49	East: Berlin 2, Dresden 51, Leipzig 41, Magdeburg 91; West: Berlin 30, Bonn 228, Frankfurt 69, Munich 89	+6
Ghana 233	Accra 21, Koforidua 81, Kumasi 51, Takoradi 31	+5
Greece 30	Athens (Athinai) 1, Iraklion (Kritis) 81, Larissa 41, Piraceus Pireefs 1	+7
Guatemala 502	Guatemala City 2, all others 9	−1
Guinea 224	Conakry 4, Kindia 61, Labe 51 Mamou 68	+5
Guinea-Bissau 245	None required; all numbers 6 digits beginning with 20, 21, 22, or 25	+5
Guyana 592	Bartica 5, Georgetown 2, New Amsterdam 3	+2
Haiti 509	Cap-Haitien 3, Cayes 5, Gonaive 2, Port-au-Prince 1	0
Honduras 504	None required	−1
Hungary 36	Budapest 1, Derbrecen 52, Gyor 96, Miskolc 46	+6
Iceland 354	Akureyri 6, Keflavik Naval Base 2, Reykjavík 1	+5
India 91	Bombay 22, Calcutta 33, Madras 44, New Delhi 11	$+10^{1/2}$
Indonesia 62	Jakarta 21, Medan 61, Semarang 24	+12
Iran 98	Esfahan 31, Mashad 51, Tabriz 41, Tehran 21	$+8^{1/2}$
Iraq 964	Baghdad 1, Basra 40, Kerbela 32, Kirkuk 50, Mousil 60, Najaf 33	+8
Ireland 353	Cork 21, Dublin 1, Galway 91, Limerick 6 or 61	+5
Israel 972	Haifa 4, Jerusalem 2, Ramat Gan 3, Tel Aviv 3	+7

Italy 39	Florence 55, Genoa 10, Milan 2, Naples 81, Rome 6	+6
Ivory Coast (Cote d'Ivoire) 225	None required	+5
Japan 81	Kyoto 75, Osaka 6, Sapporo 11, Tokyo 3, Yokohama 45	+14
Jordan 962	Amman 6, Irbid 2, Jerash 4, Karak 3, Ma'an 3	+7
Kazakhstan 7	Alma-Ata 3272, Chimkent 3252, Guryev 31222	+11
Kenya 254	Kisumu 35, Mombasa 11, Nairobi 2, Nakuru 37	+8
Kirghizia (Kyrgyzstan) 7	Osh 33222, Pishpek 3312	+11
Kiribati 686	None required	+17
Korea (South) 82	Inchon 32, Pusan (Busan) 51, Seoul 2, Taegu (Daegu) 53	+14
Kuwait 965	None required	+8
Latvia 7	Riga 0132	+8
Lebanon 961	Beirut 1, Juniyah 9, Tripoli 6, Zahlah 8	+7
Lesotho 266	None required	+7
Liberia 231	None required	+5
Libya	Benghazi 61, Misuratha 51, Tripoli 21, Zawai 23	+7
Liechtenstein 41	All points 75	+6
Lithuania 7	Vilnius 0122	+8
Luxembourg 352	None required	+6
Madagascar 261	Antananarivo 2, Diego Suarez 8, Fianarantsoa 7, Moramanja 4, Tatatave 5	+8
Malawi 265	Domasi 531, Makwasa 575, Zomba 50	+7
Malaysia 60	Ipoh 5, Johor Bahru 7, Kajang 3, Kuala Lumpur 3	+13
Maldives 960	None required	+10
Mali 223	None required+5	
Malta 356	None required+6	

Marshall Islands 692	Ebeye 871, Majuro 9	+17
Mauritania 222	None required	+5
Mauritius 230	None required	+9
Mexico	Acapulco 748, Cancún 988, Celaya 461, Cordoba 271, Culiacan 671, Guadalajara 36, Hermosillo 621, Jalapa 281, Leon 471, Mérida 99, Mexico City 5, Monterrey 83, Tampico 121, Tijuana 66, Toluca 721, Torreon 17, Veracruz 29	−1 (Mexico City)
Micronesia 691	Kosrae 370, Ponape 320, Truk 330, Yap 350	+16
Moldova 7	Kishinev 0422	+8
Monaco 33	All points 93	+6
Mongolia 976	Ulan Bator 1	+13
Morocco 212	Agadir 8, Beni-Mellal 48, El Jadida 34, Casablanca— none required	+5
Mozambique 258	Beira 3, Chokwe 21, Maputo 1, Nampula 6	+7
Namibia 264	Grootfontein 673, Keetmanshoop 631, Mariental 661	+7
Nauru 674	None required	+17
Nepal 977	None required	$+10^{1/2}$
The Netherlands 31	Amsterdam 20, Rotterdam 10, The Hague 70	+6
New Zealand 64	Auckland 9, Christchurch 3, Dunedin 24, Hamilton 71	+17
Nicaragua 505	Chinandega 341, Diriamba 42, Leon 311, Managua 2	−1
Niger 227	None required	+6
Nigeria 234	Lagos 1	+6
Norway 47	Bergen 5, Oslo 2, Stavanger 4, Trondheim 7	+6
Oman 968	None required	+9

Pakistan 92	Islamabad 51, Karachi 21, Lahore 42	+10
Panama 507	None required	0
Papua New Guinea 675	None required	+15
Paraguay 595	Asunción 21, Concepción 31	+2
Peru 51	Arequipa 54, Callao 14, Lima 14, Trujillo 44	0
Philippines 63	Cebu City 32, Davao 82, Iloilo City 33, Manila 2	+13
Poland 48	Crakow (Krakow) 12, Gdansk 58, Warsaw 22	+6
Portugal 351	Coimbra 39, Lisbon 1, Porto 2, Setubal 65	+5
Qatar 974	None required	+8
Romania 40	Bucharest 0, Cluj-Napoca 51, Constanta 16	+7
Russia 7	Magadan 41300, Moscow 095, St. Petersburg 812	+8
Rwanda 250	None required	+7
San Marino 39	All points 549	+6
São Tomé 239	All points area code 12 plus 5 digits	+5
Saudi Arabia 966	Hofuf 3, Jeddah 2, Makkah (Mecca) 2, Riyadh 1	+8
Senegal 221	None required	+5
Seychelles 248	None required	+9
Sierra Leone 232	Freetown 22, all other points 232	+5
Singapore 65	None required	+13
Solomon Islands 677	None required	+16
South Africa 27	Cape Town 21, Durban 31, Johannesburg 11	+7
Spain 34	Barcelona 3, Madrid 1, Seville 54, Valencia 6	+6
Sri Lanka 94	Colombo Central 1, Kandy 8, Kotte 1	$+10^{1/2}$

Suriname 597	None required	+2
Swaziland 268	None required	+7
Sweden 46	Goteborg 31, Malmo 40, Stockholm 8, Vasteras 21	+6
Switzerland 41	Basel 61, Bern 31, Geneva 22, Zurich 1	+6
Syria 963	Aleppo 21, Damascus 11, Halab 21, Hama 331, Homs 31	+8
Taiwan 886	Kaohsiung 7, Tainan 6, Taipei 2	+13
Tajikistan 7	Dushanbe 3772	+11
Tanzania 255	Dar es Salaam 51, Dodoma 61, Mwanza 68, Tanga 53	+8
Thailand 66	Bangkok 2, Burirum 44, Chanthaburi 39	+12
Togo 228	None required	+5
Tonga 676	None required	+18
Tunisia 216	Bizerte 2, Kairouan 7, Msel Bourguiba 2, Tunis 1	+6
Turkey 90	Adana 711, Ankara 4, Istanbul 1, Izmir 51	+7
Turkmenistan 7	Ashkhabad 3632, Chardzhou 37822	+10
Tuvalu 688	None required	+17
Uganda 256	Entebbe 42, Jinja 43, Kampala 41, Kyambogo 41	+8
Ukraine 7	Kharkiv 0572, Kyiv 044, Lviv 0322	+8
United Arab Emirates 971	Abu Dhabi 2, Ajman 6, Al Ain 3, Dubai 4, Sharjah 6	+9
United Kingdom	Belfast 232, Birmingham 21, Edinburgh 31, Glasgow 41, London (inner) 71, London (outer) 81, Manchester 61	+5
Uruguay 598	Canelones 332, Mercedes 532, Montevideo 2	+2
Vanuatu 678	None required	+16
Venezuela 58	Barquisimeto 51, Caracas 2, Maracaibo 61, Valencia 41	+1

Vietnam 84	Hanoi 4, Ho Chi Minh City 8	+12
Western Samoa 685	None required	–6
Yemen 967	Amran 2, Sanaa 2, Taiz 4, Yarim 4, Zabid 3	+8
Yugoslavia 38	Belgrade (Beograd) 11, Sarajevo 71, Zagreb 41	+6
Zaïre 243	Kinshasa 12, Lubumbashi 222	+6
Zambia 260	Chingola 2, Kitwe 2, Luanshya 2, Lusaka 1, Ndola 2	+7
Zimbabwe 263	Bulawayo 9, Harare 4, Mutare 20	+7

INFORMATION SOURCES

Extensive information about countries and regions is available, and the following publications and organizations are only a few examples. In addition, certain schools and training programs specialize in international communication and foreign languages (check your local *Yellow Pages*), and audio- and videocassettes are available (inquire at your local bookstore or library).

Books and Pamphlets

The following titles illustrate the type of material that is available for specific countries and regions. The list also includes general studies on international communication and language.

Background Notes: U.S. Government Printing Office, Washington, D.C., short country profiles of selected countries available by single copy, by set of about 160 countries, or by subscription, with irregular updates and new profiles.

The Complete Word Book, by Mary A. De Vries: Prentice Hall, Englewood Cliffs, New Jersey, 1991.

Culturgram: Brigham Young University, Provo, Utah, four-page country profiles of selected countries available by single copy or by set of about one hundred countries.

Do's and Taboos Around the World, edited by Roger E. Axtell, compiled by the Parker Pen Company: John Wiley & Sons, New York, 1990.

The Do's and Taboos of International Trade: A Small Business Primer, by Roger E. Axtell: John Wiley & Sons, New York, 1991.

Encountering the Chinese: A Guide for Americans, by Hu Wenzhong and Cornelius L. Grove: Intercultural Press, Yarmouth, Maine, 1991.

European Customs and Manners, by Nancy L. Braganti and Elizabeth Devine: Meadowbrook Press, New York, 1992.

Exporters' Guide to Federal Resources for Small Business: U.S. Government Printing Office, Washington, D.C., 1992.

Foreign Consular Offices in the United States: U.S. Government Printing Office, Washington, D.C., updated periodically.

From Nyet to Da: Understanding the Russians, by Yale Richmond: Intercultural Press, Yarmouth, Maine, 1992.

Information Please Almanac: Houghton Mifflin Company, Boston, updated annually.

Intercultural Communication, by Larry A. Samovar and Richard E. Porter: Wadsworth Publishing Company, Belmont, California, 1991.

International Business Communication, by David A. Victor: HarperCollins Publishers, New York, 1992.

The International Businesswoman of the 1990s, by Marlene L. Rossman: Praeger Publishers, New York, 1990.

International English Usage, by Loreto Todd and Ian Hancock: New York University Press, New York, 1987.

Japanese Etiquette and Ethics in Business, by Boye De Mente: NTC Business Books, Lincolnwood, Illinois, 1990.

Japanese Language and Culture for Business and Travel, by Kyoko Hijirida and Muneo Yoshikawa: University of Hawaii Press, Honolulu, 1987.

Key Officers of Foreign Service Posts: Guide for Business Representatives, Publication 7877: U.S. Government Printing Office, Washington, D.C., available by single copy or subscription.

Letitia Baldrige's Complete Guide to Executive Manners: Rawson Associates, New York, 1985, Chapter 5: "International Business Manners."

MRI Bankers' Guide to Foreign Currency: Monetary Research International, Houston, updated quarterly.

The Practical Writer's Guide, by Mary A. De Vries: New American Library, New York, 1986.

The Statesman's Year-Book, edited by Brian Hunter: St. Martin's Press, New York, updated annually.

The Travelers' Guide to Latin American Customs and Manners, by Elizabeth Devine and Nancy L. Braganti: St. Martin's Press, New York, 1988.

Understanding Arabs, by Margaret K. Nydell: Intercultural Press, Yarmouth, Maine, 1987.

The Universal Almanac: Andrews and McMeel, Kansas City, updated annually.

The World Almanac and Book of Facts: Pharos Books, New York, updated annually.

The World Factbook: World Bank Publications, Washington, D.C., profiles of two hundred countries updated annually.

World Travel Guide: Columbus Press Limited, London, updated annually.

Organizations

Numerous organizations provide information on other countries and regions, and the following are only a few examples of such useful sources. Contact those of interest and request a description of their services and publications.

Following this list are the names and addresses of U.S. embassies around the world and a list of telephone extensions and room numbers of Department of Commerce country desk officers.

American University, The BCIU [Business Council for International Understanding] Institute, 3301 New Mexico Avenue, N.W., Washington, DC 20016.

David M. Kennedy Center for International Studies, Brigham Young University, Publication Services, 280 HRCB, Provo, UT 84602.

Export-Import Bank of the United States, 811 Vermont Avenue, N.W., Washington, DC 20571.

Overseas Private Investment Corporation, 1615 M Street, N.W., Washington, DC 20527.

SIETAR [International Society for Intercultural Education, Training, and Research], 1505 22nd Street, N.W., Washington, DC 20037.

U.S. Department of Commerce, United States and Foreign Commercial Service, Room 3810, HCH Building, 14th and Constitution Avenue, N.W., Washington, DC 20230.

U.S. Department of Education, Center for International Education, Room 3053, ROB-3, 7th and D Streets, S.W., Washington, DC 20202.

U.S. Department of State, Bureau of Economic and Business Affairs, 2201 C Street, N.W., Room 6822, Washington, DC 20520.

U.S. Small Business Administration, Office of International Trade, 409 Third Street, S.W., Washington, DC 20416.

U.S. Trade and Development Program, 1621 North Kent Street, Room 309, Rosslyn, VA 22209.

U.S. Embassies

For convenience in locating quickly the country you want, the country name is stated first in the following address list. In your envelope address, however, it should be positioned on the last line as explained in the section on international mail earlier in this appendix:

Name of Person (if any)
Embassy of the United States of America
1054 Budapest
Szabadsagter 12
HUNGARY

Most of the addresses are those of an embassy. For Cuba, however, the address is for the U.S. Interests Section; for Malaysia, it is the U.S. High Commission; for Maldives, it is the U.S. Consulate.

Afghanistan: Wazir Akbar Khan Mina, Kabul.

Algeria: 4 Chemin Cheich Bachir Ibrahimi, BP 549, Alger-Gare 16000, Algiers.

Antigua and Barbuda: Queen Elizabeth Highway, St. John's (FPO Miami 34054, St. John's).

Argentina: Avenida Colombia 4300, Palermo, 1425 Buenos Aires.

Australia: Moonah Place, Canberra, ACT 2600.

Austria: Boltzmanngasse 16, A-1091 Vienna.

Bahamas: P.O. Box N-8197, Mosmar Building, Queen Street, Nassau.

Bahrain: P.O. Box 26431, Sheikh Isa Road, Manama.

Bangladesh: GPO Box No. 323 Ramna, Madani Avenue, Baridhara Model Town, Dhaka 1212.

Barbados: P.O. Box 302, Canadian Imperial Bank of Commerce Building, Broad Street, Bridgetown.

Belgium: Boulevard du Regént 27, B-1000 Brussels.

Belize, C.A.: Gabourel Lane and Hutson Street, Belize City.

Benin: BP 2012, Rue Caporal Anani Bernard, Cotonou.

Bolivia: Casilla 425, Edificio Banco Popular del Perú, Calle Colón 290, La Paz.

Botswana: P.O. Box 90, Gaborone.

Brazil: Lote 3, Setor de Embaixadas Sul, Avenue das Nações, 70.403 Brasília DF.

Brunei Darussalam: Teck Guan Plaza, 3rd Floor, Bandar Seri Begawan 2085.

Bulgaria: Boulevard A. Stamboliiski 1, Sofia.

Burkina Faso: 01 BP 35, Ouagadougou 01.

Burundi: BP 1720, Avenue des Etats-Unis, Chaussée Prince Rwagasore, Bujumbura.

Cameroon: BP 817, Rue Nachtigal, Yaoundé.

Canada: 100 Wellington Street, Ottawa, Ontario K1P 5T1.

Cape Verde: CP 201, Rua Hoji Ya Yenna 81, Praia, São Tiago.

Central African Republic: BP 924, Avenue President Dacko, Bangui.

Chad: BP 413, Avenue Félix Eboué, N'Djamena.

Chile: Agustinas 1343, Santiago.

China, People's Republic of: 3 Xiu Shui Bei Jie, Beijing 100600.

Colombia: Calle 38, No. 8-61, Bogotá.

Congo: BP 1015, Avenue Amílcar Cabral, Brazzaville.

Costa Rica: Pavas Frente Centro Comercial, Apartado 920-1200 Pavas, San José.

Cuba: U.S. Interests Section, Calzada entre L y M, Vedado, Havana.

Cyprus: Dositheos Street and Therissos Street, Lykavitos, Nicosia.

Czech Republic: Trziste 15, 125 48 Prague.

Denmark: Dag Hammarskjölds Allé 24, 2100 Copenhagen Ø.

Djibouti: BP 185, Villa Plateau du Serpent, Boulevard Maréchal Joffré.

Dominican Republic: Calle César Nicolás Pensón, Santo Domingo, DN.

Ecuador: Avenida 12 Octubre y Patria 120, Quito.

Egypt: 5 Sharia Latin America, Garden City, Cairo.

El Salvador: 25 Avenida Norte 1230, San Salvador.

Ethiopia: Entoto Street, P.O. Box 1014, Addis Ababa.

Fiji: P.O. Box 218, 31 Loftus Street, Suva.

Finland: Itäinen Puistotie 14A, 00140 Helsinki.

France: 2 Avenue Gabriel, 75008 Paris.

Gabon: BP 4000, Boulevard de la Mer, Libreville.

The Gambia: P.O. Box 19, Kairaba Avenue, Fajara, Banjul.

Germany, Federal Republic of: Deichmanns Avenue 29, W-5300 Bonn 2.

Ghana: P.O. Box 194, Ring Road East, Accra.

Greece: Leoforos Vassilissis Sofias 91, 106 60 Athens.

Grenada: P.O. Box 54, Point Salines, St. George's.

Guatemala: Avenida La Reforma 7-01, Zona 10, Guatemala City.

Guinea Republic: BP 603, Conakry.

Guinea-Bissau: CP 297, Avenida Domingos Ramos, 1067 Bissau Cedex.

Guyana: 31 Main Street, Georgetown.

Haiti: Boulevard Harry Truman, Cité de l'Exposition, Port-au-Prince.

Honduras, C.A.: Apartado Postal 26 C, Avenida La Paz, Tegucigalpa.

Hungary: 1054 Budapest, Szabadság tér 12.

Iceland: Laufásvegur 21, Reyjkavík.

India: Shanti Path Chanakyapuri, New Delhi 110 021.

Indonesia: Jalan Merdeka Selatan 5, Jakarta.

Iraq: P.O. Box 2447, 929/7/57 Hay Babel, Masba, Alwiyah, Baghdad.

Ireland: 42 Elgin Road, Ballsbridge, Dublin 4.

Israel: 71 Rehov Hayarkon, Tel Aviv 63903.

Italy: Via Vittorio Veneto 119A, 00187 Roma.

Ivory Coast (Côte d'Ivoire): BP 172, 5 Rue Jesse Owens, Abidjan 01.

Jamaica: Mutual Life Centre, 2 Oxford Road, Kingston 5.

Japan: 10-1, Akasaka 1-chrome, Minato-ku, Tokyo 107.

Jordan: P.O. Box 354, Jabal, Amman.

Kenya: P.O. Box 30137, Corner of Moi and Haile Selassie Avenues, Nairobi.

Korea, Republic of: 82 Sejong-no, Chongno-ku, Seoul.

Kuwait: P.O. Box 77, 13001 Safat, Arabian Gulf Street, Kuwait City.

Laos: Boite Postale 114, Rue Bartholonie, Vientiane.

Lebanon: Avenue de Paris, Imm. Ali Reza, Beirut.

Lesotho: P.O. Box 333, Maseru 100.

Liberia: P.O. Box 98, 111 United Nations Drive, Mamba Point, Monrovia.

Luxembourg: 22 Boulevard E Servais, 2535.

Madagascar: BP 620, 14-16 Rue Rainitovo, Antsahavola, 101 Antananarivo.

Malawi: P.O. Box 30016, Area 40, Flat 18, Lilongwe 3.

Malaysia: U.S. High Commission, P.O. Box 10035, 376 Jalan Tun Razak, 50700 Kuala Lumpur.

Maldives: U.S. Consulate, Rasheeda Mohamed Didi, Mandhu-Edhurage, Violet Magu, Malé.

Mali: BP 34, Angle Rue de Rochester NY et Rue Mohamed V, Bamako.

Malta: Development House, St. Anne Street, Floriana, Valletta.

Marshall Islands: P.O. Box 680, Majuro, 96960.

Mauritania: BP 222, Nouakchott.

Mauritius: Rogers House, President John F. Kennedy Street, Port Louis.

Mexico: Paseo de la Reforma 305, Col. Cuauhtemoc, 06500 Mexico City DF.

Micronesia: P.O. Box 1286, Kolonia, Pohnpei 96941.

Mongolia: Ulan Bator.

Morocco: BP 120, 2 Charia Marrakech, Rabat.

Mozambique: Caixa Postal 783, Maputo.

Myanmar (formerly Burma): P.O. Box 521, 581 Merchant Street, Yangon.

Nepal: Panipokhari, Kathmandu.

The Netherlands: Lange Voorhout 102, 2514 EJ The Hague.

New Zealand: P.O. Box 1190, 29 Fitzherbert Terrace, Wellington.

Nicaragua: Apartado 327, Km 4.5, Carretera Sur, Managua.

Niger: BP 11201, Yantala, Niamey.

Nigeria: 2 Eleke Crescent, Victoria Island, Lagos.

Norway: Drammensvn 18, 0255 Oslo 2.

Oman: P.O. Box 50202, Medinat Qaboos.

Pakistan: P.O. Box 1048, Diplomatic Enclave, Ramna 5, Islamabad.

Panama: Apartado 6959, Avenida Balboa, Entre Calle 37 y 38, Panama City 5.

Papua New Guinea: P.O. Box 1492, Port Moresby.

Paraguay: Casilla 402, Avenida Mcal López 1776, Asunción.

Peru: Apartado 1995, Avenida Garcilaso de la Vega 1400, Lima 100.

Philippines: 1201 Roxas Boulevard, Metro Manila.

Poland: Al. Ujazdowskie 29/31, 00-540 Warsaw.

Portugal: Avenida das Forças Armadas, 1600 Lisbon Codex.

Qatar: P.O. Box 2399, Doha.

Romania: Strada Tudor Arghezi 7-9, Bucharest.

Russian Federation: Novinsky Boulevard 19/23, Moscow.

Rwanda: BP 28, Boulevard de la Révolution, Kigali.

Saudi Arabia: P.O. Box 9041, Riyadh 11413.

Senegal: BP 49, Avenue Jean XXIII, Dakar.

Seychelles: P.O. Box 251, Victoria House, Victoria, Mahé.

Sierra Leone: Walpole and Siaka Stevens Streets, Freetown.

Singapore: 30 Hill Street, Singapore City 0617.

Solomon Islands: P.O. Box 561, Honiara.

South Africa: Thibault House, 7th Floor, Pretorius Street, Pretoria.

Spain: Serrano 75, 28006 Madrid.

Sri Lanka: P.O. Box 106, 210 Galle Road, Colombo 3.

Sudan: P.O. Box 699, Ali Abd al-Latif Avenue, Khartoum.

Suriname: P.O. Box 1821, Dr Sophie Redmondstraat 129, Paramaribo.

Swaziland: P.O. Box 199, Central Bank Building, Mbabane.

Sweden: Standvägen 101, 115 89 Stockholm.

Switzerland: Jubiläumsstrasse 93, 3005 Berne.

Syria: BP 29, Rue al-Mansour 2, Damascus.

Tanzania: P.O. Box 9123, Laibon Road, Dar es Salaam.

Thailand: 95 Wireless Road, Bangkok 10330.

Togo: BP 852, Angle Rue Pelletier Caventou et Rue Vauban, Lomé.

Trinidad: P.O. Box 752, 15 Queen's Park West, Port of Spain.

Tunisia: 144 Avenue de la Liberté, Tunis.

Turkey: Atatürk Bulvar 110, Ankara.

Uganda: P.O. Box 7007, Kampala.

United Arab Emirates: P.O. Box 4009, Abu Dhabi.

United Kingdom: Grosvenor Square, London, W1A 1AE.

Uruguay: Lauro Muller 1776, Montevideo.

Venezuela: Avenida Principal de La Floresta, Esquina Francisco de Miranda, La Floresta.

Western Samoa: P.O. Box 3430, Apia.

Yemen, Republic of: P.O. Box 1088, Sa'awan, Sana'a.

Yugoslavia: Box 5070, Belgrade.

Zaïre: BP 697, 310 Avenue des Aviateurs, Kinshasha.

Zambia: P.O. Box 31617, Independence and United Nations Avenues, Lusaka.

Zimbabwe: P.O. Box 3340, Arax House, 172 Herbert Chitepo Avenue, Harare.

Country Officer Desk List

The Department of Commerce provides a variety of information about specific countries and regions and employs country desk officers who can be reached by telephone or letter. To contact a country desk officer responsible for the countries of interest to you, call area code 202, the number 482, and the appropriate extension listed below, such as 202-482-2425 for Japan. Address letters as follows: Country Desk Officer, Name of Country or Region, Room Number, U.S. Department of Commerce, International Trade Administration, 14th Street and Constitution Avenue, N.W., Washington, DC 20230.

Country	Extension	Room
Afghanistan	2954	2029B
Albania	4915	3413
Algeria	1870	2039
Angola	4228	3317
Anguilla	2527	3021
Antigua and Barbuda	2527	4322
Argentina	1548	3017
Aruba	2527	3020
Association of Southeast Asian Nations (ASEAN)	3875	2308
Australia	3646	2308
Austria	2920	3029
Bahamas	2527	3021
Bahrain	5545	2039
Baltic Republics	3952	3318
Bangladesh	2954	2029B
Barbados	2527	3021
Belgium	5041	3046
Belize	2527	3021
Benin	4228	3317
Bermuda	2527	3021
Bhutan	2954	2029B
Bolivia	2521	2038
Bosnia-Herzegovina. See Yugoslavia.		
Botswana	4228	3317
Brazil	3871	3017
Brunei Darussalam	3875	2308
Bulgaria	4915	3413
Burkina Faso	4388	3317
Burundi	4388	3317
Cambodia (formerly Kampuchea)	3875	2308
Cameroon	5149	3317
Canada	3101	3033
Cape Verde	4388	3317

Caribbean Basin	1648	3025
Caymans	2527	3020
Central African Republic	4388	3317
Chad	4388	3317
Chile	1495	3017
China	3583	2317
Colombia	1659	2036
Comoros	4564	3317
Congo	5149	3317
Costa Rica	2527	3021
Croatia. See Yugoslavia.		
Cuba	2527	3021
Cyprus	3945	3044
Czechoslovakia	2645	6043
Denmark	3254	3413
Djibouti	4564	3317
Dominica	2527	3021
Dominican Republic	2527	3021
East Caribbean	2527	3021
Ecuador	1659	2036
Egypt	4441	2039
El Salvador	2527	3021
Equatorial Guinea	4228	3317
Ethiopia	4564	3317
European Community	5276	3036
Finland	3254	3413
France	6008	3042
Gabon	5149	3317
The Gambia	4388	3317
Germany	2434	3409
Ghana	5149	3317
Greece	3945	3044
Grenada	2527	3021
Guadeloupe	2527	3021

Guatemala	2527	3021
Guinea	4388	3317
Guinea-Bissau	4388	3317
Guyana	2527	3021
Haiti	2527	3021
Honduras	2527	3020
Hong Kong	3932	2317
Hungary	2645	6043
Iceland	3254	3037
India	2954	2029B
Indonesia	3875	2308
Iran	1810	2039
Iraq	4441	2039
Ireland	2177	3039
Israel	1870	2039
Italy	2177	3045
Ivory Coast (Côte d'Ivoire)	4388	3317
Jamaica	2527	3021
Jordan	1857	2039
Kenya	4564	3317
Korea	4957	2308
Kuwait	1860	2039
Laos	3875	2308
Lebanon	4441	2039
Lesotho	4228	3317
Liberia	4388	3317
Libya	5545	2039
Luxembourg	5401	3046
Macao	2462	2323
Macedonia. See Yugoslavia.		
Madagascar	4564	3317
Malawi	4228	3317
Malaysia	3875	2308
Maldives	2954	2029B
Mali	4388	3317

Malta	3748	3049
Martinique	2527	3021
Mauritania	4388	3317
Mauritius	4564	3317
Mexico	0300	3022
Mongolia	2462	2323
Montenegro. See Yugoslavia.		
Montserrat	2527	3021
Morocco	5545	2039
Mozambique	5148	3317
Myanmar (formerly Burma)	3875	2308
Namibia	4228	3317
Nepal	2954	2029B
The Netherlands	5401	3039
Netherlands Antilles	2527	3021
New Zealand	3647	2308
Nicaragua	2527	3021
Niger	4388	3317
Nigeria	4228	3317
Norway	4414	3037
Oman	1870	2039
Pacific Islands	3647	2308
Pakistan	2954	2029B
Panama	2527	3021
Paraguay	1548	3017
Peru	2521	2038
Philippines	3875	2308
Poland	2645	6043
Portugal	4508	3044
Puerto Rico	2527	3021
Qatar	1870	2039
Romania	2645	6043
Russia	0354	3318
Rwanda	4388	3317
São Tomé and Príncipe	4388	3317

Saudi Arabia	4652	2039
Senegal	4388	3317
Serbia. See Yugoslavia.		
Seychelles	4564	3317
Sierra Leone	4388	3317
Singapore	3875	2308
Slovak Republic. See Czechoslovakia.		
Slovenia. See Yugoslavia.		
Somalia	4564	3317
South Africa	5148	3317
Spain	4508	3045
Sri Lanka	2954	2029B
Saint Bartholemey	2527	3031
Saint Kitts and Nevis	2527	3021
Saint Lucia	2527	3021
Saint Martin	2527	3021
Saint Vincent and the Grenadines	2527	3021
Sudan	4564	3317
Suriname	2527	3021
Swaziland	5148	3317
Sweden	4414	3037
Switzerland	2920	3039
Syria	4441	2039
Taiwan	4957	2308
Tanzania	4228	3317
Thailand	3875	2308
Togo	5149	3021
Trinidad and Tobago	2527	3021
Tunisia	1860	2039
Turkey	5373	3045
Turks and Caicos Islands	2527	3021
Uganda	4564	3317
United Arab Emirates	5545	2039
United Kingdom	3748	3045

Uruguay	1495	3017
Venezuela	4303	3029
Vietnam	3875	2308
Virgin Islands (United Kingdom)	2527	3021
Virgin Islands (United States)	2527	3021
Yemen	1870	2039
Yugoslavia	2645	6043
Zaïre	5149	3317
Zambia	4228	3317
Zimbabwe	4228	3317

Index of
Terms to
Avoid or
Consider
Carefully

Subject Index